Exploring Sufi sites and seminaries, Professor Aljunied vividly describes how a dialogic tradition facilitated the formation of a Sufi habitus and life form across Muslim-majority Southeast Asia. The work deftly articulates the synergies between Sufis and the wider public, showing how such dynamics infused increasingly powerful mediums and popular forms of mass mobilization during the colonial and post-colonial eras.

Armando Salvatore
Barbara and Patrick Keenan Chair in Interfaith Studies, McGill University, Canada

At once personal and scholarly, this book shows how Sufis were engaged in dual dialogues—with themselves and their surroundings—that made them agents of social change in Southeast Asia's past and present alike. Paying equal attention to devotion and miracles, and no less, the political and martial aspects of Sufi activism, Aljunied explains why Islam remains so important in the region today.

Nile Green
Ibn Khaldun Endowed Chair in World History at the University of California, Los Angeles

Splendidly written and accessible, Khairudin Aljunied tells a lively and engaging story of Muslim piety, metaphysics, and politics as an integral part of Islamic thought and practice in Southeast Asia. Readers will gain a profound and nuanced understanding of Islam in a region with the world's largest Muslim population. A compelling read!

Ebrahim Moosa
Mirza Family Professor of Islamic Thought and Muslim Societies at the University of Notre Dame, USA

This book expands the study of Sufism by examining its historical and social impact in Southeast Asia. Aljunied provides a compelling methodology, deepening our understanding of the factors contributing to Sufism's lasting presence in the region. An excellent resource for anyone interested in a field often overlooked by scholars of Islam.

Osman Bakar
Al-Ghazali Chair of Epistemology and Civilizational Studies and Renewal at the International Islamic University of Malaysia

Aljunied presents an elegant, sobering, and masterly account of Sufism in Southeast Asia. Informed by the author's deep understanding of Muslim societies, he introduces an innovative approach – contemplative histories – that transcends biased views of Islamic spirituality. Highly original and Ghazalian in spirit, *Contemplating Sufism* is a guide and roadmap for anyone interested in historical Islam and Sufi expressions across several centuries.

Salih Çift
Professor of Islamic Studies at Bursa Uludağ University, Turkey

Contemplating Sufism

Dialogue and Tradition Across Southeast Asia

KHAIRUDIN ALJUNIED

WILEY Blackwell

This edition first published 2025
© 2025 John Wiley & Sons Ltd

All rights reserved, including rights for text and data mining and training of artificial intelligence technologies or similar technologies. No part of this publication may be reproduced, stored in a retrieval system, or transmitted, in any form or by any means, electronic, mechanical, photocopying, recording or otherwise, except as permitted by law. Advice on how to obtain permission to reuse material from this title is available at http://www.wiley.com/go/permissions.

The right of Khairudin Aljunied to be identified as the author of this work has been asserted in accordance with law.

Registered Office(s)
John Wiley & Sons, Inc., 111 River Street, Hoboken, NJ 07030, USA
John Wiley & Sons Ltd, New Era House, 8 Oldlands Way, Bognor Regis, West Sussex, PO22 9NQ, UK

For details of our global editorial offices, customer services, and more information about Wiley products visit us at www.wiley.com.

The manufacturer's authorized representative according to the EU General Product Safety Regulation is Wiley-VCH GmbH, Boschstr. 12, 69469 Weinheim, Germany, e-mail: Product_Safety@wiley.com.

Wiley also publishes its books in a variety of electronic formats and by print-on-demand. Some content that appears in standard print versions of this book may not be available in other formats.

Trademarks: Wiley and the Wiley logo are trademarks or registered trademarks of John Wiley & Sons, Inc. and/or its affiliates in the United States and other countries and may not be used without written permission. All other trademarks are the property of their respective owners. John Wiley & Sons, Inc. is not associated with any product or vendor mentioned in this book.

Limit of Liability/Disclaimer of Warranty
While the publisher and authors have used their best efforts in preparing this work, they make no representations or warranties with respect to the accuracy or completeness of the contents of this work and specifically disclaim all warranties, including without limitation any implied warranties of merchantability or fitness for a particular purpose. No warranty may be created or extended by sales representatives, written sales materials or promotional statements for this work. This work is sold with the understanding that the publisher is not engaged in rendering professional services. The advice and strategies contained herein may not be suitable for your situation. You should consult with a specialist where appropriate. The fact that an organization, website, or product is referred to in this work as a citation and/or potential source of further information does not mean that the publisher and authors endorse the information or services the organization, website, or product may provide or recommendations it may make. Further, readers should be aware that websites listed in this work may have changed or disappeared between when this work was written and when it is read. Neither the publisher nor authors shall be liable for any loss of profit or any other commercial damages, including but not limited to special, incidental, consequential, or other damages.

Library of Congress Cataloging-in-Publication Data Applied for:

Paperback: 9781394270453

Cover Design: Wiley
Cover Image: © James Strachan/Getty Images

Set in 12/14pt STIXTwoText by Straive, Pondicherry, India

SKY10097349_012825

For the children of Palestine.

You will be free.

Contents

Acknowledgements	viii
Abbreviations	xi
Glossary	xii
List of Photos	xvi
Timeline of Sufism in Southeast Asia	xviii
Introduction: A Dialogical Tradition	1
CHAPTER 1 Feelings	18
CHAPTER 2 Miracles	50
CHAPTER 3 Institutions	77
CHAPTER 4 Struggles	107
CHAPTER 5 Politics	134
Epilogue: Contemplating Sufism	165
Bibliography	171
Index	196

Acknowledgements

Writing this book has been my most challenging and rewarding endeavour to date. It is the result of decades living with Sufis and lengthy discussions with fellow travellers who share my fascination with the inner aspects of faith. This is the fifth in a series of monographs offering fresh perspectives on Islam in Southeast Asia. It challenges the common perception of Sufism as an esoteric, passive, and other-worldly creed that is detached from worldly issues and societal problems.[1] I question the dominant idea of Sufis as reclusive mystics, swirling dervishes, and wandering hermits. They were much more than that. Sufis were catalysts of social change and prime movers of political transformations. They shaped the ideological landscapes of their societies, created lasting memories, influenced economies, and defended liberties. I hope readers of this book will embrace this alternative view of Sufism in Southeast Asia and raise more probing questions about the contributions of Sufis to the shaping of historical Islam.

The book was mostly written in buses and trains, cabs and planes, cafes, and coffee shops, and it bears the marks of friends and fraternities. I would like to thank Bruce Lawrence, Martin van Bruinessen, Julian Millie, and Engseng Ho for their generous inputs during the early stages of writing. Bruce encouraged me to consider the interactions between global and local expressions of Sufism. He read the entire manuscript and made it sharper. Martin pointed to many useful works on the topic. Julian connected me with scholars working on interesting and emerging lines of enquiry. Engseng questioned the tentative structure of the book and forced me to rethink my approaches to Sufi pasts. I spent weeks mulling over his simple point: rethink Sufism in Southeast Asia in ways that would truly capture its innate uniqueness. I hope this book live up

---

[1] The following series of books provides revisionist interpretations of Islam in Southeast Asia: Khairudin Aljunied's *Muslim Cosmopolitanism: Southeast Asian Islam in Comparative Perspective* (Edinburgh University Press, 2017), *Hamka and Islam* (Cornell University Press, 2018), *Islam in Malaysia: An Entwined History* (Oxford University Press, 2019), and *Shapers of Islam in Southeast Asia* (New York: Oxford University Press, 2022).

Acknowledgements ix

to his hopes as well as the hopes of other scholars who have contributed through their writings in the making of this book.

The year I spent as full professor at the University of Brunei Darussalam (UBD) in 2022 was very productive in conceptualizing this project. I received financial support from UBD to collect data in several countries. Asbol Mail, Muhammad Rafee, Siti Norainna, Tassim Abu Bakar, Stephen Druce, Zulhimi Jaidin, Khairul Rejal, Ampuan Brahim, Hairul Azrin, Noralipah Mohamed, and Vincent Ooi were very supportive. Abdoh Abdul Salam and Jaafar Bakar were always there to offer their assistance. Noor Azam, Norkhalbi Wahsalfelah, Shaikh Sultan, Abdillah Noh, Iftekhar Iqbal, Masridah Mahmud, Amirrizal Mahmud, Ahsan Ullah, Rommel Curaming, Hafiizh Hashim, Abdul Hai, Afroz Ahmad, Hilmy Baihaqy, Abdul Waliyuddin, Khairul Adli, Katrina Daud, and Hamizah Haidi added spice to life. Amin Aziz, Emin Poljarevic, Khalil Ahmad, Shaikh Abdul Mabud, and Senad Mrahorovic furthered my thoughts and corrected many presumptions.

Kind souls across oceans have patiently listened to my ramblings and reflections on Sufi themes. John Esposito, Tamara Sonn, and Jonathan Brown at Georgetown University are dependable comrades. Ermin Sinanovic, Younos Mirza, and Yaqoub Mirza at the Center for Islam in the Contemporary World (CICW) made my research trips more fulfiling. Brothers at the Herndon Halaqah were always welcoming and helpful, making long sojourns bearable. Maria Dakake, Martin Nguyen, Atif Khalil, Abdoulaye Ndiaye, Ismail Alatas, and Huseyin Yilmaz were excellent interlocutors during seminars on "Islam in Southeast Asia and Muslim spaces" held at George Mason University and later at the University of Sarajevo. The Ilahiyat Faculty at the University of Uludag included me along many other scholars of global Sufism in a highly engaging conference on "Sufism and Politics." There, I met Salih Cift whom I now regard as my teacher and friend. Discussions with Alexander Knysh, Laila Khalifah, Tanvir Anjum, Bulent Senay, and Takyettin Karakaya made the days in Turkey heart-warming. Alexander Wain and Brendan Wolfe at the University of St. Andrews arranged for a seminar on the Islamic Civilization where some ideas found in the following pages were presented. Abu Bakar Assiddiq kindly toured me around Edinburgh and read a full draft of this book.

In Malaysia, Anthony Milner, Hamdi Abdul Shukor, Danny Wong, Farish Noor, Zulkarnain Abdul Rahman, Arba'iyah Mohd Noor, and friends at the University of Malaya kept me cheerful. Maszlee Malik, Ahmad Badri, and the staff at the International Institute of Advanced Islamic Studies (IAIS) welcomed me into their dynamic organization.

Professor Redzuan at University Selangor (UNISEL) arranged for a fellowship position with the assistance of Eda Suhana. Saliha Farid and Nadia Khan read parts of this book and provided useful pointers. Outside the workplace, Tengku Baderul Zaman, Hidayah Wan Ismail, Azaliah Aljunied, Aasil Ahmad, Norhayani Mohd Noor, and Abang Rosli made Malaysia feel like home. Shamsul Amri Baharuddin, Anis Yusoff, Kartini Khalid, Azharudin Mohd Dali, Arfah Abdul Majid, Syakir Hashim, Shafiq Sahruddin, Danial Abdul Rahman, and Haroon Alshatrie were great sounding boards. Nazirul Mubin, Syahmi, and others in the Cendekia fraternity were companions in the path of knowledge. Shazani Masri read the book with his usual sparkle and brilliance. Ahmed Inan, Tayfun Akgun, and Mehmet Ozay made for fun *teh tarik* mates, always helpful and living up to Turkish hospitality and brotherhood. Professor Osman Bakar is a sage and a soother in challenging times.

I am blessed with wonderful neighbours, close acquaintances, and empathetic institutions in Singapore and the United Kingdom. The National University of Singapore granted me leave to complete the writing of this book. The families of Omar Moad, Abdul Hai, Jamil Chisti, Fadhil Ismail, Taufik Mohamed, Rozi Naser, Norimah Abdul Ghani, and Siti Nur'ain Yuza have become my own. Azri Mokhtar, Kamaludeen Nasir, Hafiz Othman, Damanhuri Abas, Faizal Mohammad, Rudie Asmara, Sujuandy Supa'at, Shaharudin Ishak, Deary Rahmayanto, Abbas Khan, Wasim Chiang, Liao Bowen, and Abbas Karim were always encouraging me to keep writing, offering unstinting assistance whenever I needed it most. I am deeply grateful for having been endowed with supportive parents and in laws. Marlina and my six children, Inshirah, Fatihah, Yusuf, Muhammad, Yasin, and Furqan, have all become part of my writing journeys. Life as a scholar would have been less meaningful without their love and affection.

Abbreviations

GOLKAR	Golongan Karya (Functional Groups)
JIB	Jong Islamieten Bond
Masyumi	Partai Majelis Syuro Muslim Indonesia (Council of Indonesian Muslim Associations)
MUI	Majelis Ulama Indonesia (Indonesian Ulama Council)
NII	Negara Islam Indonesia
NU	Nahdlatul Ulama (Revival of the Ulama)
PAKEM	Pengawas Aliran Kepercayaan Masyarakat (Coordinating Board for Monitoring Mystical Beliefs in Society)
PAS	Parti Islam se-Malaysia (Islamic Party of Malaysia)
PERTI	Persatuan Tarbiyah Islamiyah (Islamic Education Organization)
PKMM	Parti Kebangsaan Melayu Malaya (The Malay Nationalist Party)
PNU	Partai Nahdlatul Ummah (The Revival of the Ummah Party)
PULO	Patani United Liberation Movement
SI	Sarekat Islam (Islamic Association)

Glossary

adab	manners
adat	traditional customs
ahlul bait	family of the prophet
ahlus sunnah wal jama'ah	The People of the Sunnah and the Majority
ahwal	states
Al-Insanul Kamil	The Perfect Human Being
aql	intellect
akhlaqul karimah	noble character
amal	praxis
ashiq	burning love for the divine
azimat	amulet
batin	inner
bay'ah	oath of allegiance
barakah	blessings
bid'ah	innovations in Islam
Dajjals	deceitful messiahs
da'wa	the preaching of Islam
dhawq	tasting
dhikr	remembering
dihliz	threshold position
dosa	sins
du'a	invocations
fana'	annihilation of the self
faqr	poverty
fasiq	one who violates Islamic law
fatwas	religious edicts
fuqaha	jurists
ghaflah	heedlessness
ghaib	supernatural
habaibs	beloved ones with genealogical connections to the Prophet
hadrat al-nabi	Prophet's presence
hajj	pilgrimage to Mecca
hajji	pilgrim

Glossary xiii

halal	permissible
hadith	Prophetic sayings
halaqah	study circle
haqiqah	mystical truths
hikayat	rhythmic prose stories
hijab	veil
hikmah	wisdom
ibadah	acts of worship
ihsan	excellence
ijazah	licenses
ijtihad	independent reasoning
ikhlas	sincerity
'ilmu laduni	direct knowledge from God
'ilm al-yaqin	the knowledge of certainty
imam	leader
ishara	signs
islah	reform
ittihad	union with God
jihad	holy struggle
jihad fisabilillah	struggling in the path of Allah
Jawi or *Jawah*	Malay-Indonesian scholars in Makkah
kafir	disbelief
kafirun	disbelievers
karamah	miracles
kashf	unveiling
kauman	religious community
kebatinan	search for inner truth
khalafi	followers of the later generations
khalwat	solitude
khauf	fear
khurafat	superstition
kitab	learned treatises
kraton	Javanese royalty
kyai	religious teachers
laqab	honorific
ma'rifah	interior knowedge
ma'siyah	contravening Islamic law
madhab	school of Islamic jurisprudence
mahabbah	love
majlis ta'lim	Islamic forum
manaqibs	hagiographies
maqam	shrine

maqamat	spiritual station
martabat tujuh	seven stages of being
maudhu	fabricated
mi'raj	ascension
mubah	permissible
mufti	expounder of Islamic laws
muhsinun	those who achieve the highest ranks in deeds
mujahadah	utmost striving
muraqabah	mediation
murids	novices
murshids	spiritual guides
mustahabb	recommended
musyahadah	witnessing
muzakarah/munadharah	lengthy debates and consensus building
nafs	carnal self
Nur Muhammad	Light of Muhammad
penghulus	headmen
perasaan	feelings
pondok	Islamic boarding school
qalb	heart
qanaah	contentment
qiyam	standing
rabithah	relationship forged with a spiritual guide
raja'	hopefulness
ratib	collection of litanies and supplications
redha	acceptance
riyadhah	spiritual practices
ruh	soul
ruqyah	psycho-spiritual healing and spirit exorcism
sabr	patience
sadaqah	charity
sakti	magical powers
salafi	followers of predecessors
sanad	lineage
santri	religious-educated Muslim
sesat	wayward
shahadah	profession of faith
shaykh	master
Shaykhul Islam	Chief Judge
sharh	commentary
shari'a	Islamic legal and ethical code
sha'ir	narrative poem

shaykhs	masters
shirk	idolatrous polytheism
shura	consultation
silat	Malay combative art
silsilah	spiritual genealogy
siyasa	statecraft/governance
solat	prayer
suluk	journey
Sunnah	words and acts of Prophet Muhammad
suraus	prayer halls
tafakkur	contemplation
tajdid	renewal
ta'lim	teaching
tamassuh	touching
taqlid	blind obedience
taqwa	piety
tarbiyah	cultivating
tariqah	Sufi order
tariqah sufiyah mu'tabarah	legitimate Sufi brotherhoods
tasawwur	worldview
tasbih	rosary
tawbah	repentance
tawheed	oneness of God
tasawwuf	Sufism
tawakkal	trust in God
tawassul	intercession
tok guru	respected teacher
turath	heritage of Muslim thought
ulama	Muslim scholars
ummah	global Muslim community
usul al-fiqh	principles of Islamic jurisprudence
uzlah	seclusion
wahdatul wujud	unity of existence
wahyu	revelation from God
wali	saint
waqf	endowments
wara'	scrupulousness
yaqazah	waking visions
zakah	compulsory tax
zahir	outer
zawiya	integrated devotional complex
ziyarah	visitation
zuhud	renunciation of the world

List of Photos

Chapter 1:
Illuminated frontispiece of the manuscript of *Al-Kawakib al-durriyya* by Al-Busiri made for the Sultan Qaitbay: https://en.wikipedia.org/wiki/Al-Burda#/media/File:Frontispiece_of_%22Al-Kawakib_al-duriyya%22_by_Al-Busiri_(CBL_Ar_4168,_f.2a).jpg

Malaysian Muslims participate in a Maulidur Rasul parade in Putrajaya, also known as Mawlid, the birthday of Prophet Muhammad, at Putrajaya Putra Mosque: https://en.wikipedia.org/wiki/Mawlid#/media/File:Maulidur_Rasul_(8413657269).jpg

Chapter 2:
Tombstone of Sultan Bolkiah, the fifth ruler of Brunei (1485–1524) in Kota Batu, Brunei: https://en.wikipedia.org/wiki/Bolkiah#/media/File:Tombstone_of_Sultan_Bolkiah,_June_2015.jpg

Keramat Habib Noh at Palmer Road in the early twentieth century: https://en.wikipedia.org/wiki/Keramat_Habib_Noh#/media/File:Keramat_Habib_Noh.jpg

Chapter 3:
A Quranic school in colonial Java: https://en.wikipedia.org/wiki/Pesantren#/media/File:COLLECTIE_TROPENMUSEUM_Een_Koranschool_op_Java_TMnr_10002385.jpg

The Silsilah of Hashimiyyah-Alawiyyah-Darqawiyyah-Shazliyyah order.

Chapter 4:
Fighting between Diponegoro's forces and the Dutch colonial forces in Gawok (1900 drawing): https://en.wikipedia.org/wiki/Diponegoro#/media/File:Aanval_van_de_colonne_Le_Bron_de_Vexela_op_Dipo_Negoro_nabij_Gawok.jpg

Portrait of Tuanku Imam Bonjol (1772–1864): https://en.wikipedia.org/wiki/Tuanku_Imam_Bonjol#/media/File:Portret_van_Tuanku_Imam_Bonjol.jpg

Chapter 5:
Solawatul Burdah by Raihan viewed by 882k views: https://www.youtube.com/watch?v=7NvYDCUaFwE

K.H. Hasyim Asy'ari, the founding father of NU organization: https://en.wikipedia.org/wiki/Hasyim_Asy%27ari#/media/File:Hasyim_Asyari.jpg

Timeline of Sufism in Southeast Asia

7th–10th Centuries: Initial Contacts

Muslim travellers and traders from the Arabian Peninsula and Persianate world journeyed through maritime trade routes and the Silk Road into Southeast Asia. Islamic spirituality and practices interacted with local cultures and beliefs.

11th–13th Centuries: Gradual Spread

1028: A Muslim tombstone was discovered by archaeologists which provides evidence of a growing presence of Muslims at Pulau Tambun, Pahang, and possibly in other Malay states.

1136: Muzaffar Shah I, the Sultan of Kedah, became the earliest Southeast Asian ruler to convert to Islam.

1267: Samudra-Pasai established as the first Islamic polity in region. The rulers were active in the spread of Islam in the region. They attracted scholars and traders and established diplomatic alliances with non-Muslim states and relations with Arabian, Turkic, and Persian-Islamic powers.

1281: Chinese chronicles register the arrival of two Muslims in Sumatra to the Mongol court.

1292: Marco Polo reports the existence of Muslim communities in Perlak, northern Sumatra, who lived peacefully with non-Muslims.

1270s–1310s: A Southeast Asian Sufi scholar, Abu Abdullah Mas'ud al-Jawi, is recorded to have taught in Arabia, pointing to the circulation of scholars from Southeast Asia to the Arab World.

14th–17th Centuries: Rapid Expansion

Late 14th century: Syaikh Karimul Makhdum preached Islam in the Sulu Archipelago and other parts of the Filipino islands.

1326/1386: Terengganu stone inscribed with Arabic letters confirms the lively existence of Islam in northern Malaysia. Evidence of synthesis between Hindu-Buddhist ideas with Islam is present in this historical relic.

Timeline of Sufism in Southeast Asia **xix**

1400–1511: Melaka rose to become one of the most influential Muslim maritime power in Southeast Asia responsible for the spread of Islam in the region and the diffusion of the Malay language as lingua franca.

1405–1433: Chinese Muslim Admiral Zheng He expeditions to Southeast Asia strengthened ties between Muslims in the region and the wider Muslim world. His visits led to the establishment of Chinese Muslim communities in Malay Peninsula, Sumatra, Java, and the Philippines.

15th–16th centuries: The Wali Songo (Seven Saints) spread Sufism in Java using performative arts and creative preaching.

1511: Sultan Ali Mughayat Syah established the Acehnese Islamic kingdom, furthering Melaka's role as the leading Islamizing force in the region. Aceh became the hub of Islamic learning, a conduit for Sufism, and a powerhouse of Jawi literature.

1511: The fall of Melaka to the Portuguese paved way for Johor, Brunei, and Aceh to compete for regional dominance and to be the foremost propagator of Islam.

1560s–1590s: Hamzah Fansuri of Barus wrote Sufi poetic texts that led to the spread of Ibn 'Arabi's Sufi metaphysics into the Southeast Asia.

1607–1676: Makassar and Champa rulers converted to Islam and aided in the expanding networks of Muslim societies in Sulawesi and mainland Southeast Asia.

1637–1644: Sufi scholar, Nuruddin Al-Raniri, promoted scholarly Sufism and wrote against heretical Sufi doctrines purveyed by the followers of Hamzah Fansuri. The Rifa'iyyah order spread through Al-Raniri's active promotion of its teachings.

1613–1645: Sultan Agung, a devout Sufi, a votary of Javanese mysticism, and a gifted war strategist, expanded the kingdom of Mataram by waging holy war against Hindu-Buddhist polities.

1650s: European encroachment into Southeast Asia triggered a variety of responses from Sufis, from armed rebellions to intellectual combat to strategic cooperation. Prominent Sufis such as Yusuf al-Makassari led revolts and were sent for exile.

18th–21st Centuries – Modernity and Renewal

Early 18th century: Names of female Sufis from Java and Cirebon were recorded in the silsilah of the Shattariyah order.

18th–19th centuries: The flowering of Sufi literary productions in many Southeast Asian vernacular languages, especially in Bugis, Tausug, Minang, Makassarese, Sundanese, Sasak, and Acehnese dialects. The works were usually written in the Arabic script.

1750s–1800s: Muhammad Arshad Al-Banjari from South Kalimantan attacked the corrupting influences of the martabat tujuh and wahdatul wujud ideologies.

1807–1837: Sufis, known as the Padris, returned to West Sumatra from their studies in Makkah and campaigned for aggressive reforms against local customs and esoteric Sufism.

1825–1830: Sufi prince of the Yogyakartan court, Diponegoro, waged war against the Dutch and their collaborators. These years saw the intensification of Sufi resistance against colonialism in Southern Thailand and Southern Philippines.

1820s–1890s: Founding of hundreds of pondoks and pesantren across Southeast Asia in reaction to Siamese and European intervention into Muslim affairs.

1850s–1870s: Raja Ali Haji a prominent member of the Naqshbandiyyah tariqah in Riau wrote influential poems to attract the masses to Sufism and ethical conduct.

1869: The opening of Suez Canal and invention of steamships heighten contacts between Sufis in Southeast Asia and their brethren across the Indian Ocean. This period saw increased influence of Arab Hadramis in Southeast Asian Sufism and other reform movements.

1890: Habib Nuh mausoleum was constructed in Singapore. It became a site visited by Muslims and non-Muslims.

1890–1913: Moros in the Philippines fought wars against the United States, claiming thousands of lives on both ends.

1905: Al-Imam journal which was modelled on the Egyptian periodical, Al-Manar, was published. Seeds of reformist ideas were planted in the minds of many Sufi orders despite resistance by the conservative ulama.

1907: The founding of Madrasah Al-Iqbal by Syed Shaikh al-Hadi ushered modernist reforms in the running of Islamic educational institutions.

1926: Sufi-led Nahdlatul Ulama (NU) was created as a rival to the modernist Muhammadiyah movement established more than a decade earlier.

1928–1930: The shaykhs of the Tijaniyyah, Naqshbandiyyah, and Qadiriyyah in Cirebon fought over followership leading to mutual accusations of heresy.

1939: Haji Abdul Malik Abdul Karim Amrullah (Hamka) published *Tasauf Moderen* (Modern Sufism). It became a best seller for decades to come and promoted the idea of individualized Sufism.

1945–1949: Sufi groups participated in the revolution against the Dutch which eventually brought about Indonesia's independence.

1950s–1980s: Religious authorities and Islamic movements across Malaysia and Indonesia announced their lists of legitimate Sufi brotherhoods and passed laws to clamp down deviant Sufi teachings.

1962: Demise of the Darul Islam militant movement in Indonesia upon the execution of Kartosuwiryo.

1977: The Philippines recognised twelfth of Rabiulawal, the day of the birth of Prophet Muhammad, as one of the official holidays.

1987: Nada Murni Group released nasyid albums filled with Sufi messages. Most of the songs by bands such as Raihan, Rabbani, Hijjaz, Inteam, and Snada became hits across Southeast Asia.

1994: The banning of the messianic-Sufi movement, Darul Arqam.

1999: NU Chairman, Abdurrahman Wahid, was elected as Indonesia's fourth president and the first president in the world with physical disabilities.

2011: The Ministry of Religion in Indonesia listed over 25,000 pesantren in Indonesia, most of which taught tasawwuf.

2013: Mega Mawlid event featuring Habib Syech Assegaf was organized at Putrajaya, Malaysia, and attended by hundreds of thousands.

2019: NU Chairman, Ma'ruf Amin, became the vice president of Indonesia at 76 years old, the world's oldest vice president.

2021: King of Brunei couched ratibs as "divine vaccines (*vaksin ketuhanan*)" and daily readings of these litanies were strongly encouraged to ward off COVID-19 infection.

Introduction: A Dialogical Tradition

To embark on the path of *tasawwuf* (Sufism) is to embrace a journey of constant learning, constant ruminating, constant forbearing, constant reinventing, constant nurturing, and constant struggling, in an ever-constant process of self-actualizing. Through unceasing dialogues with the divine, with nature, with fellow mortals, and with oneself, a Sufi may one day be honoured and remembered in the annals of history. One such Sufi traveller whose legacy is etched in the pages of Southeast Asian history was Yusuf Al-Makassari (1626–1699).

After close to three decades roaming in search of religious knowledge and spiritual wisdom in Aceh, Gujarat, Hadramaut, the Haramayn (Makkah and Madinah), Damascus, and Istanbul, in 1672, Yusuf returned to the Javanese port town of Banten, where he briefly called home. As a respected spiritual leader of multiple *tariqahs* (Sufi brotherhoods) in Java, he married into the royal family, was appointed chief judge, and became a commander in the Bantanese army. Yusuf's upturn in fortunes was not to last. The intrigues between Sultan Ageng Tirtayasa (1631–1695) and his son, Sultan Haji (1660s–1720s), reached a deadly impasse. Yusuf and his legions of faithful followers backed Sultan Ageng whom they believed was the rightful ruler of Banten. Defeated on the battlefields when the Dutch intervened in the civil war in support of Sultan Haji, Yusuf called for a *jihad* (holy struggle) against the traitors and unbelievers. Months into the conflict with Sultan Ageng now imprisoned and his forces depleting, Yusuf ultimately surrendered in exchange for his captured family. But the Dutch reneged on their promise. In 1684, the Sufi master was condemned to exile.[1]

---

[1] Abu Hamid, *Syeikh Yusuf: Seorang Ulama, Sufi, Dan Pejuang* (Jakarta: Yayasan Obor Indonesia, 1994), 106.

Contemplating Sufism: Dialogue and Tradition Across Southeast Asia, First Edition. Khairudin Aljunied.
© 2025 John Wiley & Sons Ltd. Published 2025 by John Wiley & Sons Ltd.

Thus began, once again, the transformative journeys he had embarked early in his life. This time to a colony in Ceylon (Sri Lanka) designated for fugitives from Dutch-controlled territories. Yusuf was destined never to return. During the nine years there with his wives, children, and several followers, he wrote numerous treatises on Sufism and other Islamic sciences. These books were read out to his students who faithfully copied and distributed his works to pilgrims en route to *hajj* (pilgrimage to Makkah) and travellers from other parts of the oceanic-linked Islamic world. Yusuf's exile never broke him. Instead, it allowed him to focus on teaching and devotions. In moments of contemplation, Yusuf counselled those in need of sagely advice in the face of life's trials and tribulations:

> Therefore, if the seeker does all of that and implements everything that we have mentioned with sincerity of intention, seeking only the pleasure of Allah, and remembers Allah abundantly without being heedless of Him, not even for a moment, and completely follows the Messenger of Allah, having patience in everything and being serious in his seeking with high aspirations, then he will be a visionary through the will of Allah, and one of the friends of Allah and amongst the knowers of Allah, the Most High.[2]

Yusuf's influence grew and so did Dutch apprehensions over the looming possibility of revolts. In his late sixties, Yusuf was deported to the Cape of Good Hope, where indentured slaves became his devoted disciples and his most energetic missionaries. They developed networks bounded together by memories of a fearless anti-colonial Sufi.[3] By the time Yusuf breathed his last on 23 May 1699, Islam had spread widely. Revered and immortalized, his tombs could now be found in both the Cape of Good Hope and Makassar. Yusuf's piety, valour, and a life dedicated to Islamic scholarship became the stuff of legends. In at least two countries today, the warrior-saint is celebrated as a national hero.[4]

---

[2] Yusuf Al-Maqassari, "Tuhfat al-Abrar li Ahl Al-Asrar," in *Spiritual Path, Spiritual Reality: Selected Writings of Shaykh Yusuf of Macassar*, eds. Yousuf Dadoo and Auwais Rafudeen, (Durban: University of South Africa, 2021), 121–122.

[3] Saarah Jappie, "Between Makassars: Site, Story, and the Transoceanic Afterlives of Shaykh Yusuf of Makassar" (PhD Dissertation, New Jersey, Princeton University, 2018).

[4] Muzdalifah Sahib, *Sheikh Yusuf Al-Makassary, His Life Story as a National Hero from Gowa, South Sulawesi to Cape Town, South Africa and a Reformer in Islamic Mystic World* (Makassar: Alauddin University Press, 2011).

Introduction: A Dialogical Tradition

This book begins with this enthralling story because it exemplifies how Sufis and Sufism have profoundly impacted communities across non-Arab-speaking world. Looked upon in isolation, Yusuf's adventurous life may seem extraordinary, bordering in the realm of fiction, fit for an action novel or a blockbuster movie. Yet his journey mirrors the experiences of many Sufis who harmonized and globalized Islam through various roles and in various localities. If we accept that Muslims planted their roots in Southeast Asia[5] as early as the eleventh century, it is safe then to regard Sufis as among the most enduring purveyors of the Islamic faith, shaping its interpretation and practice in that quarter of the Muslim civilization.[6]

In the following chapters, I interrogate several key questions lingering in my mind and perhaps in the minds of scholars riveted by Islam's global expansion: Why has Sufism asserted such a powerful presence and influence in Southeast Asia for so long? How did Sufis respond to and navigate the forces of change that have unremittingly challenged their beliefs and practices? From what angle of vision, what methodology should we study the complex history of Sufism to reveal its resilience and contributions to the making of Southeast Asia as one of the most densely populated Muslim regions in the world?

I address the last question first. Several approaches to understanding how Sufism embedded and shaped Southeast Asia over many generations can be discerned. The first can be termed as the "devout advocate" approach, characterized by faithful followers and passionate exponents of the Sufi tradition. They are "insiders" to the Sufi tradition.[7] Devout advocates position Sufism as something to be experienced, internalized, and realized, not merely studied. They believe in the extraordinary

---

[5] By Southeast Asia, I am focusing specifically to "Muslim Southeast Asia," "Island Southeast Asia," or "the Malay World." It includes geography that is known today as Indonesia, Malaysia, Singapore, South Thailand, and South Philippines. That said, Muslim/Island Southeast Asia or the Malay world is not a reified object. It is a region that was always in dialogue with mainland Southeast Asia and other parts of Asia and other far-flung areas. Exchanges between Muslim and non-Muslim communities throughout Southeast Asia have remained lively for over a millennium. This book therefore uses the term "Southeast Asia" in order to capture such connections thereby showing how the Sufis functioned within the capillaries of relationships that characterized the region as a whole.

[6] I have discussed the roles of different purveyors of Islam in Southeast Asia in my recent books. Khairudin Aljunied, *Muslim Cosmopolitanism: Southeast Asian Islam in Comparative Perspective* (Edinburgh University Press, 2017); Khairudin Aljunied, *Hamka and Islam* (Cornell University Press, 2018); Khairudin Aljunied, *Islam in Malaysia: An Entwined History* (Oxford University Press, 2019).

[7] Alexander Knysh, *Sufism: A New History of Islamic Mysticism* (New Jersey: Princeton University Press, 2017), 1–39.

qualities of tasawwuf and the potency of its teachings, rituals, and practices. Integral in this standpoint is an unwavering belief in the miracles of saints, the power of tombs, and the remarkable stories of Sufis such as one who can teleport from one place to another within the twinkle of an eye, and the other who could cure all ailments except death.[8] No study of Sufism is complete without bringing to the fore its calmative, curative, and constructive prowess. And for the same reason, this approach has given birth to a variety of *manaqibs* (hagiographies) and texts highlighting the virtues and extraordinary *karamah* (miracles) of Sufi scholars and missionaries in Southeast Asia. Marvels won over sceptics, wonders captivated the curious, so the reasoning goes. In describing a prominent Hadrami-Arab Sufi once based in Java, a devout advocate writes: "Habib Soleh bin Muhsin al-Hamid is known by his moniker Habib Soleh Tanggul (Jember), renowned for having his invocations answered. He was respected and loved by many. His prayers were sincere and untainted by worldly affairs. Because of this, his petitions were swiftly granted by Allah."[9]

In contrast, the "reflexive admirer" approach problematizes such claims without denouncing or ardently promoting Sufism. They view Sufism's attributes and promises absorbing, enigmatic, and noteworthy. In the same vein as the devout advocate, they register the inventive capacities of Sufis in infusing Islam and transforming Southeast Asia into a region inhabited by among the largest Muslim population in the world. But reflexive admirers recognize Sufism's strengths and weaknesses, its merits and demerits, its moderating effects, and its excesses. They highlight its contributions to the advancement of Muslims, and its aversion to change. Saints, *tok gurus* (respected teachers), or *habaibs* (beloved ones with genealogical connections to the Prophet), to the reflexive admirer, can be appraised. They view Sufis as ordinary mortals affected by errors and inconsistencies, warranting meticulous scrutiny to appreciate their historical contributions. The reflexive admirer methodology is one that sits at the border of being a complete outsider and an estranged stranger. She is an enthusiast looking at a subject she accepts as part of her everyday encounters and shared heritage. Naquib Al-Attas, whose landmark studies on Sufism among the Malays are now regarded as classics and whose writings will feature glaringly in this book, is one such reflexive admirer,

---

[8] Muhammad Ghouse Khan Surattee, *The Grand Saint of Singapore: The Life of Habib Nuh Bin Muhammad Al-Habshi* (Singapore: Masjid Al-Firdaus, 2008).

[9] Muhadir Bin Haji Joll As-Sanariy, *Pesona Ahli Syurga* (Petaling Jaya: Galeri Ilmu, 2016), 91.

par excellence.[10] The famed Malay-Indonesian scholar, Haji Abdul Malik bin Abdul Karim Amrullah (acronym "Hamka," 1908–1981) sums up the reflexive admirer's worldview which he avowedly belonged to:

> We have studied tasawwuf since its genesis during the time of the prophet and its expansion in Indonesia. This analysis goes beyond objective reasoning and has become a subjective experience. That is to say, the one who teaches and studies Sufism may consciously or unconsciously be affected by it. He begins to lead his life with humility and becomes an ascetic.[11]

The third yet no less noteworthy approach is the "critical appraiser," which has two guises. One type maintains a disinterested stance, explaining the evolution of various forms of spiritualities as a matter of fact. On this score, the critical appraiser agrees with the reflexive admirer. The difference between them rests on their subjective relationship with Sufism. For the critical appraiser, Sufism in Southeast Asia is an intellectual passion or else a career. Many illuminating works have emerged from this approach and probably the most definitive is by Martin van Bruinessen. His analyses of the tariqahs, their institutions, and their roles in the making of monarchies and nation-states are now standard texts for anyone working on the topic.[12] Alternatively, there is yet another type of critical appraiser, a value-laden, norm-oriented type aimed at distinguishing orthodox Sufism from heretical practices. This approach, often linked to state or quasi-governmental institutions, and religious movements are driven by methodological confessionalism. They scrutinize Sufi orders from the perspective of normative piety, emphasizing valid practices while condemning deviant teachings. They distinguish,

---

[10] See for examples: Syed Muhammad Naquib Al-Attas, *Prolegomena to the Metaphysics of Islam* (Kuala Lumpur: ISTAC, 2001); Syed Muhammad Naquib Al-Attas, *The Mysticism of Hamzah Fansuri* (University of Malaya Press, 1970); Syed Muhammad Naquib Al-Attas, *Some Aspects of Sufism as Understood and Practised among the Malays* (Singapore: Malaysian Sociological Research Institute, 1963); Syed Muhammad Naquib Al-Attas, *A Commentary on the Hujjat Al-Siddiq of Nur Al-Din Al-Raniri* (Kuala Lumpur: Ministry of Culture, 1986).

[11] Hamka, *Tasauf: Perkembangan Dan Pemurniannya* (Seventh Edition) (Medan: Yayasan Nurul Islam, 1978), 234.

[12] Martin van Bruinessen, *Kitab Kuning: Pesantren Dan Tarekat* (trans. Farid Wajidi and Rika Iffati) (Yogyakarta: Gading Publishing, 2012); Martin van Bruinessen, "Controversies and Polemics Involving the Sufi Orders in Twentieth-Century Indonesia," in *Measuring the Effect of Iranian Mysticism on Southeast Asia*, ed. Imtiyaz Yusuf (Bangkok: Cultural Centre, 2004), 129–162.

in strict terms, the *tariqah sufiyah mu'tabarah* (legitimate Sufi orders) as against those that promote *ajaran sesat* (deviant teachings).[13]

Imagining these three approaches in dialogue reveals their convergences and divergences. The devout advocate might find the reflexive admirer and critical appraiser too detached and judgemental of spiritual and other epiphenomenal experiences. The reflexive admirer and critical appraiser might fault the devout advocate for being overly engrossed in all things noble and honourable in the lives of Sufi *shaykhs* (masters), blinding them of moral failures. The critical appraiser is sceptical and sometimes cynical of the conclusions made by the other two standpoints, questioning their lack of objectivity. Although divergent in their scope and visions, these ways of approaching Sufism share some affinities. They are on the same page in recognizing Sufis in Southeast Asia as virtuosos in synthesizing beliefs, cultures, and creeds. They study Sufism in its textual as well as historical contexts and the interplay between both in the habituation of Islam in Southeast Asia. Together, these bodies of works throw light on Sufi networks in the region and in the wider *ummah* (global Muslim community). They direct our eyes to the sacred connections and the intellectual transformations that Sufis have inspired, accelerated, and sustained Sufism in Southeast Asia for close to a millennium.[14]

I situate myself within the *dihliz* of three preceding positions. Drawing from the works of the Sufi polymath, Abu Hamid Al-Ghazali (1058–1111), Ebrahim Moosa defines *dihliz* as "espousing a subjectivity that celebrates a threshold position, shares certain features with life in exile. It is about being out of place, being neither insider nor outsider, but rather occupying a permanent in between-ness."[15] By adopting this *dihliz* position, I transcend the ideological and analytical enclosures found in the works of the devout advocate, the reflexive admirer, and the critical appraiser. I propose here a whole new methodology, a fresh approach. I call it "contemplative histories" to explain undying Sufi dialogical tradition in Southeast Asia. As is well-known, contemplation or *tafakkur* is a central term in Islamic psycho-spiritual heritage.[16] In Arabic as it

---

[13] Kementerian Agama, *Mu'tabara Tariqas (Notable Sufi Orders) in Indonesian Islam* (Jakarta: Badan Litbang Agama dan Diklat Keagamaan, 2011).

[14] Azyumardi Azra, *The Origins of Islamic Reformism in Southeast Asia* (Honolulu: University of Hawai'i Press, 2004).

[15] Ebrahim Moosa, *Ghazālī and the Poetics of Imagination* (Chapel Hill: University of North Carolina Press, 2005), 275.

[16] Malik Badri, *Contemplation: An Islamic Psychospiritual Study* (Herndon: International Institute of Islamic Thought, 2018).

Introduction: A Dialogical Tradition **7**

is in the Malay-Indonesian languages, the concept of tafakkur signifies reflection, pondering, or to be in deep thought. Sufis of all places and ages gave primacy to this practice. To Al-Ghazali, contemplation fosters greater awareness and reflection on divine creations, revealing the principles governing life.[17]

Building on Al-Ghazali's ideas, contemplative histories offer a critical approach that transcends mere chronological account of events and epochs in Muslim pasts. Such diachronic accounts of Sufism in Southeast Asia are numerous, perhaps too many.[18] Contemplative histories transcend the event-centred approach without downplaying the importance of crucial episodes in Sufi pasts. The methodology of contemplative histories acknowledges the plurality of the past and of human experiences. It rests on three key modalities: empathy towards the spiritual and the suprarational; recognition of patterns of Sufi experiences across different times and spaces; and comprehension of the interchange between pious endeavours and secular dynamics.

Much of what Sufis articulate, think, and act may seem at odds to the modern mind. Animated by the Enlightenment conceptualization of reason and rationality, decades of orientalist scholarship on the subject tended to ascribe the terms "superstitious," "irrational," "emotional," and "eccentric" upon Sufis.[19] These appellations were also adopted by reformist and modernist Muslims.[20] The rise of "methodological atheism" in the humanities and social sciences has ruled out "metahuman explanations" or "supernatural reasonings." Ideologized by such approach, many scholars dismiss spiritual and mystical experiences as sheer projections of worldly or socially constructed realities.[21] Contemplative histories mandate a balanced consideration of what may appear "absurd" and "outlandish" to better understand why Sufis believe and

---

[17] Megawati Morris, *Al-Ghazzali's Influence on Malay Thinkers: A Study of Shaykh 'Abd-Samad Al-Palimbangi* (Islamic and Strategic Studies Institute Berhad, 2016); Abu Hamid Al-Ghazali, *The Book of Contemplation: Book 39 of the Ihya' 'Ulum al-Din* (Louisville: Fons Vitae, 2021).

[18] Among the most notable and oft-cited is Michael F. Laffan, *The Makings of Indonesian Islam: Orientalism and the Narration of a Sufi Past* (Princeton University Press, 2011).

[19] Jennifer W. Nourse, "The Meaning of Dukun and Allure of Sufi Healers: How Persian Cosmopolitans Transformed Malay–Indonesian History," *Journal of Southeast Asian Studies* 44, no. 3 (2013): 400–422; Martin van Bruinessen, "Sufism, 'Popular' Islam and the Encounter with Modernity," in *Islam and Modernity: Key Issues and Debates*, eds. Muhammad Khalid Masud, Armando Salvatore and Martin van Bruinessen (Edinburgh: Edinburgh University Press, 2009), 125–127.

[20] Mark Sedgwick, *Western Sufism: From the Abbasids to the New Age* (New York: Oxford University Press, 2017), 152.

[21] Douglas V. Porpora, "Methodological Atheism, Methodological Agnosticism and Religious Experience," *Journal for the Theory of Social Behaviour* 36, no. 1 (2006): 57–75.

act in certain ways. Myths, legends, and seemingly illogical pronouncements and actions of Sufis contained rationales of their own, even if they may come into conflict with our concerns with historical accuracy and scientific validity. Understanding these beliefs and practices requires looking at them from within, through the internal logic that Sufis use to make sense of the world.

This does not imply that an analyst and observer can completely transcend their biases towards spiritual experiences and expressions. Religious, secular, ethnic, class, gender, or cultural prejudices can impede objective analysis. What is needed is empathy towards the spiritual and suprarational claims of Sufis. Borrowing from the American psychologist Carl Rogers, we must see Sufism "as if it were your own, but without ever losing the 'as if' quality.... To sense the client's anger, fear, or confusion as it were your own, yet without your own anger, fear, or confusion getting bound up in it, is the condition we are endeavoring to describe."[22] In being empathetic, we must assign equal importance to what is considered as mythological with the scientific and empirical, showing the connections and congruency between the two. For example, rather than dismissing *ruqyah* – a psycho-spiritual healing and spirit exorcism technique frequently employed by the Sufis – as mere magic and shamanic ritual in contradistinction with modern medicine, we might perhaps find it more useful to view these curative strategies in their own terms, through their unique reasoning as one of the means to resolve illnesses linked to the soul, which is often overlooked by mainstream medical practitioners.

By unearthing Sufi assumptions about human nature and the relationships between humans, the environment, and unseen beings, we can appreciate why these healing strategies made sense to the communities and why some challenges in life were resolved through scientific and others through supra-scientific means.[23] Katherine Ewing, in her study of dreams and visions within Sufi communities in Pakistan, underscores this point: "Instead of bracketing these sources of significance and hence, the subjects of our research, we should take them seriously and allow them to play a role in shaping what are ultimately realities we share as participants in a global human community."[24]

---

[22] Carl Rogers, *On Becoming a Person: A Therapist's View of Psychotherapy* (Boston: Houghton Mifflin, 1995), 284.

[23] Mohd Faizal Harun, *Tasawuf Dan Tarekat Sejarah Perkembangan Dan Alirannya Di Malaysia* (Kedah: UUM Press, 2017), 317.

[24] Katherine P. Ewing, "Dreams from a Saint: Anthropological Atheism and the Temptation to Believe," *American Anthropologist* 96, no. 3 (1994): 579.

Introduction: A Dialogical Tradition **9**

The second element of contemplative histories sensitizes us to various patterns of Sufi thoughts, actions, and legacies. John Gaddis contends that the purpose of historical writing is to identify:

> patterns that extend across time. These are not laws, like gravity or entropy; they are not even theories, like relativity or natural selection. They are simply phenomena that recur with sufficient regularity to make themselves apparent to us. Without such patterns, we'd have no basis for generalizing about human experience... surprising patterns of regularity can exist within what appear to be chaotic systems.[25]

In exploring Sufism in Southeast Asia, the challenge lies in detecting recurring thoughts and behaviours from an abundance of historical data, across various times and places. Consider, as an illustration, Sufi resistance to colonial rule. Yusuf Al-Makassari's jihad was not an isolated incident but replicated in different forms with similar patterns. Interesting parallels and lessons can be drawn from these separate events, be it in terms of motivations for resistance, the mobilizing ideologies, and unifying idioms, as well as the structures of command and control. Viewed in this sense, Sufi resistance should not be studied only as unique events with their own contextual peculiarities. Rather, they form an ensemble of confrontations against foreign rule, reappearing in different situations throughout Southeast Asia, but sharing many common attributes.[26] In bringing to light these patterns, we must also pay close attention to certain internal variations. The forest is just as important as the trees. The thrust of contemplative histories is to make the forest more apparent, more vivid, and to tease out trends from diverse cases. In identifying these patterns within Sufism in Southeast Asia, we become more observant of certain tendencies that may have been overlooked. Many Sufis, for example, did not belong or at least were not known to be a formal member of any tariqah. But they equally affiliated themselves to the Sufi tradition. This individualized or non-institutionalized Sufism had existed for generations in Southeast Asia and, yet, has rarely been studied by scholars in the field as enduring patterns of Sufi praxis.

Further, contemplative histories unveil the interchange between pious endeavours and secular dynamics. It problematizes the casting

---

[25] John Lewis Gaddis, *The Landscape of History* (New York: Oxford University Press, 2002), 6 and 84.
[26] Sartono Kartodirdjo, *Protest Movements in Rural Java: A Study of Agrarian Unrest in the Nineteenth and Early Twentieth Centuries* (Singapore: Oxford University Press, 1973), 3.

of Sufis as fervent worshippers such that they were least interested in worldly quests, material gains, and power politics. The realities of Sufi lives were more complex. While some embrace austerity and renounced the profane world, there were many Sufis who interfaced pious aspirations with secular enterprises. This included callous competition to augment followership, siding with the despotic elites regardless of faiths, and repressing fellow Sufis to gain paramountcy over privileges and resources.[27] Faithfulness to the divine was fused with earthly pursuits. Many Sufis deemed indulging in secular affairs as equally important in ensuring that Islam and their personal interests could be preserved. Talal Asad is instructive here: "the 'religious' and the 'secular' are not essentially fixed categories."[28] They flow into each other and structure one another. Sufis in Southeast Asia attempted to strike a balance between the two, hoping to get the best of both. They, like other human beings, struggled to reach this balance. Many became more worldly than they would readily admit, and others retreated into asceticism and anonymity.

Using contemplative histories as my framework, I argue that Sufis have maintained a presence in Southeast Asia because of their capacity for creative and spirited dialogues with themselves and their surroundings. To put it more sharply and succinctly, Sufism in Southeast Asia is a dialogical tradition. In developing this argument, I am indebted to the works of two key thinkers whose understanding of the two concepts of "dialogical" on the one hand, and "tradition" on the other, can aid in our understanding of Sufism in Southeast Asia. I use the term "dialogical" used by the German philosopher, Hans-Georg Gadamer. To Gadamer, human beings are dialogical creatures, imbued with a unique horizon that enables us to view the world from a particular viewpoint. This horizon is not purely abstract or philosophical. It shapes human interactions, their mode of being, and their conduct in society. We need dialogues with others to reach wider understandings of what Gadamer calls the "fusion of horizons." The fusion of horizons emerging from dialogical processes enhances thought and experience. As he puts it:

> If anything does characterize human thought, it is this infinite dialogue with ourselves which never leads anywhere definitively and which differentiates us from that ideal of an infinite spirit for

---

[27] See for example: Ach. Fatchan and Basrowi, *Pembelotan Kaum Pesantren Dan Petani Di Jawa* (Surabaya: Yayasan Kampusina, 2004).
[28] Talal Asad, *Formations of the Secular: Christianity, Islam, Modernity* (Stanford University Press, 2003), 25.

which all that exists and all truth lies open in a single moment's vision. It is in this experience of language – in our growing up in the midst of this interior conversation with ourselves, which is always simultaneously the anticipation of conversation with others and the introduction of others into the conversation with ourselves – that the world begins to open up and achieve order in all the domains of experience.[29]

Dialogue, to Gadamer, enriches tradition and "to be situated within a tradition does not limit the freedom of knowledge but makes it possible."[30] Here, I find it useful to bridge and expand Gadamer's conceptualization with Talal Asad's idea of tradition. For Asad, tradition consists of two components: the discursive and the embodied. Both components influence one another. The discursive aspect is "a process in which one learns/ relearns 'how to do things with words,' sometimes reflexively and sometimes unthinkingly, and learns/relearns how to comport one's body and how to feel in particular contexts." The embodied aspect, in turn, "help in the acquisition of aptitudes, sensibilities, and propensities through repetition until such times as language guiding practice becomes redundant. Through such practices one can change oneself – one's physical being, one's emotions, one's language, one's predispositions, as well as one's environment."[31]

The Sufis manifest Gadamer's idea of dialogue and Asad's concept of tradition, and much more. Gadamer brackets dialogue within the dialectics of querying and answering. A close study of Sufis in Southeast Asia reveals that they barely regarded discourses as *the* most important aspect of dialogue. Dialogue is not limited to the realms of speech, writing, or rhetorical arguments. Dialogue encompasses all realms of human life including prayer and meditation, discursive engagements, and memory-making. Dialogue includes reformation of societies, enactment of laws, entanglements with politics, among many others. To be dialogical is to converse with oneself and with others in thought and action, in the realm of the material as well as the metaphysical, in the boulevards of culture, the halls of power, and through multiple networks, local, regional, and global. Dialogue from the point of view of Sufis in Southeast Asia

---

[29] Gadamer Hans-Georg, *Truth and Method* (trans. Joel Weinsheimer and Donald G. Marshall) (London: Continuum, 2006), 547.

[30] ibid., 354.

[31] Talal Asad, "Thinking About Tradition, Religion, and Politics in Egypt Today," *Critical Inquiry* 42, no. 1 (2015): 166–214.

includes connecting with communities and the natural environment around them. Dialogue necessitates percolating into the hearts of places and populations. Sufis in Southeast Asia therefore personify the discursive and embodied aspects of tradition, as Asad adroitly delineates it.

It follows then that, as a dialogical tradition in Southeast Asia, Sufis have defined Sufism as an authoritative branch of Islam that derives its primary source of inspiration from the Qur'an, *sunnah* (words and acts of Prophet Muhammad), and the *turath* (heritage of Muslim thought). Sufis in Southeast Asia have diverse interpretations. This is perhaps not a place to review all interpretations. Many Sufis I have interacted with remarked that any attempts at providing a fixed definition of the things they solemnly do, their structures of thought, and their methods of instruction melt into thin air as something artificial and meaningless. Sufism is to be tasted (*dhawq* or *rasa* in Malay), not just be talked about. Sufism is Islam. Sufism is in line with the Shari'a. There can be no Sufism outside these two imperatives. Most Sufis shy away from being called "Sufi" because the term is a privilege reserved for those who have reached the highest level of spirituality. Alexander Knysh's observation is useful in this regard. There is an absence of a "uniformly accepted, transregional metanarrative about Sufism and Sufis in the premodern and modern Muslim world. There were, of course, numerous textbooks of Sufism or even dynastic histories composed from a Sufi perspective, but they were socially, linguistically, and culturally specific to the regions where they originated and, to boot, hardly representative of the internally diverse Sufi movement in Islam as a whole."[32]

Be that as it may, Sufis in Southeast Asia have explained and exemplified their dialogical tradition through key terms explicated and epitomized by scholars whose works they regard as sages. Among them was Al-Qushayri (986–1072) who explained: "The people of this community (Sufis) use these terms among themselves with the goal of unveiling their meaning to one another, achieving concision and concealing them from those who disagree with their method, so that the meaning of their words would be hidden from outsiders."[33] Yet, these terms are seldom unknown to the masses. Communicated and textualized by classical Sufi masters and scholars, Sufis in Southeast Asia culled from such works to render tasawwuf digestible and legible to the common people.

---

[32] Alexander Knysh, *Sufism: A New History of Islamic Mysticism* (New Jersey: Princeton University Press, 2017), 3.

[33] Abu'l Qasim al-Qushayri, *Al-Qushayri's Epistle on Sufism* (trans. Alexander D. Knysh) (Reading: Garnet Publishing Limited, 2007), 75.

Introduction: A Dialogical Tradition **13**

They often used Sufi terms in their Arabic original and sometimes in Persian but explained them in languages and meanings understandable to Southeast Asian audiences.[34]

For Sufis in Southeast Asia, Sufism rests on three foundations – the transcendental, the transmittal, and the transformational – which they explicated using specific vocabularies. The transcendental goal of Sufis is to attain *ma'rifah* (interior knowledge) of Allah's wisdom and *tawheed* (oneness of God). This can be achieved by traversing the *suluk* (journey) that lays bare the exoteric meanings of the shari'a and *haqiqah* (mystical truths). Syamsuddin Al-Sumatra'i (d. 1630) analogizes in the following way: "What is called shari'a is the skin, what is called tariqah is what it contains [that is the muscles], what is called haqiqah are the sinews, what is called ma'rifah are the bones."[35] The journey is ridden with obstacles, stemming primarily from the temptations of the *nafs* (carnal self) and corruption of the *qalb* (heart), *aql* (intellect), and the *ruh* (soul). There is no easy escape from the allures of base desires. Muhammad Nawawi Al-Jawi (1813–1897),[36] whose works are still studied in many seminaries across Southeast Asia, describes carnal self "as the source of all sins. The carnal self is part of the soul that steers bodily desires and that prompts the self towards various pleasures. And the carnal self is the mainspring of evil and debased behaviour."[37] All aspiring Sufis must therefore be guided by those who are acquainted with perils along the journey to the afterlife.

Therein lies the transmittal aspect of Sufism. "Sufi writings," Seyyed Hossein Nasr asserts, "are at once the 'horizontal' continuation of a transmitted knowledge that has passed from one generation to another going back to the origin of Islam and a 'vertical', fresh vision of the Truth, which stands at the same time at the origin and beginning of

---

[34] Among these scholars are Junayd Al-Baghdadi (830–910), Abu Hamid Al-Ghazali (1056–1111), Ibn 'Ata Allah Al-Iskandari (1260–1306), Muhyiddin Ibn 'Arabi (1165–1240), Abdul Karim Al-Jili (1366–1408 or 1417), and Abdallah Alawi al-Haddad (1634–1720). The Andalusian Sufi Ibn 'Arabi, occupies a highly contentious place in Southeast Asian Sufism. His concept of *wahdatul wujud* (Oneness of Being) have been used and contested by many Sufi scholars, some have approved only selected aspects of Ibn 'Arabi's ideas that were in line with the shari'a. See: Azra, *The Origins of Islamic Reformism in Southeast Asia,* 50; Syed Muhammad Naquib Al-Attas, *Raniri and the Wujudiyyah of 17th Century Acheh* (Singapore: Malaysian Branch of the Royal Asiatic Society, 1966).

[35] C.A.O. van Nieuwenhuijze, *Samsu'l-Din van Pasai: Bijdrage Tot de Kennis Der Sumatraansche Mystiek* (Leiden: Brill, 1945), 138.

[36] Or more commonly remembered as "Shaykh Nawawi Al-Bantani."

[37] Syaikh Muhammad Nawawi ibnu Umar Al-Jawi, *Nashaihul 'Ibad* (trans. Abu Mujaddidul Islam Mafa) (Surabaya: Gitamedia Press, 2008), 102.

the revelation and at the Centre of our being here and now."[38] For Sufis in Southeast Asia, *ilm al-yaqin* (the knowledge of certainty) and *kashf* (divine disclosure) can be reaped not only through personal rumination but also through transmission from *murshids* (spiritual guides) who command almost absolute authority over the *murids* (novices). In Southeast Asia, murshids are also dubbed as *shaykhs* (masters), tok guru or tuan guru, or habaibs. They are experts of various Islamic sciences. They trace their *silsilah* (lineage) to a long list of venerated scholars and saints back to the Prophet Muhammad. Upon obtaining the *bay'ah* (oath of allegiance) from seekers and accepting them as murids, the murshids and murids form part of a tariqah. Among the tariqahs with substantial following in Southeast Asia were Ahmadiyyah-Idrisiyyah, Qadiriyyah, Sammaniyyah, Shattariyyah, Naqshbandiyyah, Rifa'iyyah, Khalwatiyyah, Rashidiyyah, Shadhiliyyah, Chistiyyah, and 'Alawiyyah. Some Southeast Asian Sufi shaykhs founded a few orders or hybrid orders, among the most popular was the Qadiriyyah wa-Naqshbandiyyah established by the Makkan-based, Ahmad Khatib (1803–1875) from Sambas in west Borneo in the later part of the nineteenth century.[39]

The murshids' task is to transmit their knowledge and experience of spiritual life. The dialogue between the master and novice takes place through indefatigable vigilance. Murshids are constantly watching over their students' *ahwal* (states), cautioning them against falling into *ghaflah* (heedlessness), and reorienting them away from digressions and distractions that disturb their *muraqabah* (meditation). Yet, as part of a dialogical tradition, Sufis in Southeast Asia are equally adept to the ways of the world. Nik Abdul Aziz Bin Haji Nik Mat (1931–2015) was the *Murshidul 'Am* (Spiritual Guide) of the Islamic Party of Malaysia (Parti Islam se-Malaysia, PAS) and the leader of the Ahmadiyyah tariqah in Kelantan. He served as the Chief Minister of Kelantan for a few terms between 1995 and 2008. Founder of a *pondok* (Islamic boarding school), he encouraged the *ulama* (Muslim scholars) to participate in democratic politics to actualize the dream of an Islamic state and to transmit the teachings of Islam to the rest of Malaysia.[40]

The third foundation of Sufism in Southeast Asia pertains to transformations achieved through a dialogical process. Sufis stress the importance of abiding wholeheartedly to the demands of the shari'a towards

---

[38] Seyyed Hossein Nasr, *Living Sufism* (London: Unwin Paperbacks, 1980).

[39] Wan Mohd Shaghir Abdullah, *Penyebaran Thariqat-Thariqat Shufiyah Mu'tabarah Di Dunia Melayu* (Khazanah Fathaniyah, 2000).

[40] Tuan Guru Nik Abdul Aziz, *Peranan Ulama Dalam Politik* (Kuala Lumpur: GG Edar, 1994).

Introduction: A Dialogical Tradition **15**

becoming *muhsinun* (those who achieve the highest ranks in deeds). This is but one small part of the transformational journey. Throughout, they commit themselves to a lifetime of tafakkur, *muhasabah* (self-examination), *dhikr* (remembering), beseeching for *barakah* (blessings) from God, *ziyarah* (visitations) to holy places, and displaying *akhlaqul karimah* (noble character). In their *mujahadah* (utmost striving) to be close to God and gain His mercy, every aspiring Sufi continuously engages in *ibadah* (acts of worship) and *tawbah* (repentance).[41] They are expected to embrace the virtues of *sabr* (patience), *mahabbah* (love), *wara'* (scrupulousness), *ihsan* (excellence), *ikhlas* (sincerity), *qana'ah* (contentment), *redha* (acceptance), *zuhud* (renunciation of the world), *taqwa* (piety), and *tawakkal* (trust in God). Abdullah Alwi Al-Haddad – the teacher of many Sufi masters in Southeast Asia – enjoins his readers that the transformational edge of Sufism can only be felt when a seeker ceases to cherish "hopes of prolonging life in this world, and through this, you will not neglect your devotions."[42]

Through *riyadhah* (spiritual practices) and *uzlah* (seclusion), Sufis rise through different *maqamat* (spiritual stations) and are progressively strengthened by *iman* (faith) and *nur* (divine light). The *hijab* (veil) concealing humankind to the secrets of divine attributes and majesty would sooner or later be unveiled to them, by God's Grace. They would be empowered to effect changes in their families and societies. A sixteenth-century Javanese Muslim text written and taught by one of the nine saints of Java, Sunan Bonan (or Bonang), exhorts all Sufis to commit fully to the transformational element of Sufism: "Enjoin all your children and grandchildren to follow what is laid down by my teachings, lest they should follow the teachings of heretics...Fear the Lord, do not swerve from the right path but strive after perfection!"[43] Sunan Bonan's exhortation underscores the dialogical dimensions of Sufism. Sufism "is not just about an individual's transrational experiences and transformation, but includes interpersonal interaction within a person's socio-cultural environment," as Arthur Buehler astutely observes.[44]

---

[41] For a detailed and pioneering study of the concept of tawbah in Sufi thought, see: Atif Khalil, *Repentance and the Return to God: Tawba in Early Sufism* (Albany: State University of New York Press, 2018).

[42] Abdullah Alwi Al-Haddad, *Nasihat Agama Dan Wasiat Iman* (trans. Anwar Rasyidi and Mama' Fatchullah) (Semarang: Thoha Putra, 2012), 685.

[43] Sunan Bonan, *The Admonitions of Seh Bari* (ed. and trans. G.W.J. Drewes) (Martinus NIjhoff: The Hague, 1969), 101.

[44] Arthur F. Buehler, *Recognizing Sufism* (London: I.B. Tauris, 2016).

Crucially, the transcendental, transmittal, and transformational foundations of Sufism in Southeast Asia are not to be seen as a linear process but interwoven in a dialogical and orbitual modus operandi. Sufis emulate the greatest Sufi – Prophet Muhammad – whom they view as the *Al-Insan Al-Kamil* (The Perfect Human Being). To walk in thoroughfares of Sufism is to place oneself in a perpetual state of becoming, an incessant zeal of *tazkiya* (purifying) the self. To be a Sufi is to be attuned to the metaphysical without disregarding material realities. To be a Sufi is to be a conscientious Muslim who neither abandon the world nor be engulfed by its seductions.

Many other concepts that Sufis used to express their worldview will be covered in the ensuing chapters. Suffice is it to say that any personalities or collectives not accepting the Qur'an, the Sunnah, the heritage of Muslim thought, and key terms Sufis used as edifices for their beliefs and practices will be regarded in this book as "Sufi-inflected mysticism." It is a type of Sufism that is usually less attentive to doctrines and texts: "the cosmology of the ordinary."[45] Adaptive to the everyday practices of the masses, followers and propagators of Sufi-inflected mysticism sometimes flaunted Islamic rules and norms. They embed Islam into the heart of locals using cultural tools and folk beliefs, blurring the lines between what is Islamic and supra-Islamic. Sufi-inflected mysticism is therefore distinct from the scholarly and textualist Sufism, as the latter emphasizes strict compliance to Islamic rules and norms. These expressions of Sufism have existed contemporaneously. They have interacted with one another and colluded in times of need. In many moments in Southeast Asian history, dialogues between these two strands of Sufism clashed, when scholars and reformers from mainstream Sufism hoped to set aright what they saw as heterodoxies emerging from the wells of Sufi metaphysics. Sufi shaykhs fought not only against anti-Sufis but also against fellow Sufis who they viewed as "extravagant" in their promotion of syncretic practices and speculative doctrines.[46] Still, they all contributed to the growth of Sufism as a dialogical tradition, often channelled through networks.

This concise book is divided into five chapters that enumerate a multitude of factors, forces, and figures that shaped Sufism in Southeast Asia as a dialogical tradition. I bring to light the emotional, monumental,

---

[45] A. Kevin Reinhart, *Lived Islam: Colloquial Religion in a Cosmopolitan Tradition* (New York: Cambridge University Press, 2020), 32.

[46] Azyumardi Azra, *Islam in the Indonesian World An Account of Institutional Formation* (Jakarta: MIzan Press, 2006), 135.

institutional, martial, and political undercurrents influencing the fates of the Sufis. I include in this bundle of contemplative histories my ethnographic observations and personal experiences living, listening, and learning about all things Sufi. As you travel with me on a journey to uncover why and how Sufism became an energetic force in Southeast Asian history, I hope you will see the inventiveness of the Sufis in purveying their ideas and routines. Be it as warriors or reformers, scholars or politicians, social movement leaders or celebrities, Sufis have spawned a multitude of ideological, cultural, political, social, and aesthetical changes in Southeast Asia. Coloured with contradictions, paradoxes, and a host of demanding circumstances, the paths and choices Sufis fostered have generated a self-renewing dialogical tradition. I invite you to join me in contemplating over these captivating pasts.

CHAPTER 1

Feelings

It is impossible to write the history of Islam without referencing how the faith appealed to the feelings of those it touched. The Qur'an's rhythmic prose enchanted the Arabs. The enigmatic arrangement and tempo of its verses melted the hearts of the staunchest enemies of Islam. Although the Makkans loathed Muhammad's message of unity, egalitarianism, and humanism, they were entranced by the beauty and simplicity of the revelations sent through him. The aesthetics of the Qur'an facilitated the rapid growth of Islam. Artistic and literary works produced centuries after Muhammad's demise communicated the Qur'an's exquisiteness, winning converts from all walks of life within the expanding Muslim civilization. Sufis were perhaps the most passionate recipients of the divine word. They wept at the recitals of the Qur'an. Some suffered from fits, and others died in states of extreme emotion.[1]

In Southeast Asia, Sufis used the term *rasa* to express their internalizations of Islam's sacred sources. Rasa, a Sanskrit term denoting taste or flavour, is an emotive and affective concept widely used by poets and mystics in India. The term permeated everyday conversations of societies within the Sanskrit cosmopolis, which spanned the waterways and land routes linking South Asia and Southeast Asia.[2] In Java, local mystics used rasa to describe earnest internalizations of divine revelations, pointing to a profound recognition of the inner

---

[1] Navid Kermani, *God Is Beautiful: The Aesthetic Experience of the Quran* (trans. Tony Crawford) (Cambridge: Polity, 2015), 293–345.

[2] Ricci Ronnit, *Islam Translated: Literature, Conversion, and the Arabic Cosmopolis of South and Southeast Asia* (Chicago: University of Chicago Press, 2011), 83–95.

Contemplating Sufism: Dialogue and Tradition Across Southeast Asia, First Edition. Khairudin Aljunied.
© 2025 John Wiley & Sons Ltd. Published 2025 by John Wiley & Sons Ltd.

Feelings 19

powers of charismatic persons and unravelling the "intuitive aspects of reality."[3] Sufis in other parts of Southeast Asia used rasa similar to the Arabic term *dhawq*, which literally means tasting. In Sufi cosmology, it refers to experiencing the divine fully via the senses, sensibilities, and the soul. Dhawq connotes an ardent awareness of all things transcendent and unseen.

Sufis in Southeast Asia stressed *merasakan* (to feel) divine presence in their writings. Such feelings were intended to go beyond the personal to the social, beyond the inner conscience to touching other hearts. Using rasa as their missionizing tool, Sufis in Southeast Asia generated a whole array of textual, visual, auditory, and performative arts. As Annemarie Schimmel observes: "Thanks to their experiences, new nuances of 'the language of love' developed in Arabic. Persian is unthinkable without the Sufi flavor, even in very worldly parts of its literature; Turkish, Urdu, Sindhi, Panjabi and Pashto were all used as literary media first by the Sufis in order to preach to the people in an idiom which they could easily understand."[4]

The same could be said about Malay-Indonesian, the languages of Southeast Asia, which are widely spiced with Sufi inflections. Southeast Asian Sufis were innovators and inventors of poetical works. Adept with Hindu-Buddhist metaphysics, acquainted with Indic epics, and skilled at appropriating Arab-Persian mystical prose, they introduced a new genre of poetics that was at once Islamic and yet indigenous in character and concerns. By introducing new vocabularies and reinterpreting existing ones into Malay-Indonesian poetical writings, Sufis ushered two major transformations.

First, they altered local concepts and made these concepts congruent with the spirit of Islam. Ancient and Hindu-Buddhist keywords were reinterpreted to reflect the Islamic *tasawwur* (worldview). Hence, *sembahyang* which literally means "to pray to the divine" was retained because it has the same connotation as *solat* in Arabic. Sufis, however, changed the interpretation of sembahyang from entreating many deities to praying to the One True God, Allah. *Dosa*, a Sanskrit word that could be translated as "something which causes harm," was reinterpreted to mean sins. As they did in South Asia, the Sufis in Southeast Asia

---

[3] Paul Stange, "The Logic of Rasa in Java," *Indonesia* 38 (1984): 4.
[4] Annemarie Schimmel, "Aspects of Mystical Thought in Islam," in *The Islamic Impact*, ed. Yvonne Y. Haddad, Byron Haines, and Ellison Findly (Syracuse: Syracuse University Press, 1984), 113–136.

vernacularized Islam to fit local needs, embedding primordial beliefs within the faith's universal message.[5]

Second, due to the imaginative stimulus afforded by the Sufis, Southeast Asian literary works once penned in Kawi, Sasak, Pallava, and Nagari scripts gradually transitioned to Jawi, a writing system based on Arabic script. A "Jawi ecumene" encompassing most of island Southeast Asia, and stretching north into Thailand and Cambodia, became dominant in the sixteenth and seventeenth centuries when the kingdoms of Malacca, Aceh, and Patani morphed into intellectual and literary powerhouses.[6] Sufism did not completely undo the creative legacies of non-Muslims in Southeast Asia. Rather, they made these artistic vestiges "deeper, more complex, and utterly fascinating."[7]

This chapter examines how Sufis utilized and fashioned emotions through oral, artistic, and literary works filled with significant meanings. Products of *perasaan* (feelings), these works shaped the feelings of the people as well. I call them "aesthetical mediums" inspired by Islam's sacred sources, with the Qur'an being the most dominant. Sufi dialogical tradition in Southeast Asia was reproduced by aesthetical mediums, used to engage with the masses and bring about a new brand of religious universalism. For clarity, I have divided the mediums into supplicative and figurative forms.

SUPPLICATIVE MEDIUMS

Sufis produced and used supplicative mediums to direct the masses' feelings towards divine grace and to epitomize the magnificent qualities of His Messenger, the Prophet Muhammad. I use the word "supplicative" because these mediums were not for vain entertainment but for generating the remembrance of all things sacred. Supplicative mediums were transcendental in character, linking human beings to God through pleasurable and memorable words, acts, and sounds. The most influential

---

[5] Tanvir Anjum, "Vernacularization of Islam and Sufism in South Asia: A Study of the Production of Sufi Literature in Local Languages," *Journal of the Research Society of Pakistan* 54, no. 1 (2017): 190–207.

[6] Michael Francis Laffan, *Islamic Nationhood and Colonial Indonesia: The Umma Below the Winds* (Routledge, 2003), 11–36; Leonard Y. Andaya, *Leaves of the Same Tree: Trade and Ethnicity in the Straits of Melaka* (Honolulu: University of Hawai'i Press, 2008), 125; Philipp Bruckmayr, *Cambodia's Muslims and the Malay World : Malay Language, Jawi Script, and Islamic Factionalism from the 19th Century to the Present* (Leiden: Brill, 2019), 21.

[7] David D. Harnish and Anne K. Rasmussen, "Introduction," in *Divine Inspirations: Music and Islam in Indonesia*, eds. David D. Harnish and Anne K. Rasmussen (New York: Oxford University Press, 2011), 18.

supplicative mediums popularized by the Sufis in Southeast Asia are called *burdah*, *mawlid*, and *ratib*, all originating from the Arab-Persian worlds and have been translated in many parts of Asia for centuries. These mediums included dhikr, *du'a* (invocations), and Prophetic panegyrics.

The importance of dhikr and du'a in Sufi praxis is well-documented. Numerous books and treatises discussing the types of dhikrs and du'a to be read by any aspiring Muslim have been published across Southeast Asia, some claiming to provide cures for a host of illnesses such as cancers.[8] Both dhikr and du'a were read in tandem either individually or in gatherings, with the use of different instruments performed in either monophonic or polyphonic rhythms.[9] Dhikr and du'a were also part of a long assemble of *wirid* (litanies) put together to beseech God's succour, praising the Prophet, his family, and companions, and petitioning for the well-being of oneself and the community of believers. For the Sufis, dhikr and du'a are inseparable as means to attain the highest forms of love and to enter into the abode of serenity.[10]

As a child, I used to attend congregations to read these texts, eagerly anticipating the feasts that followed these highly emotive sessions. Such gatherings served many purposes. They were occasions of blessed remembrance, communal solidarity, and generous hospitality as kindreds and the needy converge to enjoy sumptuous meals. The texts read by the congregants were arranged and read in ways to ease memorization. Kenneth Honerkamp captures the functions of these supplicative mediums well:

> Through these litanies and invocations, which were recited and memorized from childhood, even those who had neither the time nor the means to pursue a mystical path had the opportunity to reflect upon the essential teachings of Islam as they were filtered through the litanies, invocations, and devotional texts of the faith, and through the inherited wisdom and shared understanding of the community as a whole.[11]

Burdah, mawlid, and ratib have been read in one sitting and interlaced with three other supplicative mediums: *zikrzamman* (remembrance of

---

[8] H.M. Amin Syukur, *Zikir Menyembuhkan Kanker* (Jakarta: Emir, 2016).

[9] Patricia Matusky and Tan Sooi Beng, *The Music of Malaysia: The Classical, Folk and Syncretic Traditions* (London: Routledge, 2017), 237–250.

[10] Sri Mulyati, *Tasawuf Nusantara: Rangkaian Mutiara Sufi Terkemuka* (Jakarta: Kencana, 2017), 144–145.

[11] Kenneth Lee Honerkamp, "The Spirituality of Invocations and Litanies in Islam," in *The Wiley Blackwell Companion to Islamic Spirituality*, eds. Vincent J. Cornell and Bruce B. Lawrence (Chichester: Wiley-Blackwell, 2023), 71.

the time), *hadrah* (presence), and *qasidah rebana* (poetic tambourine songs).[12] In Kerala, South India, where many Muslim missionaries in Southeast Asia hailed from, burdah, mawlid, and ratib were recited to guard against and relieve oneself from evils and ailments caused by evil spirits, snake bites, and burns.[13] Similarly, Sufis in Southeast Asia incorporated beautiful sounds and rhythms appealing to local ears as they read these mediums. They termed it as *sama'* (listening), where music, chanting, singing, and melodious recitations were used to achieve spiritual states and devotional experiences.[14] Burdah, mawlid, and ratib filled the transcendental thirst of the Sufis and those who promoted and participated in the remembrance of God and his Prophet. These supplicative mediums cemented communitarianism among Southeast Asians while heightening feelings about Islam and revered Muslim figures.

The *Qasidah al-Burdah* (Poem of the Cloak) was one of the earliest supplicative mediums that captivated the rasa of Southeast Asians.[15] Written by Sharaf al-din al-Busiri (1211–1294), an adherent of the Shadhiliyyah Sufi order, it is part of longer poem entitled *Al-Kawakib al-Durriyya fi Madh Khair al-Bariyya* (The Shining Stars in Praise of the Best of Creation), consists of ten parts and over 160 lines. Al-Busiri enjoins his audience to suppress their egos and lusts in order to fully discern and internalize the merits, message, and mission of Prophet Muhammad. Known to Southeast Asians as *kasidah burdah*, this supplicative medium was possibly introduced by Sufis from Makkah, Egypt, and India who travelled into the region. Well into the nineteenth century, the burdah was recited during festive gatherings or during the pinnacle of every *majlis ta'lim* (or *majelis taklim,* Islamic forum). The Dutch orientalist, Snouck Hurgronje recorded the recital of the burdah in nineteenth-century Makkah in a congregation led by a famous Southeast Asian Sufi shaykh, Ahmad Khatib Sambas (1803–1875). An émigré to the holy land, Ahmad Khatib Sambas' followers comprised students and pilgrims from many parts of Southeast Asia who disseminated his teachings and institutionalized burdah recitals in their hometowns.[16]

---

[12] David D. Harnish, "Tensions between Adat (Custom) and Agama (Religion) in the Music of Lombok," in *Divine Inspirations: Music and Islam in Indonesia,* eds. David D. Harnish and Anne K. Rasmussen (New York: Oxford University Press, 2011), 93–96.

[13] V. Kunhali, *Sufism in Kerala* (Calicut: University of Calicut, 2004), 75.

[14] Kenneth S. Avery, *A Psychology of Early Sufi Sama: Listening and Altered States* (Abingdon: RoutledgeCurzon, 2002).

[15] Ph. S. van Ronkel, "Account of the Six Malay Manuscripts of the Cambridge University Library," *Bijdragen Tot de Taal-, Land- En Volkenkunde van Nederlandsch-Indië* 46, no. 1 (1996): 49–50.

[16] C. Snouck Hurgronje, *Mekka in the Latter Part of the 19th Century: Daily Life, Customs and Learning. The Moslims of the East-Indian Archipelago*, (trans. J. H. Monahan) (Leiden: Brill, 2007), 300.

The poem's allure and power lie in its autobiographical confessions, its clever play of words, and the cadence of its rhyming couplets. Read in Arabic and vernacular languages at mosques and homes, the burdah oscillates between the personal and the prophetic. The poet expresses his innermost weaknesses, portraying himself as a wretched and insignificant soul when compared with the impeccable figure of Muhammad. The contrast drawn between the lowly self and the notable ideal, between self-effacement and eulogizing a perfect figure, between regretting one's heedlessness and beseeching divine guidance, struck a high chord among Southeast Asians who had for centuries been attuned to poetic religious literature. The burdah echoed aspects of Southeast Asian Hindu-Buddhist inclinations towards humility and fine manners and their constant admiration of saintly and deity-like figures.[17] The burdah's emphasis on love and the beloved, lynchpins of rasa, made the poem even more mesmerizing for its listeners.[18] A close reading of burdah underlines this point:

> A token of love in hope of getting a glimpse of you,
> Then spending my days and nights with you for eternity;
> A word of praise for the Praised, O you,
> the Praiseworthy One,
>
> ...
>
> Yes, sights of my love have come at night and kept me awake;
> How love repels all delights and comforts with agony!
>
> ...
>
> He is the loved one whose intercession we're hopeful of,
> At every horror to hit—yes, every calamity.
>
> ...
>
> He is the one with perfected essence and outward form
> Picked as the love of the Maker of all humanity.
>
> ...
>
> O my beloved, I beg of you in life and in death,
> To wrap your Burdah of special care and love over me.[19]

---

[17] G. W. J. Drewes, *Een 16de Eeuwse Maleise Vertaling van de Burda van Al-Būsiri: Arabisch Lofdicht Op Mohammad* (Nijhoff:'s-Gravenhage, 1955), 27–30.

[18] Wazir Jahan Karim, "Prelude to Madness: The Language of Emotion in Courtship and Early Marriage," in *Emotions of Culture: A Malay Perspective, ed. Wazir Jahan Karim* (Singapore: Oxford University Press, 1990), 21–63.

[19] Sharaf al-din al-Busiri, *The Burdah: The Singable Translation of Busiri's Classic Poem in Praise of the Prophet* (trans. Mostafa Azzam) (Atlanta: Al-Madina Institute, 2016), 1, 4, 9, and 30.

Illuminated frontispiece of the manuscript of *Al-Kawakib al-durriyya* by Al-Busiri made for the Sultan Qayt Bay: https://en.wikipedia.org/wiki/Al-Burda#/media/File:Frontispiece_of_%22Al-Kawakib_al-duriyya%22_by_Al-Busiri_(CBL_Ar_4168,_f.2a).jpg

These emotive lines were amplified by music instruments. In West Kalimantan, for example, the burdah has been read in various local dialects and tunes to mark different occasions, accompanied by drums and tambourines. In recent times, electric guitars and other

Feelings

25

modern musical instruments have replaced percussions. The burdah took centerstage during weddings and childbirth. It has been read as a fulfilment of one's vow. For the Malays in West Kalimantan, burdah retains its place as a marker of their identity, memorized by young and old. Parents send their children to study with religious teachers to perfect their reading of the text while learning the rules of the Qur'an.[20] In Bali and the Celebes islands, the burdah has been sung with the use of *rebana* (frame drums). The Bugis community claimed to be the first to popularize the burdah in Southeast Asia, although such claims cannot be verified with written sources. Oral histories paint the burdah in glowing terms as one of the efficacious mediums used by Sufi saints to convert the Hindu-Buddhists to Islam. Burdah is an established and venerable tradition handed down *turun-temurun* (from one generation to another).[21]

The burdah has also been recited during Mawlidur Rasul (or simply *mawlid*), a day of observance for the birth of Prophet Muhammad on the twelfth of Rabiulawal in the Muslim calendar. The mawlid's origins could be traced to the Imami Shi'ite tradition and made a state-sponsored event by the Fatimid dynasty that ruled Egypt from 969 till 1171. Mawlids were celebrated annually with lavish ceremonies, public feasting, and recitals of the hagiographies of the prophet and Shi'ite imams. The Fatimids used these celebrations to underscore their hereditary status, linking back to the Prophet Muhammad. The institutionalization of the mawlid served a dual purpose: preserving the memories of the prophet and his progeny and legitimizing Shi'ite rule over the majority Sunni population.[22] Mawlids survived the restoration of Sunnism in Egypt. With support from succeeding caliphates and kingdoms, Sunni Sufi scholars removed Shi'ite elements in mawlids and disseminated the practice in other parts of the Muslim world. Numerous texts extolling the virtues of Prophet Muhammad were read during the mawlids in Southeast Asia. Among them, the ones composed by 'Abdurrahman ibn Ali Al-Dayba (1461–1537), the *Mawlid ad-Dayba'i*, and Ja'far bin Hassan al-Barzanji (1690–1766), *'Iqd al-Jawhar fi Mawlid al-Nabiyyil-Azhar* (The Jewelled Necklace of the Resplendent Prophet's Birth), were most popular.

---

[20] Yusriadi, *Identitas Orang Melayu Di Hulu Sungai Sambas* (Pontianak: IAIN Pontianak Press, 2019), 55–59.

[21] Mashino Ako, "Frame Drum Ensemble in Muslim Balinese Culture," in *Drums and Drum Ensembles Along the Great Silk Road*, eds. Xiao Mei and Gisa Jahnichen (Berlin: Logos Verlag, 2019), 119.

[22] Nico N. J. Kaptein, *Muhammad's Birthday Festival* (Leiden: Brill, 1993).

These mawlid texts have also been referred to as "Maulud Ad-Diba'i" or "Maulud Barzanji." In different places in Southeast Asia, mawlid was known as "Molud," "Mo'lot," "Perjanjen," "Berjanjen," "Berzanjen," "Marhabanan," or "Marhaban." In the Malay peninsula, where the supplicative medium remained iconic, we encounter terms such as "Sulong Maulud," "Padua (or Sengah) *Maulud*," "Peruga (or Alany) *Maulud*," and "Bongsu *Maulud*," each describing the times of the day when these mawlids were organized.[23]

Sufis in Southeast Asia also used the mawlid text written by the Andalusian scholar, Syihab al-Din Ahmad bin Ali al-Bukhari. Entitled *Syaraf al-Anam* (The Glory of Humanity), it was the first Islamic book to be printed on lithographed paper at Surabaya in 1853. In Javanese dialect, it was called *Sarapulanam*, while in Acehnese, *Carapha anam*.[24] Southeast Asian Sufi masters in Makkah wrote commentaries on these texts to explain their inner meanings and maintain the authoritativeness of the mawlid and burdah in the hearts and minds of Muslims back home. They organized mass recitals in the houses of their closest murids, who would then bring back the same practices in their homelands. The mawlids and burdah travelled along the capillaries of Sufi diasporic and trade networks.[25] Texts and their recitals moved along with communities and commodities in the heart of Southeast Asia, aiding in the spread of rasa coloured by Islamic nuances.

The origins of mawlids in Southeast Asia are difficult to trace. The earliest recorded mention of this supplicative medium was in the early seventeenth century in Makassar, South Sulawesi, where the mawlid barzanji was referred to as "Barasanji" or "Maudu'."[26] In many Makassarese villages, Sufis from the Sammaniyyah, Naqshbandiyyah-Khalwatiyyah, and Bahr ul-Nur tariqahs, led by a Hadrami-Arab Sayyid Jalaluddin al-'Aidid and his descendants, led the recitation of mawlid texts. They popularized the mawlid barzanji through networks of students and families that grew slowly into remote villages in South Sulawesi.[27] These networks were not only communities of meaning that derived inspiration from the life stories of Muhammad but also formed and fortified local

---

[23] Abdul Samad Ahmad, *Kesenian Adat, Kepercayaan Dan Petua* (Melaka: Associated Educational Distributors, 1990), 58.

[24] C. Snouck Hurgronje, *The Achehnese Vols. I* (trans. A.W.S. O'Sullivan). (Leiden: Brill, 1906), 18–20.

[25] Hurgronje, *Mekka in the Latter Part of the 19th Century*, 291–295.

[26] Muhammad Adlin Sila, *Maudu': A Way of Union with God* (Acton: ANU Press, 2015).

[27] Thomas Gibson, *Islamic Narrative and Authority in Southeast Asia: From the 16th to the 21st Century* (Basingstoke: Palgrave Macmillan, 2007), 120–122, 151–152.

Muslim identities. As villages congregated regularly to show their love for the Prophet, they affirm their faithfulness to his teachings. Such networks also led to the construction of authoritative practices, influencing policies relating to everyday lives of societies. Miriam Cooke and Bruce Lawrence theorize such networks as having the potential of reinforcing "norms and orthodoxies even as they submit them to constant scrutiny and challenge... They both sustain and contest the systems of which they are a part."[28]

From the nineteenth century onwards, mawlids were institutionalized and normalized. The Acehnese declared it obligatory for all Muslims to celebrate mawlids on the month of Rabiulawal and the two months that followed. In the Philippines, on 14 February 1977, Article 169 of the "Code of Muslim Personal Laws of the Philippines" was passed to recognize Prophet Muhammad's birthday as one of the official holidays.[29] Outside these specific months, the mawlid was read on occasions of a child's birth, circumcision, or during weddings.[30]

Local animistic rituals and Hindu-Buddhist beliefs and practices were sometimes blended in mawlid recitals, making these texts creolized supplicative mediums readily accepted by Muslims and non-Muslims alike. At the same time, such melding of influences have been denounced by the ulama. In many parts of Indonesia, for example, the mawlid was recited at the tombs of Sufi saints, with men and women dancing to the beats of loud music and animal sacrifices made during these events.[31] In South Philippines, the Tausugs have an established tradition of arranging palm leaves on banana stalk pillars and placing these artistic objects around mosques to symbolize Prophet Muhammad. These objects, called *telian-telian,* have been the centre of attraction with different Muslim tribes reciting the mawlid according to their unique vocal traditions (*lugu* or *luguh*) and regional melodies.[32] Since the last four centuries, the royal courts of Yogyakarta celebrated the birth of the Prophet for an entire week. The main feature of the celebration is the "Garebeg Maulid."

---

[28] Miriam Cooke and Bruce B. Lawrence, "Introduction," in *Muslim Networks from Hajj to Hip Hop,* eds. Miriam Cooke and Bruce Lawrence (Chapel Hill: The University of North Carolina Press, 2005), 9 and 28.

[29] "Presidential Decree No. 1083" (1977), accessed March 25, 2023 https://pcw.gov.ph/assets/files/2020/03/PRESIDENTIAL-DECREE-No-1083.pdf.

[30] Hurgronje, *The Achehnese Vols. I* (trans. A.W.S. O'Sullivan), 18.

[31] Thomas Gibson, *Islamic Narrative and Authority in Southeast Asia: From the 16th to the 21st Century* (Basingstoke: Palgrave Macmillan, 2007), 151–152.

[32] Peter G. Gowing, *Muslim Filipinos: Heritage and Horizon* (Manila: New Day Publishers, 1979), 124; Elmer I. Nocheseda, "Palapas Vernacular: Towards An Appreciation of Palm Leaf Art in the Philippines," *Philippine Quarterly of Culture and Society* 32, no. 1 (2004): 10.

A *gunungan* (Javanese for "mountain") model made up of various local foods and fruits is built prior to the start of the ceremony. With sounds of the gamelan filling the air, Javanese rulers, their royal guards, and hundreds of followers carrying the gunungan marched towards the Great Mosque. Upon arrival, men, women, and children eagerly take parts of the gunungan, a ritual carried over from the pre-Islamic era. For many Javanese Muslims, the objects on the gunungan are blessed, providing protection from mishaps and seen as sources of prosperity.[33]

Indeed, mawlids in Southeast Asia were always a symphonic affair. Led by those with melodious voices, men, women, and children alternated readings of the text in vernacular and Arabic languages, creating a highly emotive mixture of staccato, legato, and vibrato sounds. Reading the mawlid was a form of art in itself, perfected through constant practice.[34] Some contents of the mawlid deserve close attention here. I highlight verses that strongly appealed to Southeast Asians' love for stories of the incredible and extraordinary, the miracles associated with the Prophet, and his conspicuous superiorities. These virtues, narrated in hyperbolic ways bordering between fact and fantasy, set the messenger apart from the rest of humankind.

> It was announced in the Heavens and the Earth that Sayyidah Aaminah was carrying the blessed Noor. Every ardent lover turned towards this scented breeze of the Most Beloved. After a long barren spell, the earth was clothed with a lush green carpet, fruits ripened, the trees bowed their heavy-laden loads so that fruits became easy pickings. Every animal from the Quraish tribe, spoke in pure Arabic of his arrival. The idols fell flat on their faces. The animals of prey from east to west exchanged this good news. The whole world drank pure wine from this cup of great joy. The jinns announced his coming, the soothsayers foretold, and the monks became afraid. Every learned scholar was eager to hear the news of his coming and became lost in astonishment by the display of his beauty.
>
> ...
>
> Upon the Blessed birth, miraculous and strange events appeared in order to announce His Prophethood and to notify the world

---

[33] Herman Beck, "Islamic Purity at Odds with Javanese Identity: The Muhammadiyah and the Celebration of the Garebeg Maulud Ritual in Yogyakarta," in *Studies in Ritual Behaviour*, ed. Jan Platvoet and Jan van der Toorn (Leiden: Brill, 1995), 261–284.

[34] Anna M. Gade, *Perfection Makes Practice: Learning, Emotion, and the Recited Quran in Indonesia* (Honolulu: University of Hawai'i Press, 2004), 11–12.

Feelings   **29**

that He is Allah's Chosen One. The sky was shielded; the evil and mischievous devils and jinn were driven away from it. The luminous stars struck every accursed one and then lowered themselves to the Beloved out of love. By their light, the valleys and hills of the Ḥaram (Makkah) were illuminated. Upon the Blessed Birth such a bright light appeared with Him, illuminating the Roman castles of Shaam, and these were seen by those who resided in the valleys of Makkah. The high and extremely strong Persian palace at Mada'in built by Nausherwan cracked and crumbled and fourteen of its high balconies fell. This event, which had such a devastating effect on the palace, had the same effect on his kingdom. Upon the appearance of the Blessed illuminating face, by the illuminating rays of this beautiful full moon, the fires worshipped by the Persian kingdoms extinguished.[35]

Massive in scale, no part of Southeast Asia was spared by the charms of the burdah and mawlid. These recitals had permeated every corner of the region by the mid-nineteenth century. However, the rise of modern reformists brought critiques and calls for purification. Influenced by the Salafiyyah movement figures like Muhammad Abduh (1849–1905) and Rashid Rida (1865–1935), the modern reformists (also known as the "Kaum Muda (Young Faction)" or "Golongan Sunnah (Sunnah Group)") in Southeast Asia argued that these practices deviated from true Islamic teachings. They viewed elements of the burdah and mawlid as innovations (bid'ah) that strayed from the Prophet's tradition.[36] Modern reformists' reproaches were a continuation of reservations expressed by medieval *fuqaha* (jurists). Both contested the contents and extravagant performances associated with many supplicative mediums. The fuqaha viewed burdah and mawlids as *bid'ah dalalah* (innovations that deviate from the truth). Although some took a softer position of categorizing supplicative mediums as *bid'ah hasanah* (good innovations), most fuqaha singled out the *Nur Muhammad* (Light of Muhammad) ideology found in most of these texts, which depicts the Prophet as the source

---

[35] Ja'far bin Hassan al-Barzanji, *The Barzanji Mawlid: The Jewelled Necklace of The Resplendent Prophet's Birth* (trans. Muhammad Shakeel Qaadari Ridawi) (London: Self-Publishing, 2018), 15 and 22.

[36] Most prominent among which were comprised of personalities such as Syed Sheikh Al-Hadi (1867–1934), Shaykh Tahir Jalaluddin (1869–1957), Shaykh Muhammad Djamil Djambek (1860–1947), Haji Abdul Karim Amrullah (1879–1945), Haji Abdullah Ahmad (1878–1933), Mohd Asri Zainul Abidin and Rozaimi Ramle. *Hukum Sambut Maulid Nabi - Dr Rozaimi / Dr Maza / Maulana Asri / Maulana Fakhrurrazi*, 2022, https://www.youtube.com/watch?v=1_KqyjI1RkI.

of all creation. To them, this ideology amounted to pantheism.[37] In Chapter 5, I will delve more deeply into the controversy over the concept of Nur Muhammad among Sufis in Southeast Asia.

The fuqaha and modern reformists highlighted other ills accompanying the mawlids and burdahs. The depraved atmosphere during these events was apparent to all. Men and women intermingled freely, opening doors to illicit relationships. The boundaries of Islamic morality and decency were usually breached. Wastage of food and lavish spending on processions and performances were common.[38] The modern reformists censured the practice of *qiyam* (standing) midway during the mawlid, a collective ritual that came with the belief that divine and prophetic *hadrah* (presence) could be achieved during these sessions. They opposed the incorporation of music as well as elements of pre-Islamic cultures.

Controversies over burdah and mawlids became so heated that Southeast Asians requested for fatwas from the ulama residing in Makkah. Sufi scholars such as Shaykh Nawawi Al-Bantani and Ahmad Dahlan regarded qiyam and the use of tambourines during mawlids as *mustahabb* (recommended). Ahmad Dahlan, however, forbade the use of phrases like "Oh Muhammad, Oh my beloved" when referring to the Prophet and railed against those who used mawlids for scandalous entertainment. At the same time, he highlighted the iniquities found in these gatherings, prominent among which was smoking hookahs.[39] The modern reformists went further. The Al-Imam periodical regarded mawlids as a deviation from the prophetic tradition. Minangkabau scholar Abdul Karim Amrullah and Ahmad Hassan (1887–1958) from the Persatuan Islam (PERSIS) rebuked the use of tambourines and the belief in *hadrat al-nabi* (Prophet's presence) during mawlids. They labelled Muslims who made such claims as *fasiq* (one who violates Islamic law).[40]

To the modern reformists, Sufi scholars who justified the celebration and reading of mawlid and burdah were methodologically unsound. Noble in intention and no doubt well-meaning, most mawlids have,

---

[37] Marion Holmes Katz, *The Birth of the Prophet Muhammad Devotional Piety in Sunni Islam* (Abingdon: Routledge, 2007), 169–205.

[38] Samuli Schielke, "Hegemonic Encounters: Criticism of Saints-Day Festivals and the Formation of Modern Islam in Late 19th and Early 20th-Century Egypt," *Die Welt Des Islams* 47, no. 3/4 (2007): 319–355.

[39] Nico N. J. Kaptein, "The Berdiri Mawlid Issue among Indonesian Muslims in the Period from circa 1875 to 1930," *Bijdragen Tot de Taal-, Land- En Volkenkunde* 149, no. 1 (1993): 124–153; Nico N. J. Kaptein, *The Muhimmat Al-Nafa'is: A Bilingual Meccan Fatwa Collection for Indonesian Muslims from the End of the Nineteenth Century* (Jakarta: Indonesian-Netherlands Cooperation in Islamic Studies (INIS), 1997), 156.

[40] Kaptein, *The Berdiri Mawlid Issue*, 133–149.

however, violated the foundational teachings of Islam and have strayed from the *usul al-fiqh* (principles of Islamic jurisprudence). Even the founder of the Sufi-based organization, the *Nahdlatul Ulama* (Revival of the Ulama), saw mawlids organized in the 1930s as veering into *ma'siyah* or *maksiat* (contravening Islamic law). For Muhammad Hasyim Asy'ari (1871–1947), if done in line with the shari'a, mawlids can deepen one's "love, respect, and exaltation towards the Prophet, while displaying gratitude."[41] The Muhammadiyah movement held the same position. The mawlid is *mubah* (permissible) if done for the sake of remembering the Prophet and instilling love for him.

This tolerant attitude towards mawlids saw a shift from the 1970s onwards. The onset of Salafism from Saudi Arabia into Southeast Asia brought about a new wave of denunciation towards mawlids. Mawlid texts, to the Salafis, contained exaggerated allegories and metaphors that barely represented the sober career and message of the Prophet. Ostentatious mawlids transgressed the proper manner to which Muslims should honour the messenger of Islam. The Salafis, in sum, imposed limits on the scope of enchanting rasa so often acculturated by the Sufis. Rasa must be tamed by what was historically factual and what is legally permissible in Islam.[42]

Anti-mawlid diatribes have hardly lessened its allure among Southeast Asians. In response to these criticisms and the pressures of modernization, Sufis have continuously repackaged, reinvented, and represented mawlids. Under colonial rule, *perarakan mawlid* (mawlid marches) were akin national-day parades. Contingents of men and women walked from street to street carrying flags and uniforms to symbolize specific families, organizations, and tariqahs. Attended by thousands, such events were also a public show of Muslim unity and hence have had the potential of becoming platforms for political and other forms of mobilization. In Singapore on 21 July 1964, for example, more than twenty thousand Muslims came out to join mawlid marches. The overall atmosphere then was burning with passions, in the midst of heated debates regarding communal politics.

---

[41] Hasyim Asy'ari, *Koreksi Peringatan Maulid Nabi Muhammad Saw (Tanbihat al Wajibat Li Man Yashna'al Maulid Bi al Munkarat* (trans. Rosidin) (Malang: Bayu Media Publishing, 2013), 5.
[42] Muhammad As'ad, "Salafi's Criticism on the Celebration of the Birthday of Prophet Muhammad," *Teosofi: Jurnal Tasawuf Dan Pemikiran Islam* 9, no. 2 (2019): 353–379; Fadlil Munawwar Mansur, "Interpretation and Overinterpretation of Ja'far Ibn Hasan Al-Barzanji's Mawlid Al-Barzanji," *Humaniora* 29, no. 3 (2017): 316–326.

Before the mawlid procession began, highly-emotive speeches were delivered by Muslim activists and grassroots leaders. As crowds chanting praises of the Prophet marched along the eastern parts of Singapore, Chinese hooligans attacked a mawlid contingent with bottles and rocks.[43] One of the bloodiest riots in the history of the island-state broke out, killing over two dozen people and injuring hundreds of others. Sufi pugilistic groups who dubbed themselves as *pendekar* (warriors) in defense of Muslim rights played major roles in the conflict. In contrast, a pacifist segment of the Sufi fraternity established goodwill committees in the aftermath of the mayhem.[44] Haji Mohammed bin Abdul Kadir recalled how the tragic episode had spurred thousands of youths to join a *silat* (Malay pugilistic art) group helmed by Ustaz Taha bin Suhaimi (1916–1999), a notable Hadrami-Arab Sufi teacher and murshid of the Ahmadiyyah tariqah in Singapore.[45] Since then, mawlid marches were banned in Singapore, though mass celebrations are still rampant in mosques and stadiums.

In other parts of Southeast Asia, the habaibs and Sufi performers have been active in magnifying the already massive mawlid celebrations. The advent of new communication technologies and the rise of social media have widened the reach of mawlids. Digital technologies provided broader publicity and deeper penetration into the furthest reaches of societies. The 1990s saw nasyid pop groups utilizing stanzas from mawlid and burdah texts into entrancing melodies.[46] The habaibs, whose religious capital have been eroded by the advent of Salafism and modern reformism, regained their hold on the Muslim masses by organizing "Mega Mawlids," "Mawlid Concerts," "Majelis Rasulullah (Prophet's Gathering)," "Malam Cinta Rasulullah (Loving the Prophet Night)" in stadiums and convention centres. Joined by hundreds of thousands of Muslims and non-Muslims, these events were streamed live on YouTube, Facebook, and other online platforms.

One of the most popular habaibs is Syekh Abdul Qadir As Saggaf. He has over a million subscribers in his YouTube channel, an ever-expanding community collectively known as "Syekher Mania" who are awestruck by his vocal powers. Almost single-handedly, Abdul Qadir

---

[43] Alberto Lau, *A Moment of Anguish: Singapore in Malaysia and the Politics of Disengagement* (Singapore: Eastern Universities Press, 2003), 137–138.

[44] "Goodwill Committees Established in All 51 Constituencies," *The Straits Times*, July 27, 1964.

[45] Mohamed B. Haji Abdul Kadir @ S. Mohdir Haji, *Visual Arts*, Reel/Disc 9 of 20, Accession Number 003431, 2009.

[46] Wendy Mee, "The Ebb and Flow of Popular Islamic Music Forms: Zikir Maulud Amongst Sambas Malays," *Asian Journal of Social Science* 40, no. 2 (2012): 203–233.

made the "Mawlid Simtud Duror," originally written by Habib Ali bin Abdurrahman al-Habshi (or Habib Ali Kwitang, 1870–1968), a meteoric sensation. The confluence of state-of-the-art technologies, exquisite vocals, aggressive marketing, and the coming together of Sufi masters from different parts of the world transformed mawlids in Southeast Asia into huge gatherings akin to music gigs. Well into the twenty-first century, what I would call "Superstar Mawlid" has thrived and transformed into a multi-million dollar pious industry.[47]

Malaysian Muslims participate in a Maulidur Rasul parade in Putrajaya, also known as Mawlid, the birthday of Prophet Muhammad, at Putrajaya Putra Mosque: https://en.wikipedia.org/wiki/Mawlid#/media/File:Maulidur_Rasul_(8413657269).jpg

The third supplicative medium to be considered here is ratibs. They are a collection of litanies and supplications recited in congregation in praise of Allah and His beloved prophets and saints. A few ratib texts have predominated Southeast Asian Islam: the Ratib Al-Attas, the Ratib Al-Haddad, and Ratib Samman. The first two originated from Hadrami-Arab authors namely Umar Ibn Abd Al-Rahman Al-Attas (1583–1660) and Abdullah bin Alawi Al-Haddad (1634–1720). They were said to

---

[47] "Mega Mawlid 2013: Habib Syech Assegaf," accessed June 2, 2013, https://www.youtube.com/watch?v=c_Bi3Sg4t6c. See also Habib Syech Assegaf YouTube channel: https://www.youtube.com/@habibsyechbinabdulqadirassegaf.

have spread Islam into Southeast Asia through the use of ratibs. The Ratib Samman traces its roots from the Sammaniyyah tariqah whose founder, Muhammad bin 'Abd al-Karim al-Madani al-Syafi'i (1719–1775, commonly known as-Sammani), was a Makkan-based Southeast Asian Sufi scholar. His most loyal student was Abdul Samad al-Palimbani (1704–1791). Al-Palembani introduced the Ratib Samman in Sumatra before it was adopted by Sufis in other adjacent islands.[48]

Ratib sessions have been conducted weekly in mosques and *suraus* (prayer halls). In Singapore, ratib sessions organized at the Ba'alawi Mosque every Thursday served multiple audiences and motives: for sincere devotees seeking salvation, for volunteers bent on maintaining the vivacity of the house of Allah, for business people hoping to expand their networks, and for those vying for positions in the government and other elite institutions.[49] Secular and sacred, personal and political motivations intersect during these sessions. Finding a balance between these agendas is perplexing. Many Sufis have instrumentalized gatherings such as ratibs, burdahs, and mawlids for pragmatic ends and as instruments of social control and political endorsement. This utilitarian use of supplicative mediums is especially palpable in the event when Sufis anticipate many incentives – material and symbolic – from patronage by those in power, as seen in North African Sufis. Isabelle Werenfels argues:

> On the one hand, the Sufi elites have interests linked to their spiritual activities and social agendas that entice them to engage in the political arena. On the other hand, state policies have created additional incentives or increased pressure to do so ... In short, even if a Sufi sheikh's main concern simply is to spread his spiritual message, he is forced to play by the rules of the game in order to achieve his goal. Playing the game implies entering into competition with other orders or religious actors over adepts and resources and seeking protection, patronage, and a position in clientelist structures and other arrangements with national power players.[50]

---

[48] Vladimir I. Braginsky, *The System of Classical Malay Literature* (Leiden: KITLV Press, 1993), 477–478.

[49] Mona Abaza, "A Mosque of Arab Origin in Singapore: History, Functions and Networks," *Archipel* 53 (1997): 61–83.

[50] Isabelle Werenfels, "Beyond Authoritarian Upgrading: The Re-Emergence of Sufi Orders in Maghrebi Politics," *The Journal of North African Studies* 19, no. 3 (2014): 283.

Playing the game also entails managing the laity in ways that would ensure obeisance and submission to the will of Sufi and elite partnerships. Ratib is a powerful tool to achieve that end. During my conversations with mosque congregants who have been following ratib sessions for decades, they shared that there are privileged circles of politicians, businessmen, academics, and known personalities within the congregation who have reserved places in prayer halls and special rooms after the end of ratib recitals. Ordinary Muslims have no access to these designated places unless they serve as volunteers for the shaykhs and elite classes, with little (if any) practical return for themselves. Most accept such arrangements based on respect, reverence, and redemption. "Privilege" during ratib sessions is therefore enforced and reproduced through spatial favouritism, hierarchical enclosures, and differential treatment.

Equally emotive in content, ratibs, however, differ from the mawlids in several ways. First, ratibs are usually read without musical stylistics. Sombre pitches increase in pace as the reading progresses. The eyes of the congregation are usually closed midway through such recitals, and their bodies swing from side to side. There is no standing ritual in ratibs, unlike in mawlids. Furthermore, ratibs are small-scale events organized weekly in mosques, homes, and other designated places. Ratibs can also be read individually and daily after the completion of obligatory prayers or in mornings and evenings. On rare occasions, ratibs have been read during mawlids.

The third difference lies in the function of ratibs. The litanies are perceived as antidotes for many tribulations in life. In the early twentieth century, Malays read the ratibs to ward off small pox and cholera pandemics. This specific ratib was known as "ratib tubin." It was read over a hundred times during night, reflecting the infusion of a pre-Islamic form of mysticism with the use of a Sufi supplicative medium. A resurgence of ratib occurred during the Covid-19 pandemic. In Brunei, ratibs were couched as *vaksin ketuhanan* (divine vaccines). Daily readings of these litanies were strongly encouraged for all Bruneian Muslim citizens.[51]

The Ratib Samman deserves some elaboration here because it differs from other ratibs. The ratib is read exclusively by followers of the tariqah. In Aceh, this ratib incorporated local *pantun* (poems), idioms,

---

[51] Raymond LeRoy Archer, "Muhammadan Mysticism in Sumatra," *Journal of the Malayan Branch of the Royal Asiatic Society* 15, no. 2 (128) (1937): 105–107; Awang Abdul Aziz bin Juned, *Raja Brunei: Pelopor Penggunaan Vaksin Ketuhanan* (Bandar Seri Begawan: Jabatan Mufti Kerajaan, 2021).

popular music, and dance performances.[52] Divided into ten to seventeen different dhikrs, Ratib Samman sessions stretched for a few hours. The first few dhikrs were read first in *ratib duduk* (sitting ratib) then *ratib berdiri* (standing ratib). The congregation would usually make a large circle and move their bodies and hands upwards and downwards. They stamped their feet while chanting in fast sequence, *Ahum!*, then *Ahil!* and ending with *'Am! Ah! 'Am! 'Ah!* Within a few minutes, the congregation would enter a trance, regaining consciousness only after being summoned by the Sufi master.[53]

The influence of Hindu worship is noticeable here and frowned upon by the religious authorities, as observed by Naquib Al-Attas in his study of the ratib in Johore in the 1960s.[54] Some decades earlier, Hadrami-Arab scholars in Indonesia, namely, Shaykh Salim bin Sumayr (d. 1852) and his student, Sayyid Uthman bin Yahya (1822–1914), launched stinging attacks against practitioners of this ratib. Sayyid Uthman's critique rested on theological, linguistical, moral, and sociological grounds. To him, Ratib Samman should be forbidden because the Arabic words were often pronounced wrongly during recitals, corrupting the meanings of holy words. Moreover, the screaming, dancing, and clapping associated with the ratib contradicted Islamic *adab* (manners) and were reminiscent of the practices of disbelievers during the time of the Prophet. The loud noises caused by this ratib disturbed public peace. Sayyid Uthman also faulted the Sammaniyyah tariqah for prioritizing their litanies over other obligatory rituals and basic duties towards their families.[55]

Sayyid Uthman's critique was one among many attempts by Sufi scholars to reform Sufi-inflected mystic practices. Regardless, the significance of the ratib in the lives of rural communities can hardly be ignored. One reason why it has been difficult for Sufi scholars and modern reformists to steer Muslims away from this ratib has to do with the transmittal aspect of such rituals. Ratib Samman was passed on through *ijazah* (licenses) by respected teachers to students. As will be seen in Chapter 3,

---

[52] Holly S. Smith, *Aceh: Art and Culture* (Kuala Lumpur: Oxford University Press, 1997), 57.

[53] Osman Bakar, "Sufism in the Malay-Indonesian World," in *Islamic Spirituality: Manifestations,* ed. Seyyed Hossein Nasr (New York: Crossroad, 1991), 29.

[54] Syed Muhammad Naquib Al-Attas, *Some Aspects of Sufism as Understood and Practised among the Malays* (Singapore: Malaysian Sociological Research Institute, 1963), 78–88.

[55] G. W. J. Drewes, "A Note on Muhammad Al-Samman, His Writings, and 19th Century Sammàniyya Practices, Chiefly in Batavia, According to Written Data.," *Archipel* 43 (1992): 73–87; Ahmad Purwadaksi, *Ratib Samman dan Hikayat Syekh Muhammad Samman: Suntingan Naskah dan Kajian Isi Teks* (Jakarta: Yayasan Naskah Nusantara, 2004), 318–319.

the teachers and students were bound together by organic texts that were read, learnt, and reflected upon by members of a close-knit fraternity. Teachers and students were bonded by the affective ties of solidarity and commitment to preserving traditions, among which was the ratib. Ijazah has been an effective method by which the ratib was handed down from person to person, making it a novelty sought after by Muslims in certain parts of Southeast Asia to this day.[56]

FIGURATIVE MEDIUMS

David Harnish and Anne Rasmussen distinguished between *"musik Islam* with its Arabic texts" and *"musik islami* (music featuring Islamic characteristics)," which "is a category that can include all kinds of folk and popular music in regional languages and in Indonesian, as well as newly composed music and popular music hybrids."[57] This is a useful typology for differentiating between supplicative and figurative mediums. While supplicative mediums included references to God and the Prophet in the Arabic original, figurative mediums are usually written and articulated in the vernacular, with some Arabic devotional terms peppered within them. As the term suggests, figurative mediums are Sufi works that employed analogies, metaphors, similes, symbols, and allegories with the overriding objective of capturing the rasa of the masses, to bring them closer to Islam and Sufism. These texts stand in stark contrast from the more formalistic and methodical *kitab* (learned treatises). Both supplicative and figurative mediums contain allegorical elements and use wordplay to arouse the rasa of their listeners. The difference lies in the fact that figurative mediums are not meant or used for devotional purposes. They were not ritualized and read at designated times and places.

Figurative mediums produced by Sufis legitimized the power and authority of elites in Southeast Asian Muslim societies. Legitimization was achieved through narratives and proses that exhibit the extraordinary traits of the nobility and their journeys towards salvation. Figurative mediums also highlight the softer and exoteric dimensions of Islam. Themes of beauty, the refinement of character, morality, spirituality, the

---

[56] Abdul Razak Abdul Rahman, *Tradisi Ratib Al-Haddad Di Alam Melayu: Manuskrip, Sanad, Kitab Dan Pembudayaannya* (Kuala Lumpur: Akademi Jawi Malaysia, 2021); Lois Lamya Al-Faruqi, "The Mawlid," *The World of Music* 28, no. 3 (1986): 85.

[57] Harnish and Rasmussen, "Introduction", 26–27.

environment, as well as the experience of traversing through the five worlds of consciousness – *Nasut* (the Human World), *Malakut* (the Invisible World), *Jabarut* (the Highest World), *Lahut* (the Divine World), and *Hahut* (the Ipseity World) – saturate figurative mediums. Through them, Sufis articulated their affection and awe towards everything around them. They expressed their hopes to meet God and achieve deliverance from their sins. Most figurative mediums registered the "principle of mutual resemblance, or mutual correspondence, of the macrocosm (universe) and the microcosm (humanity)."[58]

Sufis refashioned these texts with local poetics and inundated them with Arabic and Persian concepts to Islamize Southeast Asians, albeit subtly and in gentle ways. There are two dominant types of figurative mediums: *sha'irs* and *hikayats*. The nine saints of Java, according to oral histories, were most active in using such mediums to purvey Islamic beliefs. They capitalized on the local penchant towards romance and miraculous tales to relate stories of legendary Muslims and Sufi figures. Sha'irs and hikayats have been included in *wayang kulit* (shadow puppet play). In East Java, festivals have been held to memorialize the astuteness of these Sufis in spreading Islam through such figurative mediums.[59]

The sha'ir (or sya'ir, derived from the Arabic shi'r) is a narrative poem. Its importance in Islam is evidenced in a *surah* (chapter) in the Qur'an, *Ash-Shu'ara* (The Poets). The prominence of sha'irs and poets in pre-Islamic societies, their persuasiveness and misdemeanors, are discussed in this surah. Sufis have mined these verses to develop beautiful poetry. The term *shu'ara* (poets) has been used as honorifics for their best prose writers. The Timurid Sufi, Nuruddin 'Abdul Rahman Jami or simply Jami (1414–1492), was described by Sufis as *Khatam al-Shu'ara* (The Seal of the Poets). During the zenith of the Mughal empire, a special graveyard was reserved for Sufis and other notable poets christened as *Mazar-i Shu'ara* (Cemetery for Poets).[60] Sha'ir shares common features with Malay pantun. Both are monorhyme quatrains offering sagely advice or recounting stories of ethical value. Many features of sha'ir are shared by other poetic compositions such as *gurindam* (rhyming couplets with free meter), *seloka* (poetry containing humour), *nazam* (thematic poem), and *teromba* (poem that contains teachings of Malay customs

---

[58] Braginsky, *The System of Classical Malay Literature*, 274.

[59] Ismatu Ropi, "Wali Songo Festival: Tracking Islamic Heritage and Building Islamic Brotherhood," *Studia Islamika: Indonesian Journal for Islamic Studies* 6, no. 3 (1999): 197–202.

[60] Sunil Sharma, *Mughal Arcadia: Persian Literature in an Indian Court* (Boston: Harvard University Press, 2017), 126.

Feelings **39**

and traditions). They were written in *untai/bait/rangkap* (stanzas) like songs. Each line of the sha'ir contains nine to thirteen syllables, and the length can be as short as five to hundreds of lines. Sufi authors would usually graft Qur'anic imageries into their sha'irs.

Scholars are divided over the evolution of the sha'ir in Southeast Asia. This is no place to discuss the history of this genre that originated from Arab-Persian lands. What is most important for our purposes is to be acquainted with the fact that the sha'ir was first introduced by the Sufis in Aceh. As one of the earliest kingdoms to accept Islam as a state religion, Aceh became the nucleus for the production of sha'irs and other figurative mediums. From the fifteenth century onwards, the kingdom developed into a centre of Sufi thought and literature. Sufism, according to Leonard Andaya, provided the inspiration for much of the religious literature written and read by Aceh's intellectual elite. The rulers' principal Islamic advisors – known as the *Shaykh al-Islam* – were mostly Sufi scholars who determined the theological direction of the country.[61]

Sha'irs were used by the Sufis to steer the rasa of Southeast Asians towards spiritual maturity and enlightenment. The most famous of them was the sixteenth-century Acehnese litterateur, Hamzah Fansuri (d. 1590). A pioneer and an avant-gardist of the kitab genre, Hamzah also introduced the sha'irs as rhymes written with four verses in each stanza. His *Asrar al-Arifin* (Secrets of the Gnostics) and *Syarab Al-Asyikin* (Drink of the Lovers) gave new forms to Arab-Persian poetics, namely the *ghazal* (amatory poem), *bait* (*poetry* with two half lines), *ruba'i* (*poetry* with four lines of rhyming *verse*), and *saj'* (rhymed prose). Hamzah melded these styles with the Malay *pantun* (Malay quatrains expressing ideas and emotions), creating a unique poetic fusion.[62] Or as Amin Sweeney explains: "Although his aim was to write Islamic poetry, his basic materials – as regards verse structure, rhyme, and number of lines in a unit – were Malay. Before Hamzah's time, however, no known genre of poetry, whether in Arabico-Persian or Malay, displayed all four defining characteristics of the Malay *sha'ir*."[63] Writing within the ambit of Islamic prosody and Sufi cosmology, Hamzah's poems were highly metaphorical covering a host of topics, imageries, and tropes, from divine love, to adventure, to romance to the splendours of nature, to unveiling

---

[61] Andaya, *Leaves of the Same Tree: Trade and Ethnicity in the Straits of Melaka*, 123.

[62] Syed Muhammad Naquib Al-Attas, *The Mysticism of Hamzah Fansuri* (University of Malaya Press, 1970).

[63] Amin Sweeney, "Some Observations on the Malay Sha'ir," *Journal of the Malaysian Branch of the Royal Asiatic Society* 44, no. 1 (219) (1971): 66.

his innermost struggles and his interrogative sense of the self. Yet the messages he was seeking to convey were not purely for entertainment's sake. His Southeast Asian audience were cajoled into appreciating and accepting Islamic devotions and ideas. Hamzah won converts to Islam just as he exchanged barbs with his Muslim dissenters.[64]

Hamzah Fansuri transformed sha'ir into a much-loved genre in Southeast Asia, read and sung in homes, palaces, and marketplaces. The themes and words he employed in *Sha'ir Burung Pingai* (Poem of the Pingai Bird), *Sha'ir Dagang* (Poem of Trade), *Sha'ir Perahu* (Poem of the Boat), and many others were adopted by later writers and musicians who kept alive Hamzah's poetic ingenuity and rhetorical flair. The sha'irs produced by Hamzah, his followers, and admirers became a famed figurative medium because it evoked the emotions of Southeast Asian audiences. These compositions were filled with detailed descriptions of personas, places, and passions. The richer the depictions, the more these sha'irs provoked the audience to engage, remember the lines, and become invested in them.[65] In the wake of Hamzah, five distinct kinds of sha'irs developed in Southeast Asia. The hagiographic type, covering the stories of prophets and saints, was predominant. There were sha'irs focusing on beliefs and devotions. The third kind touched on eschatology and the afterlife, the fourth was centred around the environment, and there were a substantial sub-genre delving into existential questions.[66]

One sample of Hamzah's stanzas must detain us for a moment since it had set the tone for Malay poetry in the centuries to come:

> If you know yourself, dear sir,
> You are the sea without compeer,
> Waves and sea are not different,
> Let this vision be steadily yours.
>
> -------
>
> Smooth is the course of the waves of benignity,
> Do not give up yourself to the waves of omnipotence,
> Earn your livelihood in an honest way,
> So that the Endless Sea be pleased.[67]

---

[64] Amin Sweeney, "Malay Sufi Poetics and European Norms," *Journal of the American Oriental Society* 112, no. 1 (1992): 89.

[65] Virginia Matheson, "Questions Arising from a Nineteenth Century Riau Syair," *Review of Indonesian and Malayan Affairs* 17 (1983): 1–61.

[66] Vladimir Braginsky, *The Heritage of Traditional Malay Literature: A Historical Survey of Genres, Writings and Literary Views* (Leiden: KITLV Press, 2004), 364.

[67] Hamzah Fansuri, *The Poems of Hamzah Fansuri* (trans. G.W.J. Drewes and L.F. Brakel) (Leiden: Royal Institute of Linguistics and Anthropology, 1986), 131 and 135.

Feelings **41**

Hamzah's poems and other treatises soon came under the condemnation of other Sufi scholars such as Nuruddin Al-Raniri (d. 1658) who flagged the poet's pantheistic inclinations. But his significance lived on for many centuries thereafter through his disciples or those who were inspired by his poetic edge. Some notable sha'ir authors who expanded Hamzah's legacy were Hasan Fansuri, Syamsuddin al-Sumatra'i, Abdul Rauf Singkel, Daud al-Sumatrani, Raja Chulan, Raja Hassan, and Raja Ali Haji. In their sha'irs, we may discern Sufi concepts relating to dhawq, ma'rifah, *ashiq* (burning love for the divine), *fana'* (annihilation of the self), *faqr* (poverty), and *musyahadah* (witnessing).

In the eighteenth century, the sha'ir sub-genres grew to cover themes of romance, dreams, and incredible tales of nobles and kings. Sufi traces were of course noticeable. The existence of Sufi ideas and symbolisms in later sha'irs can be found in *Sha'ir Tabir Mimpi* (Poem of the Interpretation of Dreams), written in the early nineteenth century and published in Singapore. Dream interpretation (*ta'bir al-ru'ya*) and dream visions (*al-ru'ya*) occupy a prominent place in Sufi thought. Used for centuries to unravel divine signs and as a means to communicate with angels and pious figures who had long passed on, dream visions were, to the Sufis, comparable to prophetic inspiration.[68] *Sha'ir Tabir Mimpi* is unique because it provides interpretations of a variety of dreams: about one's state of being and social relations, encounters with animals, and experiences with the natural environment, all pointing to the rural milieu of the author. These interpretations showed a clever redaction and reinterpretation of the work of a well-respected scholar and Sufi, Muhammad Ibn Sirin (d. 729), to fit with the Southeast Asian context. Some stanzas in the sha'ir suffice here to illustrate its Sufistic thrust:

> This is the beginning chapter,
> Of which the council of the learned says,
> Dreams should be accepted as omens,
> And should be interpreted without delay.
>
> -----
>
> If one dreams that he ascends the clouds,
> Or that another person does so, oh brethren,
> It is a sign that he will live in great ease,
> And God in his generosity will favour him.

---

[68] Elizabeth Sirriyeh, *Dreams and Visions in the World of Islam: A History of Muslim Dreaming and Foreknowing* (London: I.B. Tauris, 2015), 2.

If one dreams of storm and rain,
With pitchy darkness, so that everything becomes invisible,
It is a sign that evil is coming,
And that many people will die of illness.
That dream is most evil,
And no mercy is portended,
Many people will commit treason,
And calamity will be brought down by the angels.[69]

Modernity did little to diminish the production and impact of sha'irs. Aside from being recited and sung during mass events, in the early twentieth century, sha'irs were vehicles for Islamic missionizing. In Sumatra, a Sufi master named Abdul Wahab Rokan (1811–1926) authored the *Sha'ir Munajat* (Supplication Sha'ir) broadly used by followers of the Naqshbandiyyah tariqah to convert the Sakai tribes in Riau Islands to Islam.[70] In contemporary Malaysia, one of the most recognized popularizers of the sha'irs is Roslan Madun. He established the Anggun Performing Arts Club to keep alive the Malay and Sufi ethno-musical traditions. His efforts at giving new life to Sufi sha'irs have reached audiences globally and are now the subject of a number of studies. A recipient of the international laureate for folk singers, Roslan's *Sha'ir Berbuat Jasa* (Poem of Good Deeds), reincarnates and provides a new rendering of Hamzah Fansuri's *Sha'ir Perahu* (Poem of the Boat).[71]

Another figurative medium with Sufi nuances is the hikayat. Tales highlighting the genealogies and virtues of prophets, saints, kings, warriors, missionaries, and other extraordinary figures, and the part they played in the making of Muslim societies were common themes of hikayats. Hikayats existed before the coming of Islam in Southeast Asia. Sensitive to its significance in local life, the Sufis utilized these oral traditions for the purposes of Islamization. The hikayats provided unique visions of justice and love, with a view of reminding the masses of the importance of loyalty and faithfulness to the king, customs, and religion.

---

[69] Hans Overbeck, "Shaer Ta'bir Mimpi," *Malaysian Branch of the Royal Asiatic Society* 7, 2 (107) (1929): 338–375.

[70] U.U. Hamidy, *Pengislaman Masyarakat Sakai Oleh Tarekat Naksyahbandiyah Babussalam* (Pekanbaru: UIR Press, 1992), 37–60.

[71] Editorial, "USIM Iktiraf Sumbangan Roslan Madun Martabat Syair," *Berita Harian*, May 2, 2019; Roslan Madun, "Roslan Madun Syair Berbuat Jasa," accessed April 29, 2022, https://www.youtube.com/watch?v=AMrsaY8UibM; Victor A. Pogadaev, "Folk Singer Roslan a Hit at Russian Festival," *The New Straits Times*, August 22, 2021.

Feelings **43**

The hikayats cautioned elites of the grave consequences of tyranny and warned the masses of *derhaka* (treason), the most serious of crimes punishable by death and exile. These texts were written in a didactic style to underline the importance of Islam and the social contract between rulers and the people as lynchpins of the *kerajaan* (kingship).[72] Highly moving in tone and lacking a chronological sequence, like the sha'irs, hikayats were imbued with the concepts and doctrine of Nur Muhammad, *wahdatul wujud* (the unity of existence), and the *martabat tujuh* (seven stages of being which is a Southeast Asian rendering of the wahdatul wujud).

The British orientalist Richard Winstedt divided Malay-Islamic hikayats into "Muslim Legends" and "Cycles of Tales from Muslim sources." Sufistic elements impregnated both genres. These works were, to him, adaptations from Indian, Persian, and Arab stories.[73] But such argument seems too far-fetched. Most hikayats had original plots. Even if some adaptations from outside sources are indeed present, they were highly modified. Even if these texts were, to the orientalists, uninventive in form and content, they were no less impactful in Southeast Asia up until mid-twentieth century. The hikayats were read aloud by traders during their long journeys, by storytellers and performers as sources of entertainment, by missionaries to spread Islam, by educators and parents to nurture the young, and by soldiers in the face of battles.[74] The hikayats were texts of passion, persuasion, pontification, and provocation. These texts certainly provoked Hadrami-Arab Sufi scholars who regarded most hikayats, notably those about the Prophet Muhammad, as works "compiled by heretics (*Rafidi*): do not believe it."[75]

I divide the hikayats into two broad categories, Sufi centred and Sufi-imbued. Sufi-centred hikayats are texts which manifestly indicate Sufi origins and messages. A few significant examples of Sufi-centred hikayats are in order here. The most well-known of them all is the Hikayat Rabi'ah. A tale based on the ninth-century female mystic Rabiah al-Adawiyah who lived in Basra, Iraq, the earliest textualized version of the hikayat can be dated to the nineteenth century. That the story of a famous Sufi was retold in a Southeast Asian text suggests attempts by

---

[72] Amin Sweeney, "The Connection between Hikayat Raja2 Pasai and the Sejarah Melayu," *Journal of the Malaysian Branch of the Royal Asiatic Society* 40, 2 (1967): 94–105.

[73] Richard O. Winstedt, "A History of Malay Literature," *Journal of the Malayan Branch of the Royal Asiatic Society* 17, no. 3 (135) (1940): 58–78.

[74] Ismail Hamid, *The Malay Islamic Hikayat* (Bangi: Penerbit Universiti Kebangsaan Malaysia, 1983), 44–45.

[75] Winstedt, "A History of Malay Literature," 70.

Sufistic authors to use such a narrative for religious conversion directed primarily towards women. As is well-known, women were held in high esteem in Southeast Asian societies and played crucial roles in shaping and enforcing customs and faiths in the region. The Sufis were most likely aware of this social datum. They used stories of female mystics to connect Islamic notions of womanhood and piety with pre-Islamic matrilocal and matrilineal cultures. Rabiah's ascetic life was embellished as an embodiment of an ideal female figure which Southeast Asian women could aspire to become. The hikayat was also an oblique reminder to male audiences to be watchful of their treatment of pious women in everyday life.[76]

Standard biographies of Rabiah al-Adawiyah tell us of a mystic who remained celibate throughout her life. The Hikayat Rabi'ah narrates a different story. She is portrayed as an honourable woman. Married twice, first with an eminent Sufi master, al-Junaid al-Baghdadi (d. 910), and then with the Sultan Abu Sa'id of Baghdad, these unions heightened Rabiah's spiritual acumen. She rose to the highest *maqam* (station) of spiritual ecstasy. Such interesting twist of facts should be read as a localization of Rabiah's image to make it consonant with Southeast Asian realities. Singlehood and celibacy were frowned upon in Southeast Asia. Multiple marriages among women were fairly common even before the coming of Islam. More crucially, this hikayat made Rabiah a magnetic figure for its readers and listeners. *Rabiya* or *rubiah* are often used in Malay-Indonesian writings to point to commendable traits stemming from the teachings of Sufism: "from hermit or ascetic, living an isolated and presumably celibate life; to teacher, engaged rather than secluded; to teacher's wife, fully enmeshed in domestic and conjugal relationships."[77]

To wit, the hikayat underlines the virtue of *wara'* or *warak* in Malay-Indonesian. Wara' means scrupulousness, a moral compass guiding a Muslim to refrain from unlawful acts and things. This concept was deliberated in Hikayat Sultan Ibrahim bin Adham, a story narrated in Malay, Javanese, Sundanese, and Acehnese dialects. This tale mirrored a known Arab-Persian story of a ruler who lived in eighth-century Balkh, a territory within modern-day Afghanistan. The story of Ibrahim is somewhat reminiscent of the life of Buddha. Such a parallel should come as no surprise given the wide influence Buddhism enjoyed in Southeast Asian

---

[76] Barbara Watson Andaya, *The Flaming Womb: Repositioning Women in Early Modern Southeast Asia* (University Hawai'i Press, 2006), 87.

[77] Mulaika Hijjas, "The Trials of Rabi'a Al-'Adawiyya in the Malay World: The Female Sufi in the Hikayat Rabi'ah," *Bijdragen Tot de Taal-, Land- En Volkenkunde* 174, no. 2/3 (2018): 220.

Feelings   **45**

societies and texts many centuries before the rapid spread of Islam.[78] The new rendering of Sultan Ibrahim bin Adham's life in the hikayat fuses two streams of accounts: Arab-Persian portrait of a prominent Sufi and Indic portrayal of Buddha. There is strong evidence suggesting that a Hadrami-Arab, Shaykh Abu Bakar, was one of the authors or copiers of the hikayat.[79]

The hikayat reads like a book of counsel for Southeast Asian rulers, informing them of the dangers of worldly avarice. Renunciation is the preferred approach to attain happiness. In the hikayat, the much loved and just king, Sultan Ibrahim, became disillusioned with power and wealth. He turned to asceticism and travelled to distant lands posing as a beggar. This is a different representation of the historical Ibrahim bin Adham, who fled the onslaught of the Abbasid army, lived life as a Sufi, and died in exile after being killed in a raid.[80] The hikayat has it that Ibrahim chanced upon a lady named Siti Saleha, the owner of a pomegranate plantation. Siti Saleha had earlier on received premonition about meeting Ibrahim. Impressed by his piety, she asked for his hand in marriage, a common practice among women in Southeast Asia who held the upper hand at times in nuptial arrangements. They bore a son named Muhammad Tahir.

Years of affluent life passed but Ibrahim again saw his devotions fleeting in the face of fame and fortune. He left his family and continued his travels to Makkah. His sacrifices availed him to be with those that obtained the highest blessings from God. Muhammad Tahir, in turn, followed his father's footsteps. He travelled to Iraq where he was offered the mantle of a king. Politely refusing the position, he advised the would-be ruler to remain just. Tahir left Iraq with precious gifts for his mother and continued to receive contributions from the just king. Ibrahim's life story and that of his son underline a central message the author was sending to Southeast Asian rulers: power and wealth have no intrinsic value. Renunciation is the path to eternal bliss.

Like the Hikayat Rabiah, the overall plot of Hikayat Sultan Ibrahim bin Adham was centred around the theme of spiritual enlightenment. If Rabiah gained divine guidance and wisdom through her relationships

---

[78] Al Makin, "Unearthing Nusantara's Concept of Religious Pluralism: Harmonization and Syncretism in Hindu-Buddhist and Islamic Classical Texts," *Al-Jami'ah: Journal of Islamic Studies* 54, no. 1 (2016): 1–30.

[79] Russell Jones, *Hikayat Sultan Ibrahim Ibn Adham* (Lanham, MD: University Press of America, 1985), 85.

[80] Tsugitaka Sato, "The Sufi Legend of Sultan Ibrahim Bin Adham," *Orient* XLII (2007): 41–54.

with her loved ones, Ibrahim did so through abandonment. Both, however, established familial relations and thrived in them. Both forsook affection for material wealth and lived life in austerity as fakirs. Both symbolized Sufi emphasis on being in constant dhikr. There are many other Southeast Asian hikayats with such Sufistic essences.[81] Viewed as a corpus, these figurative mediums exhibit a synthesis of pre-Islamic and Islamic views of spirituality, the merging of local and foreign narrative traditions, and the unique creativity of the authors in using stories to advise kings and laypersons. They all place into sharp relief the importance of contemplation, the cleansing of the heart, and the presence of the divine in all things, in all happenings. They all emphasize dialogues between human beings, their environment, and their Creator.[82]

The second kind of hikayat to be considered here are Sufi-imbued. Such hikayats explained how and why Southeast Asian kingdoms accepted Islam and the miraculous circumstances leading to the Islamization of rulers. *The Sejarah Melayu* (Malay Annals), *Hikayat Iskandar Dzulkarnain, Hikayat Merong Mahawangsa, Hikayat Acheh, Hikayat Patani*, and the *Tajus-Salatin* are among many others in this inventory. The narration of the rulers' unexpected shift in beliefs, usually by way of dream visions and encounters with holy men, bear evidence of the influence of hagiographical Sufi literature.[83] The Hikayat Raja Pasai (also known as Hikayat Raja-Raja Pasai) is one of such texts. It eventually emerged as a model or template for all other Malay hikayats produced from the sixteenth century onwards.

Commissioned by a ruler in Sumatra in the mid-fourteenth century, Sufi-imbued hikayats became part of the oral culture and living tradition of the Malays. The stories in it were refashioned and recast as they reached new audiences in the rest of Southeast Asia. An ensemble of romance and incredible tales, the episodes, characters, themes, and

---

[81] To name a few: *Hikayat Luqman al-Hakim, Hikayat Syekh Abd al-Qadir Jilani, Hikayat Abu Yazid al-Bistami, Hikayat Syah Mardan, Hikayat Syaikh Muhammad Samman, Hikayat Inderaputra, Hikayat Isma Yatim, Hikayat Badr al-'Asyiq, Taj al-Muluk, Hikayat Nabi Lahir* (Tale of the Prophet's Birth), *Hikayat Nur Muhammad* (Tale of the Light of Muhammad), Hikayat Kejadian *Baginda Rasulullah* (Tale of the origins of God's Blessed Messenger), *Hikayat Nabi Mi'raj* (Tale of the Prophet's Ascent), *Hikayat Nabi Wafat* (Tale of the Decease of the Prophet), *Hikayat Nabi Mengajar Fatimah* (Tale of the Prophet teaching Fatimah), and *Hikayat Nabi Mengajar Ali* (Tale of the Prophet teaching Ali).

[82] Hamid, *The Malay Islamic Hikayat.*

[83] Russell Jones, "Ten Conversion Myths from Indonesia," in *Conversion to Islam*, ed. Nehemia Levtzion (New York: Holms and Meier, 1979), 154.

Feelings **47**

lessons in the Hikayat Raja-Raja Pasai were often repeated in other courtly texts found in Southeast Asia, testifying to the intense intellectual networks that existed among the Malays and between locals and the rest of the world from the eleventh century until the eve of colonial rule. The hikayats' references to Indian, Chinese, Arab, and European kingdoms and personas show how globally oriented the Malays were during those times and the extent to which Sufi circulations have affected their thinking.[84]

The Hikayat Raja-Raja Pasai narrates the metamorphoses of the first non-Muslim ruler in Southeast Asia – Merah Silu (or Silau) – his conversion to Islam, and his role as a pioneering propagator of his newfound faith. Like most Sufi-inspired stories of Muslim kings, Merah Silu's life story is traced to the Prophet Muhammad. The prophet had somewhat been informed of Pasai's fame, more commonly known to the Arabs by its pre-Islamic name, "Samudera." The prophet envisioned Samudera as a place filled with *wali Allah* (saints of Allah) who would spread Islam throughout Southeast Asia. No authoritative book other than this hikayat can verify whether the prophet knew of Samudera's existence.[85] This was a clear indication that the author of this text was either a Sufi or was familiar with Sufism, according to Ismail Hamid.[86] Beyond Southeast Asia, the amalgamating of fiction and fact has been a common aspect of many Sufi tales across the Muslim world. Fabricated sayings of the Prophet and his companions were often included without proper reference to where these words were drawn. Fabricated sayings were powerful nonetheless as they bolstered the agency of the Sufis in the conversion of many Muslim populations, much to the consternation of Sufi scholars who specialized in the science of hadith and viewed such tales with contempt.[87]

The task of spreading Islam to Samudera, so goes the hikayat, was left to a Makkan-born Sufi preacher, Shaykh Ismail. Before Shaykh Ismail's arrival at Samudera, Merah Silu encountered the Prophet in a dream. Dreams of encounters and deriving wisdom from the prophet

---

[84] Sumit Mandal, "The Indian Ocean in a Malay Text: The Hikayat Mareskalek in Transregional Perspective," *Indonesia and the Malay World* 43, no. 120 (2013): 237–254.

[85] Anon., "Hikayat Raja-Raja Pasai, ed. and trans, by A. H. Hill," *Journal of the Malayan Branch of the Royal Asiatic Society* 33, no. 2 (190) (1960): 116–117.

[86] Hamid, *The Malay Islamic Hikayat*, 198.

[87] Yusuf Talal Delorenzo, "Translator's Introduction," in *A Sufi Study of Hadith: Haqiqat al-Tariq Min al-Sunna al-'Aniqa* (London: Turath Publishing, 2010), 17–18.

are an important part of Sufi monumentalization of their miraculous powers, as we shall see in the next chapter. The Hikayat Raja-Raja Pasai recounts:

> In his dream, he saw a person standing, his chin cupped in his hand, his eyes covered by his four fingers. The person said "Merah Silu, recite the words of the profession of faith." "I do not know how to recite them," replied Merah Silu. "Open your mouth," said the person. Merah Silu opened his mouth and the person spat into it....Then Merah Silu said "Who are you?" asked Merah Silu, and in his dream the voice answered, "I am the Prophet Muhammad the Apostle of God (may God bless him and give him peace) who was in Mecca." Then the person removed his hand from his chin.[88]

The prophet taught the king the *kalimah syahadah* (declaration of faith). He enjoined Merah Silu to eat only *halal* (permissible) meat and informed the ruler of the coming of Shaykh Ismail in forty days' time, who would instruct him about Islam. The prophet personally bestowed him a new illustrious name and title, Sultan Malikul Saleh or the "Pious King." Malikul Saleh woke up from his dream realizing that he had been miraculously circumcised. He could recite the Qur'an.[89] Sufi influences are evident here and in many other hikayats written in Southeast Asia since the sixteenth century. In drawing upon many stories from other Sufi sources and melding them creatively into the stories of kings and their conversion, the hikayats made Southeast Asian kings larger than life. The hikayats endowed the kings with Sufistic credentials and connected them into an already globalized Sufi dialogical tradition.

CONCLUSION

Using supplicative and figurative mediums, the Sufis charmed, challenged, and changed the rasa of the Southeast Asians. By introducing new musical styles and instruments, chants, and tales from elsewhere in the Muslim world and combining them with those already familiar

---

[88] Anon., "Hikayat Raja-Raja Pasai", 118.
[89] Ibid., 118.

in the region, Southeast Asians became increasingly predisposed to Sufi concepts and cosmology.

Put simply, the Sufis culturalized Islam into Southeast Asia without necessarily displacing what was already established. Soon enough, Hindus, Buddhists, and animists accepted Islam or learnt to live harmoniously with Muslims who shared their love for the arts. What came out of this process was the creation of a hybridized Hindu-Buddhist-Islamic culture expressed in vernacular languages and in many daily and devotional practices. Sufism's metaphysical and philosophical expressions, in other words, enchanted the feelings of peoples in Southeast Asia. Or as Sean Foley, in his study the Naqshbandiyyah-Khalidiyyah order, through such mediums, the Sufis struck deep into "the innermost desires" of their audiences.[90]

Contemplating over centuries of Sufi engagement with the feelings reveals to us how a dialogical tradition was stamped into the lives of Southeast Asians in ways that were at once subtle and salient. Sufis won over their audiences and maintained them within ever-expanding Islamic solidarities by captivating them with prose and poetry which they could easily relate to in their everyday lives. Sufis in Southeast Asia made play with the human need for motivation by providing them with inspirational stories of prophets, heroes, and saints whom everyone aspired to be or at least, emulate. This relentless dialogue with feelings enabled Sufis to enchant Southeast Asians all through the waves of modernization and secularization. This dialogue also provoked fellow Sufis to air their discontentment towards what they saw as creative expressions and practices that breached the shari'a. The contestations between Sufis and between Sufis and non-Sufis on how supplicative and figurative mediums ought to be appropriated seem unending. Till this day, what has become an age-old dialogical tradition of touching the feelings of Southeast Asians has gained a renewed prominence as contemporary Sufis and their interlocutors use new advances in technology to leave imprints on the cognitive and emotive landscapes of their subjects.

---

[90] Sean Foley, "The Naqshbandiyya-Khalidiyya, Islamic Sainthood, and Religion in Modern Times," Journal of World History 19, no. 4 (2008): 521–545.

CHAPTER 2

Miracles

Abdurrahman Wahid, known as Gus Dur (1940–2009), is considered today as one of the most cosmopolitan presidents of Indonesia. But he was more than that. Leader of the world's largest Muslim movement, Gus Dur frequently visited *maqams* (tombs, or makam in Malay). This practice became a lifelong hobby, evolving from his youth well into his vibrant tenure as head of state. A week before his passing, Gus Dur was deep in contemplation at the graves of his ancestors and teachers. Whether at noon or in the still of the night, his *ziyarah* (visitation) was driven by spiritual visions. He claimed to have conversed with the dead, who urged him to visit them. Gus Dur often dreamt of meeting saints who admonished him for neglecting them. Shaken by these spiritual encounters, he would immediately gather entourages of families and friends to visit known tombs. These expeditions were highly publicized events. Gus Dur's visitations prompted the revival of derelict graveyards, transforming them into heritage sites, while also provoking the indignation of reformist ulama who condemned the practice of seeking help from the dead for *tawassul* (intercession). Gus Dur's reverence for the departed came full circle with his own grave being consecrated as a sacred mausoleum. He is now held as the "tenth saint" of Java.[1] Indonesian Muslims, especially those affiliated with the Nahdlatul Ulama (NU), spend hours at Gus Dur's tomb to obtain *barakah* (*berkat* in Malay, or blessings) from Allah. The NU built a mosque in his name. Gus Dur is most remembered

---

[1] Nils Bubandt, *Democracy, Corruption and the Politics of Spirits in Contemporary Indonesia* (London: Routledge, 2014), 2–3.

Contemplating Sufism: Dialogue and Tradition Across Southeast Asia, First Edition. Khairudin Aljunied.
© 2025 John Wiley & Sons Ltd. Published 2025 by John Wiley & Sons Ltd.

Miracles   **51**

for his witty response to why he was so engrossed with graves and tombs: "I do not trust the living. The dead have no interests."[2]

The dead may have no interests, but the living certainly do employ the dead to suit theirs. This chapter examines how the interests, deeds, and aspirations of Sufis in Southeast Asia were nourished through the monumentalization of *karamah*. Literally, the Arabic term karamah (or keramat in Malay) connotes nobility, dignity, honour, and charisma. Within the Sufi vocabulary and practice, however, the term has an esoteric meaning, referring to a saint's latent capacity to perform miracles and bring barakah to people around him. The belief in karamah is widespread among Southeast Asian Muslims. Influenced by Hindu-Buddhist philosophies, karamah is believed to be present in both human beings, animals, trees, hills, mountains, and even weapons such as keris and cannons.[3] This chapter focuses on the karamah of holy persons honoured for their piety, sincerity, generosity, and nobility. Malays, for example, had other criteria to determine the presence of karamah in a person. They either had "a hairy uvula, another is a dwarf, another is short-sighted, another has half his tongue black. All have mysterious powers and some can perform miracles. One mark of a dead saint is the saffron-like fairness of his corpse: another the mysterious separation of the head and foot stones of his grave."[4]

Sufi scholars had different yardsticks. Karamah is considered a celestial privilege given to those who uphold divine law, manifest unswerving conviction in God, and refrain from committing sins, repenting almost immediately when wrongdoing is committed. Most Sufis deny having karamah, and almost none claim sainthood for fear of falling into arrogance and greed. They are conscious of the traps of *istidraj* (reaping bounties that lead to gradual destruction) and being lured unconsciously into the *al-ahwal asy-syaithaniyyah* (devilish states).[5] Karamah, so the belief goes, outlasts the mortal lives of saints. In both life and death,

---

[2] NU Online, "Mimpi Gus Dur Tentang Makam di Tengah Nusa," accessed March 29, 2012, https://nu.or.id/warta/mimpi-gus-dur-tentang-makam-di-tengah-nusa-xVxhI; Redaksi Muhammadiyah, "Hukum Dan Tuntunan Ziarah Kubur," accessed May 29, 2020, https://muhammadiyah.or.id/hukum-dan-tuntunan-ziarah-kubur/

[3] P.J. Rivers, "Keramat in Singapore in the Mid-Twentieth Century," *Journal of the Malaysian Branch of the Royal Asiatic Society* 76, no. 2 (2003): 93.

[4] Richard O. Winstedt, "'Karamat': Sacred Places and Persons in Malaya," *Journal of the Malayan Branch of the Royal Asiatic Society* 2, no. 3 (92) (1924): 264.

[5] Abdul Aziz bin Juned, *Keramat Wali-Wali Allah* (Brunei Darussalam: Jabatan Pejabat Mufti, 2011), 17–23. For discussions on the characteristics of Sufis with karamah and arguments against such claims, see: Yusuf ibn Isma'il al-Nabhani, *Jami' Karamat Al-Awliya'* (Beirut: al-Maktaba al-Thaqafiyya, 1991); Muhammad Abu l-Fadl Badran, *Adabiyat Al-Karamat al-Sufiya: Dirasa Fi l-Shakl Wal-Madmun* (al-'Ayn, United Arab Emirates: Markaz Zayid li-t-turath wa-t-tarikh, 2001).

the karamah of saints can still be felt by people around them. Karamah, therefore, has discordant dimensions. Sufis rationalize it as repeatable and verifiable occurrences similar to natural laws. Yet, in many Sufi narratives, karamah can breach the natural order of things, transcending human logic. Regardless of the view, karamah raises the status of a Sufi and elevates his posthumous significance.[6]

Mark Rees reminds us that to "monumentalize is to memorialize in grand, seemingly immovable fashion, the rebirth or reinvention of tradition."[7] Monumentalizing karamah aggrandizes an invented tradition to appear exceptional and magnificent. The monumentalization of karamah in Southeast Asia was most visible in the shape of sanctification of tombs and in incredible tales. These two paths were intertwined. Monumentalization may not necessarily be driven by spirituality or faith; financial, civic, and communal considerations often influenced the process. In other words, the monumentalization of karamah was achieved through a conscious combination and clever manipulation of worldly and transcendental apparatuses and justifications. This dialogue between the spiritual and the material and between religion and commoditization has made Sufism in Southeast Asia resilient.

SANCTIFIED TOMBS

Buildings and other features associated with Sufis and Sufism permeate and percolate the geography of Southeast Asia, often in the form of tombs and shrines, widely known as maqam or keramat. Among Tamil Indians, such shrines are called *dargah*, a Persian word meaning "portal." Thousands of graves in Java alone are reputed to have karamah. Some, such as the Wali Songo mausoleums, are considered more significant due to their roles in spreading Islam in the region. Saints with greater deeds are known to have stronger karamah.[8] In Singapore, more than seventy shrines were recorded in the 1970s. While most made way to new roads and buildings, those of Sufi origins survived

---

[6] Mark Sedgwick, *Sufism: The Essentials* (New York: Oxford University Press, 2003), 19.

[7] Mark Rees A., *Monumental Landscape and Community in the Southern Lower Mississippi Valley During the Late Woodland and Mississippi Periods*, ed. Timothy R. Pauketat (New York: Oxford University Press, 2012), 486.

[8] Henri Chambert-Loir, "Saints and Ancestors: The Cult of Muslim Saints in Java," in *The Potent Dead: Ancestors, Saints and Heroes in Contemporary Indonesia*, eds. Henri Chambert-Loir and Anthony Reid (Crows Nest, Australia: Allen and Unwin, 2002), 134.

urban development. In Malaysia religious authorities constantly guide visitors against worshipping the dead and believing in the power of shrines, often displaying signs explaining that acts are *shirk* (idolatrous polytheism) and *khurafat* (superstition).[9] Despite these policies, these buildings have transcended historical, political, religious, and ethnic boundaries, attracting millions of visitors each year. I term these sites "sanctified tombs."

Sanctified tombs' sacredness is highly contingent on human agency. The more elaborate the tombs' appearances and the more mysterious and magical stories told about them, the more prestigious they become in public eyes. If prestige confers prestige, by the same logic, then sanctity confers sanctity. The prestige of sanctified tombs in Southeast Asia was built on deliberate actions and validations by those who bestow value on them and those who contest their value. The social value of a sacred tomb heightens when recognized as a community's heritage, a mark of society's identity, a social glue uniting diverse peoples within a nation, or objects of international significance frequented by scholars, tourists, and flaneurs.

Most sanctified tombs in Southeast Asia were graves of males from Hadrami-Arab and Indian origins, though many were also resting places of local religious scholars, rulers, and respected personalities. Hadrami-Arabs and Indians were prominent in the commercial, political, and religious activities in Southeast Asia for centuries, commanding a great following and leaving deep impressions on the locals. Hadrami-Arab graves often hold higher significance due to their illustrious genealogy tracing back to the family of the Prophet Muhammad. In Vietnam, for instance, two Hadrami-Arab sanctified tombs in the Chau Doc region were the graves of Tuon Ku Umar in Koh Khoi and Tuon Kosem in Vinh Truong who originated in the sixteenth century. In local accounts, they are said to be those of Sufi saints from Kelantan who taught Islam to the Cham communities.[10]

Some Hadrami-Arab tombs were monumentalized due to watershed events associated with them, often involving struggles between underdogs and oppressive authorities, between pious locals and foreign occupiers. The maqam of Sayyid Yasin is one example. In 1823, after a

---

[9] William L. Gibson, *A Complete Catalog of Keramat in Singapore* (Singapore: National Library of Singapore, 2022), xi. See also: Angela Suen-Oltmanns, "A Historical Survey of the Keramat Phenomenon (with Special Reference to Singapore)" (Unpublished Honours Thesis, Singapore, Department of History, National University of Singapore, 1993).

[10] Philipp Bruckmayr, *Cambodia's Muslims and the Malay World: Malay Language, Jawi Script, and Islamic Factionalism from the 19th Century to the Present* (Leiden: Brill, 2019), 95–96.

dispute with another Hadrami-Arab, Syed Omar Aljunied, Yasin killed a sepoy and stabbed a British magistrate, Colonel Farquhar. Subdued and repeatedly stabbed by British soldiers, Yasin's mutilated body was hung for public viewing as a grim reminder of reprisals against those who mortally injured a white official. Documenting the monumentalization of Yasin's grave, a British popular historian wrote: "The body was then buried at Tanjong Pagar, where the result of the proceedings was (which Sir Stamford did not anticipate) that it became a place of pilgrimage and Syed Yassin was considered a great saint, because the holy Syed had only killed a Fakir (the Hindoo) and wounded a Nazarene (Colonel Farquhar)."[11]

Revered graves of female Sufis can be found in Aceh, Java, Madura, Bali, Penang, and Singapore. However, they are a minority and attract fewer pilgrims than male sanctified tombs. Monumentalization of sanctified tombs is therefore a gendered phenomenon, reserved mostly for men of high repute and piety, reflecting the dominance of men in most Muslim societies or at least in Muslim spiritual narratives. George Quinn's observations on female sanctified tombs apply to the rest of Southeast Asia: "For the most part the tombs of female saints are not showily monumental."[12] Most female saints are connected by way of silsilah or affiliation to tariqahs led by Hadrami-Arab men, such as Maknih and Wan Doneh in Aceh, who belonged to the Shattariyah tariqah and were respected as descendants of Aceh's most revered saint, Habib Abdurrahim. The second-tier female tombs in Aceh parallel those in the Muslim world.[13]

Sanctified tombs became monumentalized in Southeast Asia through their symbiotic relationship with the region's ancient pasts. These tombs display the uninterrupted influence of pre-Islamic cultures and beliefs upon Islamic ones. Writing in 1911, British writer Charles Blagden described this intermingling as

> ...survivals of the earlier phases of religious development. Scratch off the veneer of Islam and you come to a stratum of Hinduism,

---

[11] Charles B. Buckley, *An Anecdotal History of Old Times in Singapore* (Kuala Lumpur: University of Malaya Press, 1965), 97–100.

[12] George Quinn, "The Veneration of Female Saints in Indonesia," in *Encyclopedia of Women and Islamic Cultures,* eds. Suad Joseph et al. (Leiden: Brill, 2012), http://www.brill.com/publications/encyclopedia-women-islamic-cultures.

[13] Kelly Pemberton, *Women Mystics and Sufi Shrines in India* (Columbia: University of South Carolina Press, 2010); Daniel Andrew Birchok, "Women, Genealogical Inheritance and Sufi Authority: The Female Saints of Seunagan, Indonesia," *Asian Studies Review* 40, no. 4 (2016): 583–599.

where Brahma, Vishnu, and particularly Siva, together with other obsolescent half-forgotten gods of a deserted Pantheon, figure still as demonic powers unlawfully invoked in moments of supreme necessity. But these in their turn are mere shells, and at the back of them it is not difficult to detect the ancient Indonesian animism which, often masquerading under Hindu or Muhammadan forms, still remains as the core of Malay popular religion and magic.[14]

Blagden connotes that beneath the veneer of Islam, there are layers of Hinduism and ancient Indonesian animism, being Islam at the outermost. While these observations are illuminating, they are problematic. Southeast Asian Muslims, from Blagden's perspective, were token Muslims. Sanctified tombs may manifest Sufistic elements, but these were mere superficialities overlaying and garbing non-Muslim essences of such sites. To be sure, sanctified tombs exhibit the endurance of the pre-Islamic pasts albeit not in the sense Blagden envisaged. Rather than seeing sanctified tombs from the angle of different religiosities stacked over one another, with Islam being the topmost veneer, it would be more to take on a mosaic viewpoint. In other words, elements of Sufism, Hinduism, Buddhism, and animism interfaced one another, forming a blend of different practices and beliefs.

The Malay scholar-activist Mohd Taib Osman acknowledges Hindu-Buddhist and animistic influences in sanctified tombs. Many visitors attach exceptional importance to objects and animals near where Sufi saints are buried, based on the folk idea of *semangat* (spirit) in all things. Yet, "[k]eramat belief and practice among the Malay folk follow the same pattern (as the other Muslims). Into the texture have been woven threads bearing the popular Islamic notion of saints, the Brahmanical cult of wonder-working ascetics, and the belief in the powerful nature and ancestor spirits."[15] This amalgamation with the past is especially apparent in the locales where these sanctified tombs laid and in their architectural forms. Many Sufi graves were built on former non-Muslim sites, such as the graves of Shaykh Dalem Arif Muhammad, Shaykh

---

[14] Charles O. Blagden, "Review of: The Peninsular Malays. I: Malay Beliefs by R. J. Wilkinson, of the Civil Service of the Federated Malay States. (London: Luzac & Co. Leiden: Late E. J. Brill, 1906)," *Journal of the Royal Asiatic Society* 38, no. 4 (2011): 1030.

[15] Mohammad Taib Osman, *Malay Folk Beliefs: An Integration of Disparate Elements* (Kuala Lumpur: Dewan Bahasa dan Pustaka, 1989), 119.

Abdul Rahman, and Shaykh Abdul Rahim in Java, built on ruins of Hindu and Buddhist temples.[16]

Another way the karamah of sanctified tombs was monumentalized was through their external façades, manifesting different styles and projecting an enigmatic appearance. The length between the head and foot stones substantiates this point. Most graves of Sufi saints are generally longer and sometimes larger than other ordinary Muslim graves. At Pulau Besar Island near Malacca and Kusu Island close to Singapore, these "long graves" have turned the islands into hubs of spiritual tourism. Visitors, both Muslims and non-Muslims, frequent these islands to give offerings to the long graves and then spend leisurely time at nearby beaches and parks.[17] Long graves can be found at Perak, Kedah, and Penang in the Malay peninsula. In 1899, the gravestones of a local saint in Patani were observed to have made "prophetic movements" and grew longer each year.[18] Stories of long graves constantly lengthening in size is unique to Southeast Asia. I have not come across any other similar cases in other parts of the Muslim world. We may read such accounts as attempts to buttress the special status of the saints whose graves have become the stuff of popular mythology. Graves lengthening in size signifies the organicity of karamah attached to the deceased and the flowing barakah from them.

The overall architecture and aesthetics of sanctified tombs accentuate their holiness, sacramental value, and supposed power. They are mostly adorned with calligraphic inscriptions drawn from the Qur'an, Hadith, or Sufi poetry, carefully chosen to point to the theurgical and healing properties of the tombs. These inscriptions are read alongside other litanies.[19] A great saint's tomb is usually near smaller tombs, such as those of wives, children, relatives, and close acquaintances. The difference is made obvious by the gargantuan size and architectural splendour of the saints' graves. Common colours used for these buildings are shades of white, yellow, and green, denoting purity, primacy, and paradise.

---

[16] Henri Chambert-Loir, "Saints and Ancestors: The Cult of Muslim Saints in Java," in *The Potent Dead: Ancestors, Saints and Heroes in Contemporary Indonesia,* eds. Henri Chambert-Loir and Anthony Reid (Crows Nest, Australia: Allen and Unwin, 2002), 136.

[17] Betty L. Khoo, "The Land of Long Graves," *New Nation*, August 24, 1974.

[18] Walter W. Skeat, "Report of Cambridge Exploring Expedition to the Malay Provinces of Lower Siam," *The Journal of the Anthropological Institute of Great Britain and Ireland* 30 (1900): 75.

[19] Daphna Ephrat, Ethel Sara Wolper, and Paula G. Pinto, "Introduction: History and Anthropology of Sainthood and Space in Islamic Contexts," in *Saintly Spheres and Islamic Landscapes: Emplacements of Spiritual Power across Time and Place, eds. Daphna Ephrat, Ethel Sara Wolper and Paulo G. Pinto* (Leiden: Brill, 2021), 7.

The mausoleum of the fifth Sultan of Brunei, Bolkiah, or "Nakhoda Ragam," who ruled from 1485 till 1524, combines these colours. During my visit there, I notice a range of Qur'anic inscriptions, elaborated designs, mammoth head and leg stones, and a large dome form the mausoleum's overall make-up. The site mirrors other sanctified tombs in the Arab world, South Asia, and more so, in Quanzhou, China, as historical ties with the kingdoms of Brunei were strong since the fourteenth century.[20]

A distinguishing feature at the Bolkiah mausoleum is an umbrella-shaped canopy above the tomb, a symbol of royal power and prestige used for coronations and other important ceremonies in historical Southeast Asia. This Hindu-Buddhist tradition was preserved by Muslim kings to place themselves on par with their ancestors. Other Hindu-Buddhist motifs can also be found in sanctified tombs. In Patani, the tombstones of Sufi saints at Kubo Barahom were decorated with the lotus plant and images of Mount Meru, the purported home

Tombstone of Sultan Bolkiah, the fifth ruler of Brunei (1485–1524) in Kota Batu, Brunei: https://en.wikipedia.org/wiki/Bolkiah#/media/File:Tombstone_of_Sultan_Bolkiah,_June_2015.jpg

---

[20] Chen Da-Sheng, "A Brunei Sultan in the Early 14th Century: Study of an Arabic Gravestone," *Journal of Southeast Asian Studies* 23, no. 1 (1992): 1–13.

of Hindu-Buddhist gods, with the *shahadah* (profession of faith) or Qur'anic verses engraved on the tombstones. Similar fusions of Islamic and pre-Islamic features are found in North Sumatran keramats. The blending of different eras' arts and architectures in Southeast Asian history has made these sanctified tombs popular visitation sites for both Muslims and non-Muslims.[21]

Beyond their façades, the monumentalization of karamah was influenced by surrounding environments of these sanctified tombs. Located on hills, in valleys, between large rocks, in jungles, near riverbanks, beaches, and isolated paths, the routes to these graves evoke an aura of sacrality, if not, mystery.[22] The "Makam Keramat Cemare" is probably the few or else the only sanctified tomb in the world located in the middle of the sea entering into the island of Lombok. It was built sometime between the seventeenth and eighteenth centuries in honour of the contributions of a Hadrami-Arab, Sayyid Muhammad Al-Baghdadi, in spreading Islam on the island. Visitors would use small boats to reach the grave. If the site Sayyid Muhammad Al-Baghdadi grave seems anomalous, another sanctified tomb, the Makam Loang Baloq on the same island Lombok, is located within huge ficus trees. The long and thick vines hanging down from the trees and enveloping the tombs give the impression that prominent saints buried there were protected by mother nature.[23]

Many sanctified tombs are near prayer places. Similar to Central Asia since the fourteenth century, sanctified tombs in Southeast Asia "increasingly supplanted mosques as the main centres of religious activity."[24] In Penang, a local Malay saying goes, "where there is a cemetery, there is a mosque," signifying close relationship between graves of saints and places of prayer.[25] The names of the mosques sometimes replicated the names of the tombs. The mosque and tomb of Sunan Muria (Raden Umar Said (1518–1530)) located in Kudus, Central Java, is an example. Built in the late fifteenth or early sixteenth century on a mountain, visitors climb over four hundred steps to reach the graves. The sanctified tomb receives regular visitors mostly on Thursdays and Fridays.

---

[21] Wayne Bougas, "Some Early Islamic Tombstones in Patani," *Journal of the Malaysian Branch of the Royal Asiatic Society* 59, no. 1(250) (1986): 85–112.

[22] Julian Millie, "Creating Islamic Spaces: Tomb and Sanctity in West Java," *ISIM Review* 17 (2006): 12–13.

[23] "Tiga Makam Keramat Objek Wisata Religi Di Lombok," accessed June 11, 2020, https://muslim.okezone.com/read/2020/06/11/615/2228359/tiga-makam-keramat-objek-wisata-religi-di-lombok.

[24] Laurence Potter, "Sufis and Sultans in Post-Mongol Iran," *Iranian Studies* 27, no. 1–4 (1994): 78.

[25] "Mohammedan Cemeteries," *Straits Echo*, April 16, 1904.

Shops selling souvenirs and other religious products make the site a lucrative Sufi-based religious market in Indonesia.[26]

The correlation between sanctified tombs and mosques deserves further analysis. While mosques are sacred places for Muslims to connect with God, some sanctified tombs have become more revered, sometimes contesting the functions of mosques. I use "contest" not negatively but to indicate that these tombs may hold higher importance for some visitors. Many Muslims frequent sanctified tombs even if they are nominal Muslims, viewing Islam as a religion of saints who serve immediate aims more than regular devotion to the divine.

One vivid sample of this is the Makam Habib Nuh in Singapore, the mausoleum of a Hadrami-Arab named Sayyid Nuh Al-Habshi whose lineage intersected with the paternal side of my family going back three generations. Built by the Alsagoff family in the 1890s, a mosque was constructed at the foot of the hill below Habib Nuh's grave, some years later. I visited this sanctified tomb on many occasions since young. Now as an academic, I bring my students there for field trips. One of the caretakers of the site was my late uncle, Syed Hussein Aljunied. Non-Muslims have been regular visitors of this huge complex. Dozens of bottles of water would be left around Habib Nuh's grave. Some believed, much to the consternation of religious authorities, that the water was "blessed." They used it for various ailments, including for their children to excel in their studies and to redress marital problems. Initially, the tomb was separated from the mosque. After years of refurbishment, the mosque and tomb were linked seamlessly. Despite their immediacy, with exception of Friday prayers or during the two *Eids* (Islamic holidays), the mosque would not witness as many visitors as the tomb. A hagiographer of Habib Nuh supports this point. The tomb was always filled with visitors, especially on Sundays and public holidays. They would bring trays filled with *pulut kuning* (yellow rice) – offerings that trace its origins to Hindu beliefs – to honour Habib Nuh.[27]

Sanctified tombs were not always near other religious buildings. Sometimes, they are close to markets, government buildings, schools, shopping complexes, and residential areas promoting tourism. The "Makam Dato Manila" in Melaka, built in memory of a respected Sulu Muslim scholar, is placed in between shops and houses, visible to

---

[26] "Masjid Sunan Muria Kudus," accessed July 11, 2022, https://duniamasjid.islamic-center. or.id/1313/masjid-sunan-muria-kudus/

[27] Muhammad Ghouse Khan Surattee, *The Grand Saint of Singapore: The Life of Habib Nuh Bin Muhammad Al-Habshi* (Singapore: Masjid Al-Firdaus, 2008), 52.

anyone travelling along Jalan Besar Tengkara. Nearby are other famous tombs, such as Makam Habib Idros Al-Habsyi and Makam Nakhoda Nan Intan.[28] The tomb of Shaykh Burhanuddin of Ulakan has, for over a century, not only been a place for worshippers but also a haven for shoppers.[29] The sanctified tomb is part of the burgeoning "pilgrimage tourism" in Indonesia that included visits to the graves of the walis followed by museum visits, sightseeing at other historical places, and shopping in mega malls. Sacred spaces and profane interests and sites gel together during these highly commercialized pilgrimages, each conferring value on another.[30]

The inclusiveness of these sanctified tombs is noteworthy. The karamah of these tombs is appreciated by Muslims of different religious leanings and non-Muslims alike, all of whom share the same notion that there are tangible and intangible benefits to be gained from such visits. As such, sanctified tombs in Southeast Asia complicate the constructed divisions between "folk" and "high" Islam, but also perceived tensions between "normative" and "lived" Islam, and the gulf drawn between "Muslims" and "non-Muslims." Anyone could avail themselves to these sites and view it as part of their traditions. Caretakers, known as *khadim* (servant) or *juru kunci* (keeper of the keys), admit any visitors as long as they maintain decorum.[31] Similar to mausoleums in the Arab world, sanctified tombs in Southeast Asia were more than "places of retreat like early ribats where poor, needy or mystically minded people sought asylum from the world, but rather social establishments in which the place of the dead was commemorated by veneration of the living. They were attractive, lively spots, more popular than scholarly or official foundations."[32]

People with different motivations contribute to the monumentalization of these tombs. Some have supra-confessional interests, driven by curiosity about the tombs' appearances or stories: the lust of knowing. Many have documented their findings in scholarly treatises and travelogues, furthering the heritagization of these sites, which is a "process by

---

[28] Muhaimin Sulam, "Menjejak Maqam Ulama, Sejarah Yang Tenggelam Tidak Dicatat," accessed July 19, 2022, https://nextstepmalaysia.com/menjejaki-maqam-ulama/.

[29] Ph. S. van Ronkel, "Het Heiligdom Te Oelakan," *Tijdschrift Voor Indische Taal-, Land- En Volkenkunde* 56 (1914): 281–316; Pusat Data Dan Analisa Tempo, *Budaya Ziarah Makam Wali Dan Tokoh Sakti Di Jawa* (Jakarta: Tempo Publishing, 2020), 44–45.

[30] Tanti Handriana, Praptini Yulianti, and Masmira Kurniawati, "Exploration of Pilgrimage Tourism in Indonesia," *Journal of Islamic Marketing* 11, no. 3 (2020): 783–795.

[31] Abubakar Aceh, *Pengantar Sejarah Sufi and Tasawwuf* (Solo: Ramadhani, 1994), 300.

[32] Sheila S. Blair, "Sufi Saints and Shrine Architecture in the Early Fourteenth Century," *Muqarnas* 7 (1990): 45–46.

Miracles **61**

which objects and places are transformed from functional 'things' into objects of display and exhibition."[33] Heritagization was accentuated by European colonization of Southeast Asia and the decades that followed. In their efforts to map territories, to make them legible, and to profit from their existence, the Europeans introduced schemes to preserve sanctified tombs. Postcolonial states continued such high-modernist policies, designed to reap revenue out of heritage.[34] Cases in point were keramats spread across British colonies in Singapore, Melaka, and Penang. The colonial administration established endowment boards and research institutes to look into the documentation and conservation of these sanctified tombs. While the overriding concern was to maintain hegemony over the environment and the populace through the power of knowledge, the colonial state and their progenies also invented new conceptions about these places, turning them into national artefacts. Sanctified tombs were rebranded from what was originally faith-oriented to became part of the nation-state's raison d'être.[35]

The second group participating in the monumentalization of the karamah of these sanctified tombs had confessional motivations, viewing these places through the lenses of religious convictions, although many too embraced the heritagization of sanctified tombs to ensure the conservation of these sites. The ulama, imams, and the laity patronize sanctified tombs to show respect for the dead, differing in their views on the tombs' perceived power. In rural areas, Sufi saints are believed to fulfil *hajat* (wishes) and turn the course of events. Visits to sanctified tombs, especially during poor harvests or catastrophes such as social conflicts, plagues, droughts, earthquakes, and floods, involve food offerings and animal sacrifices to assuage and prevent mishaps. To quote a perceptive observer in the early twentieth century at length:

> As a Muslim, the Malay makes vows to prophets and saints imploring their aid in the hour of need. In Singapore many vows are sworn at the shrine of Habib Nuh, a humble clerk of the last century, who gave up the pride of the eye and the lusts of the flesh

---

[33] Rodney Harrison, *Heritage: Critical Approaches* (London: Routledge, 2013), 69.

[34] James C. Scott, *Seeing Like a State: How Certain Schemes to Improve the Human Condition Have Failed* (New Haven: Yale University Press, 1998).

[35] Khoo Salma Nasution, "Colonial Intervention and Transformation of Muslim Waqf Settlements in Urban Penang: The Role of the Endowments Board," *Journal of Muslim Minority Affairs* 22, no. 2 (2002): 299–315; Meng Hao Wan, *Heritage Places of Singapore* (Singapore: Marshall Cavendish, 2009), 162–163.

for religious asceticism until he could appear in several places at once. In every part of Naning are found tombs of men famed for piety, in whose names the people make vows for the prosperous termination of any project and whose burial places they honour with frequent visits and oblations... These sacred tombs, which exist throughout Malaya, bear an Arabic name (*karamat*), though the dead whose tenements they are need not be Muslim saints and may have been merely some powerful ruler or the revered founder of a settlement, or even a pagan trafficker with black magic.[36]

These confessional beliefs have been placed under serious probe even before modernization and the onset of Islamic reformism in the nineteenth century. Very early on in Southeast Asian history, Sufi scholars prohibited all forms of saint-worship and censured beliefs about saints having prophetic powers. The sixteenth-century Javanese religious text held the following view which were echoed by reformist Muslims in later years: "It is unbelief to say that the great imams are superior to the prophets, or to put the saints (*wali*) above the prophets, and even above our lord Muhammad."[37]

The monumentalization of karamah has also been made possible by the rituals conducted within the premises of sanctified tombs. Prior to the twentieth century, there were no extensive manuals on such rituals. Recently, books on how to visit sanctified tombs have mushroomed all over the region, partly revealing the emerging trend of tomb visitations especially those connected to the Wali Songo.[38] Worshippers could pick and select which rituals were most suitable in accordance to the stature of the saints. The rituals in sanctified tombs have been both individualist and collectivist in texture. It can be carried out by a single person or by groups visiting the tombs. Tomb rituals in Southeast Asia parallels with those found in the Arab-Persian worlds with some local variations. Henry Chambert-Loir document three different types of visitors to the sanctified tombs in Java, each with slightly different approaches to rituals. Such rituals and types of visitors could well be found throughout Southeast Asia. The first were *ziarah biasa* (ordinary visitors) who sought "spiritual refreshment" and usually came for short

---

[36] Richard O. Winstedt, *Shaman, Saiva and Sufi: A Study of the Evolution of Malay Magic* (London: Constable, 1925), 5–6.

[37] G. W. J. Drewes, *An Early Javanese Code of Ethics* (The Hague: Nijhoff, 1978), 38–39.

[38] I. Rofi'ie Ariniro, *Panduan Wisata Religi Ziarah Wali Sanga* (Yogyakarta: Saufa, 2016).

Miracles **63**

and organized tours. The second type of visitors were "specialists such as Muslim leaders (*ajengan*), pupils at pesantren schools (*santri*), teacher and klerik (*kiai*), and expert in Islam (*akhli hikmah*), as well as people who want to obtain particular knowledge (*ngelmu*) and those seeking solutions for their problems (*nu gaduh pamaksadan*)."[39] The third type of visitors were seasonal ones, those who visit the tombs during mawlids, during Ramadan, and the Eids.[40]

These three types of visitors share the same sequence of rituals. The first step involves having holy and *niat dan harapan suci* (hopeful intentions) This may vary from person to person and tied usually to economic, social, political, relational, and spiritual wants. Worshippers would come with the innate hope of either paying respect or seeking some special favour from the dead. Believing in the power of intercession through the saints is the first step in the rituals performed at sanctified tombs. A mental disposition borne out of belief in the blessings of the deceased, without holy and hopeful intentions, subsequent rituals have no real significance nor anticipated reward. The visit becomes a mundane tour, a tourist sightseeing, or an academic exercise.[41]

Next in the sequence of rituals was gift-giving. Visits to tombs in Southeast Asia have been regarded as akin to visits to peoples' homes in that one should not come *tangan kosong* (empty-handed). The assumption here is that the saints would be pleased by gifts and would reciprocate by bringing one's prayers and wishes to God. As noted earlier, many sanctified tombs are usually close to shops selling gifts, turning the whole complex into a religious market built around the dead. Peter Metcalf in his study of the Berawan rituals in central northern Borneo calls this the "ritual economy, the ability of a rite to telescope in scale, to expand or contract in the grandness with which it is celebrated, without any essential change in format or rationale."[42]

What were the usual gifts given to the saints to obtain their karamah and barakah? We may divide them into two, first were corporeal and second, supplicative in nature. Corporeal gifts included assorted flowers. The fragrance of these flowers was believed to be a medium that would

---

[39] Henri Chambert-Loir, "Saints and Ancestors: The Cult of Muslim Saints in Java," in *The Potent Dead: Ancestors, Saints and Heroes in Contemporary Indonesia,* eds. Henri Chambert-Loir and Anthony Reid (Crows Nest, Australia: Allen and Unwin, 2002), 170–171.

[40] Henri Chambert-Loir, "Saints and Ancestors: The Cult of Muslim Saints in Java," 134–135.

[41] Moh. Toriqul Chaer and Wahyudi Setiawan, *Ziarah, Barakah, Dan Karamah: Tinjauan Etnografi Dan Psikologi Pendidikan Islam* (Ponorogo: Wade Publishing, 2018), 29.

[42] Peter Metcalf, "Meaning and Materialism: The Ritual Economy of Death," *Man* 16, no. 4 (1981): 563.

bring the petitions and wishes of visitors to the saints then to God, a belief that has pre-Islamic origins.[43] Flowers were usually placed on top of the graves. *Air mawar* (Scented water) would be poured and incense burnt.[44] Animal sacrifice featured in the gifts presented to the dead, but this was usually reserved for special days in the Islamic calendar. Another gift, the supplicative one, were prayers read for the deceased. *Al-Fatihah* (The Opening), the first chapter of the Qur'an, remains till today the preamble recitation followed by dhikr and other litanies. Some visitors would stay for days reading this combination of prayers to maintain connection with saints.

One other ritual was *tamassuh* (touching) the tombstones, also referred to in Southeast Asia as *mengusap dan mencium batu nisan* (touching and kissing tombstones). This practice is found throughout the Muslim world, braced by the belief that by touching the tombstones, one gains blessings from and connections with the dead. In some Arab countries, visitors would roll on the ground near the tombs.[45] In the second half of the twentieth century, Southeast Asian visitors bathed and drank rainwater clogged near the tombs to cure their illnesses.[46]

Sufis have been divided over these practices. Citing the works of the Shafi'ite scholar, Abu Zakariyya Al-Nawawi (1233–1277), some Southeast Asian Sufi scholars argued such rituals were adopted from Jews and Christians and be summarily abolished. Even the saints were not assured of divine succour, how then can they assist others? The same argument has been made against circumambulation of tombs, wailing, tearing of clothes, asking for special favours (including prizes for lotteries) from the dead, and incorporating devotional elements from other religions during grave visits. Headed by Sufi-oriented scholars, the religious council of Sarawak in Malaysia and the NU in Indonesia have been particularly strict on these matters even though they were supportive of tomb visitations. In one article written by a member of the NU, it is stated that "as a general rule it can be surmised that kissing tombstones is a disavowed innovation (*bid'ah munkarah*) that is forbidden in Islamic law. This prohibition is exempted for another who

---

[43] Nelly van Doorn-Harder and Kees de Jong, "The Pilgrimage to Tembayat: Tradition and Revival in Indonesian Islam," *The Muslim World* 91 (2001): 339.

[44] Abdurrahman Misno BP, *Mari Ziarah Kubur* (Jawa Barat: Penerbit Adab, 2020), 3.

[45] Catherine Mayeur-Jaouen, "Sufi Shrines," in *Sufi Institutions,* ed. Alexandre Papas (Leiden: Brill, 2021), 149–150.

[46] Winstedt, 'Karamat': Sacred Places and Persons in Malaya, 273.

Miracles   **65**

visits the grave with the clear intention of obtaining blessings (*tabar-ruk*) from the righteous buried there."[47]

Connected to the above points, the last common ritual among Sufi visitors is asking for favours and blessings from the deceased. For some Southeast Asian Sufis, they believed in their ability to communicate with the saints at sanctified tombs during sleep, in full conviction that the dead could appear in dreams.[48] I will discuss more about this below. While camping for days at these sanctified tombs, visitors would read Ya-Sin, an oft-cited chapter in the Qur'an among Southeast Asians who held that this chapter would bring blessings to the dead. To be added to this were recital of the *tahlil* (litany in praise of God) and the hagiography of the saints. The leaders of such congregation are usually the head of a tariqah who would enter into communication with the dead during states of trance to convey the wishes from those present.[49] In Tembilahan, Riau, visitors of Shaykh Abdurrahman Siddiq Al-Banjari's tomb read his poems, *Sya'ir 'Ibarat dan Khabar Qiyamat* (The Metaphoric Poems and Messages on the Hereafter), and delivered speeches on the saint's piety and legacies. These annual sessions were usually attended by several thousand people.[50]

In other sanctified tombs, processions, flag-raising ceremonies, sword-plays, and other displays were present. The main objective of these spectacles was to display the magnificence of the dead and their continued importance of their deeds, in hearts and minds of the believers. Followers of Nagore Dargah shrine in Singapore, for example, used such processions to appease a saint named Shahul Hamid of Nagore and to pay homage to his karamah.[51] The Nagore Dargah shrine was built in the 1830s at Telok Ayer Street. Festivities were held annually in Singapore and Penang to remember the saint. The grandeur of such events has, however, tapered through time, and the processions were

---

[47] Mahbib Khoiron, "Mencium Batu Nisan Saat Ziarah, Bolehkah?," accessed November 16, 2018, https://islam.nu.or.id/jenazah/mencium-batu-nisan-saat-ziarah-bolehkah-onZfU. See also: Pejabat Mufti Negeri Sarawak, *Adab & Larangan Ketika Menziarahi Kubur* (Kuching: Pejabat Mufti Sarawak, n.d.).

[48] Elizabeth Sirriyeh, *Dreams and Visions in the World of Islam: A History of Muslim Dreaming and Foreknowing* (London: I.B. Tauris, 2015), 172.

[49] Arif Zamhari, *Rituals of Islamic Spirituality: A Study of Majlis Dhikr Groups in East Java* (Canberra: ANU E Press, 2010), 172–173; A. G. Muhaimin, *The Islamic Traditions of Cirebon: Ibadat and Adat among Javanese Muslims* (Canberra: ANU E Press, 2006), 159–201.

[50] Abd. Madjid, Hilman Latief, and Aris Fauzan, "Honoring the Saint through Poetry Recitation: Pilgrimage and the Memories of Shaikh Abdurrahman Siddiq Al-Banjari in Indragiri Hilir," *Religions* 13, no. 3 (2022): 1–12.

[51] Catherine B. Asher, "The Sufi Shrines of Shahul Hamid in India and Southeast Asia," *Artibus Asiae* 69, no. 2 (2009): 257.

subsequently stopped due to restrictions by the Penang state government and the Islamic Religious Council of Singapore.[52] Both shrines are replicas of the original tomb in Tamil Nadu. The Nagore Dargah is now designated as Singapore's national monument. The dargah, along with the tombs of Yusuf Al-Maqassari and the great Sufi of Baghdad Abdul Qadir al-Jailani, have duplicates in different parts of Southeast Asia.

INCREDIBLE TALES

Sufi tales often are filled with hyperbolic and amazing stories seen by analysts as lacking "historical objectivity to our taste."[53] Our historical tastes are certainly not what most Sufis are inclined with. Sufi tales were not tailored to meet with the standards of credible evidence. These tales set the readers on the path of imagination and the metaphysical, to encourage seekers to persist in their paths to gain God's mercy. Such stories – even if devoid of verifiability – have for many centuries served as admonitions on how to live ethical lives. Sufi tales also underline the karamah of the saints. The tales of karamah in Southeast Asia have come in two forms: narrative histories and oral stories. From the two, few sub-genres have emerged. Julian Millie categorized them into "*tadhkirah* (memorial, momento), *manaqib* (virtuous deeds), *rijal* (the men), *sirat ul-awliya'* (biographies of the saints), and *tabaqat* (ranks or classes), and a fluctuating presence in others, such as *malfuzat* (oral discourses) and *wasaya* (testaments)."[54] These tales construct images of sanctity of saints while monumentalizing their greatness through embellishments and other rhetorical strategies.

Sufi tales in Southeast Asia come in variants, such as showcasing saints' healing powers, breaching spatial and temporal barriers, and dream encounters. Stories of saints walking on water, striking rocks for water, making food and money appear, forecasting future events, and calling for rain are also common. These stories will not be discussed here as they were not as common as the earlier three variants, but they do feature in some textual and oral stories of the karamah of Sufis in

---

[52] Torsten Tschacher, *Race, Religion, and the 'Indian Muslim' Predicament in Singapore* (London: Routledge, 2018), 103.

[53] Jacqueline Chabbi, "'Abd al-Qâdir al-Djîlânî Personnage Historique: Quelques Éléments de Biographie," *Studia Islamica* 38 (1973): 77.

[54] Julian Millie, "Khâriq Ul-'Âdah Anecdotes and the Representation of Karâmât: Written and Spoken Hagiography in Islam," *History of Religions* 48, no. 1 (2008): 43.

Southeast Asia. Needless to say, such incredible tales have been used for mobilization in times of disasters, wars, and insurrections.[55] The Sufi shaykhs' propensity to do extraordinary acts beyond the grasp of human reason (*luar kebiasaan* or *khariqul-a'dah* in Arabic) give prominence to his mystic faculties and provided essential reasons why he should be unflinchingly obeyed.

Narratives of Sufi healing powers are most abundantly found in a genre of rhythmic romances called the hikayats and babads, and other texts dedicated to discussing the miracles of saints. Shaykh Abdul Qadir al-Jailani has assumed the pride of place in many of these healing tales.[56] Written sometime in the seventeenth century, the Hikayat Shaykh Abdul Qadir al-Jailani, for example, describes the lives of four saints. Their abilities were remarkable, such as restoring eyesight, treating severe skin and intestinal diseases, subduing evil spirits, and resurrecting the dead. One of the saints achieved these feats through "silence with his head looking down and asking everyone present with him to be quiet."[57] Hikayat Shaykh Abdul Qadir al-Jailani has, for many decades, been read in groups in remembrance of the karamah of the saints. Artistic impressions of the saint are still found in Muslim houses across Southeast Asia today.

Hikayat Shaykh Abdul Qadir al-Jailani and its artistic impressions have also inspired the publication of books on the miracles of Shaykh Abdul Qadir in various Malay-Indonesian languages. One recent book has it that during a cholera pandemic, Shaykh Abdul Qadir called upon villagers to eat the grass growing in the vicinity of his school. This story seems to be an indirect admonition to readers that they too can get assistance for their ailments by visiting Sufis who ran Islamic schools all over Southeast Asia. More about this is in Chapter 4. For now, the tale continues with the dearth of grass at the school as pandemic crisis heightened. Shaykh Abdul Qadir provided the penultimate solution: "Whosoever drinks water from my school will be cured by Allah."[58]

The Hikayat Patani, another popular Malay historical text written in the seventeenth century, links Sufi healing powers to the Islamization of

---

[55] Sartono Kartodirdjo, "Agrarian Radicalism in Java: Its Setting and Development," in *Culture and Politics in Indonesia,* ed. Claire Holt (Jakarta: Equinox Publishing Ltd, 2007), 80–81.

[56] G. W. J. Drewes and Poerbatjakara, *Kisah-Kisah Ajaib Syekh Abdulkadir Jailana* (trans. M. Amir Sutaarga) (Jakarta: Pustaka Jaya, 1990).

[57] Muhammad Hamidi, *Mitos-Mitos Dalam Hikayat Abdulkadir Jailani* (Jakarta: Yayasan Obor Indonesia, 2003), 124.

[58] Sahara Ramadhani and Shofia Trianing Indarti, *Kisah Penyejuk Jiwa Syaikh Abdul Qodir Jaelani* (Yogyakarta: Penerbit Anak Hebat Indonesia, 2021), 93.

kings. Sufis have functioned as traditional healers in Southeast Asia for many centuries, sometimes using magical practices.[59] In Hikayat Patani, the Sufi Shaykh Said cures Phaya Tu Nakpa, the Buddhist ruler of Patani, who was suffering from a chronic sickness that caused cracks all over his body, leading to his conversion to Islam. In Sufi literature during the medieval period, stories of bodily diseases were often used by Sufi masters as allegories for souls tainted by wrongful beliefs and excessive love of the material world. Submission to the will of the one true God was prescribed as the cure for such diseases. The Hikayat Patani adapted and localized such Sufi allegories.[60] Phaya Tu Nakpa went at great lengths to find a cure for his disease by proclaiming to everyone in his kingdom the reward for anyone who could cure to his ailment would be his daughter's hand in marriage. A Sufi from Pasai, Shaykh Said, responded to the challenge. The precondition was for the king to convert to Islam upon being cured. Phaya Tu Nakpa agreed but did not keep his promise. On two occasions after having been free of his disease, he renounced Islam. Finally, after meeting the sickly king thrice, Shaykh Said offered to sacrifice his life if the king chose to abandon his faith. Phaya Tu Nakpa was astounded by the Sufi master's preposition. He accepted Islam wholeheartedly. Healed forever, Phaya Tu Nakpa enjoined his family and subjects to follow his new faith. He took on a new name, Ismail Shah Zillullah Fil-Alam. Like all other tales of Sufis curing Southeast Asian kings, Phaya Tu Nakpa conversion to Islam was a turning point in the history of his kingdom. "Hence, Patani became peaceful and prosperous, and strangers of all sorts would come and go."[61]

Incredible tales of healing powers have been transmitted orally. Mbah Jogo, a spiritual mediator affiliated with a pesantren at Watucongol village, Java, is believed to have extraordinary healing powers, stemming from his karamah. Stories about people obtaining cures for many ailments at this grave site have been passed on for several generations, making this sanctified tomb a frequently visited site annually.[62] Similar sites with long-lasting healing abilities are found in pondoks in South Thailand in Songkhla, Patthalung, Nakorn Si Thammarak, Trang, Krabi,

---

[59] Teren Sevea, *Miracles and Material Life: Rice, Ore, Traps and Guns in Islamic Malaya* (New York: Cambridge University Press, 2020).

[60] Shahzad Bashir, *Religion and Society in Medieval Islam* (New York: Columbia University Press, 2011), 201.

[61] Anon., *Hikayat Patani,* eds. A. Teuww and D. K. Wyatt (The Hague: Nijhoff, 1970), 78.

[62] M. Dawam Rahardjo, "The Life of Santri Youth: A View from the Pesantren Window at Pabelan," *Sojourn: Journal of Social Issues in Southeast Asia* 1, no. 1 (1986): 36.

Pangnga, and Phuket.[63] The healing powers of dead saints were usually laced with stories of teleportation of extraordinary Sufis breaching spatial and temporal barriers.

The Sufis were, of course, not the first persons in Islam to have the ability to traverse across spatial and temporal spaces beyond what was humanly possible. In an event known as the Night Journey and Ascension (*Al-Isra' wal-Mi'raj*), the Prophet Muhammad was reported to have travelled from Makkah to Jerusalem and then ascent to the highest heavens within a night. This story became a "familiar trope" in Sufi tales to exhibit the prophetic traits that Sufis could imitate.[64] Manuals have been written on how to achieve the *mi'raj* (ascension) by those who manifest saintly qualities. The mi'raj was "paradigmatic for Sufi understandings of their own mystical journeys."[65] In one amazing story, a female Sufi sage was said to have teleported frequently from her home in Fes to the Saharan desert to deliver and care for her saintly husband, Ibrahim al-Zawawi.[66]

One celebrated figure in Southeast Asian Sufi writings known to have breached spatial and temporal barriers is Prophet Khidr (or Al-Khadir, Arabic for "The Green One"), depicted in Hikayat Nabi Dzulkarnain as a wise man, miracle worker, and a traveller who brought Alexander the Great to many lands and other extra-terrestrial realms.[67] This story and those of Prophet Muhammad's night journey and ascension were the templates used by creators of tales about the miraculous travels of Southeast Asian saints. The earliest known Southeast Asian teleportation story involves Sultan Agung (1593–1645), a noted Sufi scholar, conqueror, and ruler of the Kingdom of Mataram, in Central Java. He was said to have flown to Makkah for Friday prayers and returned the same day.[68] The son of the Sultan of Banten, Pangeran Dakar (or Haji Mangsur), made the same magical journeys. In a story written in the nineteenth century, Pangeran Dakar met with Shaykh Karang, a Sufi and aspirant to the

---

[63] Hassan Madmarn, "Traditional Muslim Institutions in Southern Thailand: A Critical Study of Islamic Education and Arabic Influence in the Pondok and Madrasah Systems in Pattani" (PhD Dissertation, United States, University of Utah, 1990), 118–120.

[64] Brooke Olson Vuckovic, *Heavenly Journeys, Earthly Concerns: The Legacy of the Mi'raj in the Formation of Islam* (London: Routledge, 2005), 124.

[65] Michael A. Sells (ed. and trans.), *Early Islamic Mysticism: Sufi, Qur'an, Mi'raj, Poetic, and Theological Writings* (New York: Paulist Press, 1996), 47.

[66] Scott Kugle, *Sufis and Saints' Bodies: Mysticism, Corporeality, and Sacred Power in Islam* (Chapel Hill, 2007), 104.

[67] Anon., *Hikayat Iskandar Zulkarnain* (Kuala Lumpur: Dewan Bahasa dan Pustaka, 1986).

[68] Anon., *Babad Sultan Agung* (Jakarta: Departemen Pendidikan dan Kebudayaan, 1980), 44.

throne. Shaykh Karang asked Pangeran Dakar to join him for prayers in Makkah. The story proceeds with the Sufis competing with another. As expected, the one with royal blood prevailed:

> "I can fly there, but can you?" Pangeran Dakar answered: "I can walk there." Both of them left on a Friday at 11 o'clock, Shaykh Karang flying and Pangeran Dakar underground, but Pangerang Dakar was the first-comer. They returned the same way they had come, but the next Friday the roles were reversed: Pangeran Dakar flew but at the moment Shaykh Karang's entering into the earth it closed up....Pangeran Dakar admitted his high birth, and Shaykh Karang humbly confessed that he was still out for the Banten sultanate. Pangeran Dakar said: "Alright! But first you will have to practice asceticism for a period of twenty-five years!"[69]

Such tales throw light on the imagined networks which Sufis in Southeast Asia had with their brethren based in the heartlands of Islam. Similar stories involve other Southeast Asian saints and leaders,

Keramat Habib Noh at Palmer Road in the early twentieth Century: https://en.wikipedia.org/wiki/Keramat_Habib_Noh#/media/File:Keramat_Habib_Noh.jpg

---

[69] G. W. J. Drewes, "Short Notice on the Story of Haji Mangsur of Banten," *Archipel* 50 (1995): 122.

Miracles **71**

highlighting their mystical faculties and legitimacy. Teleportation to Makkah and other similar swift journeys gave added validation to leaders of tariqahs. One example was Kyai Fuad Hasyim Buntet (1941–2014) of Cirebon. Believed to have the karamah of healing as witnessed by his students and followers, he could travel to various provinces in Indonesia within minutes when others would usually take hours or even days.[70] As for Habib Nuh discussed earlier, he was regularly imprisoned by the British for being a nuisance to the public. In shock, the colonial police would find him walking on the streets moments after he was placed in his cell. There were stories of him in Penang at the same time when he was in Singapore.[71]

Hamka, whose writings have influenced the course of Sufism in Southeast Asia, cast doubt over the historicity of these tales which, to him, were common everyday rumours. He cites the views of scholars from various schools of Islamic thought who categorically rejected such miracles which were reserved only for the prophets. To him, stories of teleportation could also be rejected based on syllogistic reasoning. "If we say a saint could fly without wings based on hearsay without providing clear evidence that it actually happened, then it is also rationally acceptable to say that such stories are simply lies or fabrications used by blinded disciples who sought to magnify the influence of their teachers."[72]

Another line of incredible tales were about dream (*mimpi* in Malay, *manam* in Arabic) encounters. As explained in the earlier chapter, dreams are crucial in Islamic beliefs and a core element within Sufi cosmology. The Prophet Muhammad regarded dreams as "the seventieth part of prophecy."[73] Carl Ernst notes that dreams are a staple part of Sufi mystical experience. "There were even some Sufis who specialized in the talent of producing dreams of the Prophet for others, in this way democratizing access to the source of spirituality."[74] Dream encounters provided divine signs (*ishara*, or *isyarat* in Malay) of things to come. They are divine rejoinders to certain hopes, requests, devotions, or deeds. Manuals and autobiographies have been written in Southeast Asia on the interpretation of dreams. A respected Sufi, Maulana Ashraf Ali Thanvi

---

[70] Samsul Munir Amin, *Karomah Para Kiai* (Yogyakarta: Pustaka Pesantren, 2008), 160–161.

[71] "The Singapore Free Press," August 2, 1866; Editorial, "The Miracle Worker of Old Singapore," *New Nation*, September 1, 1972.

[72] Hamka, *Pelajaran Agama Islam* (Jakarta: Gema Insani, 2018), 212.

[73] Muslim ibn al-Hajjaj al-Qushayri, *Sahih Muslim, Vol. 4* (Lahore: Sh. Muhammad Ashraf, 1975), 1225.

[74] Carl Ernst, "Muhammad as the Pole of Existence," in *The Cambridge Companion to Muhammad,* ed. Jonathan E. Brockopp (New York: Cambridge University Press, 2010), 136.

(1863–1943), whom many Southeast Asian Sufis studied with during their long sojourns in India, however, warned of obsession with dreams:

> Many ignorant Sufis pay too much attention to their dreams. When there is a shortage of good dreams, they consider it to be a sign of distance from Allah and therefore become disheartened and distressed. When they see good dreams, they consider it to be the height of accomplishment and grow proud. When they see an incident in a dream, they rely upon their vision implicitly. When they have a bad dream, they become caught up in its foreboding....In short, a dream is not as great as people make it out to be. The essential concern of a person should be to ask himself: When I am awake, am I acting in a way that will bring the pleasure of Allah or His displeasure?[75]

Dream encounters with the Prophet Muhammad are considered the noblest of dreams. Anyone who dreamt of meeting the prophet was destined for greatness. In placing my attention to dream encounters with the prophet here, I am not saying that dream encounters with Sufi saints are less important. Within the Sufi tradition, dreams have been viewed as important elements in maintaining the relationship between the novice and his master. Dreams and the ability to interpret dream visions may heighten a Sufi shaykh's notability.[76] This chapter begins with Gus Dur dreaming of Sufi saints. He was just one among many followers of Sufism who have for centuries encountered prominent Sufis in their dream visions. By making known these encounters, storytellers such as Gus Dur obliquely assigned prominence to themselves. Dream encounters with Sufi saints, especially with Abdul Qadir al-Jailani, connotes spiritual maturity, allowing one to rise in the pecking order of the Sufi fraternity. Such dreams were also used to nominate leaders of tariqahs.[77]

Dream encounters with the prophet have been ubiquitous especially among leaders of tariqahs, Muslim scholars, and rulers in Southeast Asia. Some claimed to have met the prophet on a number of occasions

---

[75] Maulana Ashraf Ali Thanvi, *A Sufi Study of the Hadith* (trans. Yusuf Talal DeLorenzo) (London: Turath Publishing, 2010), 280.

[76] Jonathan G. Katz, "Dreams and Their Interpretation in Sufi Thought and Practice," in *Dreams and Visions in Islamic Societies,* eds. Özgen Felek and Alexander D. Knysh (Albany: State University of New York Press, 2012), 192.

[77] Martin van Bruinessen, *Tarekat Naqsyabandiyya Di Indonesia: Survei Histories, Geografis Dan Sosiologis* (Penerbit Mizan, 1992), 191–214.

Miracles   **73**

in dreams as in *yaqazah* (waking visions). The more dream encounters with the prophet one claim to have, the higher one is elevated in the Sufi hierarchy. Dreams of the prophet, to use Pierre Bourdieu's term, is a form of "religious capital" used by specialists in that field "to modify, in a deep and lasting fashion the practice and worldview of lay people."[78] Dreams of the Prophet did more than what Bourdieu argued. These dreams justified the founding of tariqahs while expanding their reach. Dreams provided the rationalization for prescribing certain litanies. Dreams were used by leaders of tariqahs to maintain the obeisance of their followers. Only murshids, kyais, and shaykhs have been given the permission to relate their dreams to others, especially the general public. Murids were strictly prohibited from communicating their dreams to persons other than the murshids to prevent them from developing evil traits such as *riya'* (arrogance), *ujub* (self-conceit), and *takabbur* (pride). Dream encounters with the prophet could corrupt the soul when not handled with care. Conversely, for the leaders of tariqas and murshids, such dream encounters were trumpeted to inspire others.[79]

Dreams shared publicly by Sufi leaders usually have a transformational twist. The leader of the tarekat Nur Al-Mukmin in West Kalimantan, Shaykh Muhammad Effendi Sa'ad, is one sample. Stories about his early life paint him as an opponent of Sufi practices. The change in him came when he dreamt of Shaykh Abdul Qadir al-Jailani. This was followed by a series of dream encounters with the Prophet Muhammad, bestowing on Shaykh Muhammad Effendi the *silsilah* (spiritual genealogy) of his tariqa and special litanies. Genealogy has been, for the Sufis, a source of collective identity and legitimation of the authenticity of their tariqas. There are two ways to establish the silsilah. The first is through *silsilah mutassil* or *muwasalah* (Arabic for "unbroken genealogy"). This type of silsilah links generations of murshids back to Prophet Muhammad. The second one was called *silsilah barzaghi* or *uwaisi* (genealogy linked though dreams or spiritual encounters). Rejected by many Sufis and viewed with cynicism by others, Shaykh Muhammad Effendi used this second type. Sufis who were against silsilah barzaghi reasoned that such genealogical claims have no historical and scriptural basis. These claims were vulnerable to manipulation by anyone who accorded

---

[78] Pierre Bourdieu, "Legitimation and Structured Interests in Weber's Sociology of Religion," in *Max Weber, Rationality and Modernity,* eds. Sam Whimster and Scott Lash (London: Routledge, 1987), 127.

[79] Rosnaanini Hamid, *Adab-Adab Selepas Suluk: Tarekat Naqshabandiyyah* (Kedah: UUM Press, 2019), 47.

sainthood onto themselves. Some Sufis have committed immoral acts and vindicated deviant teachings based on the authority of their silsilahs.[80] Doubts expressed towards silsilah barzaghi have not stopped the expansion of tariqah Shaykh Muhammad Effendi. As of 2018, his followers were actively operating across Indonesia numbering over tens of thousands. These murids were convinced of his ability to communicate with the prophet through dreams.[81]

Some Sufi dream tales are far more dramatized, as seen in Merah Silau's conversion story in the last chapter which led to the founding of the first Islamic state in Southeast Asia. The dramatization and hagiographical hyperbole of such tales made them unforgettable and easily recounted. The famous Indonesian preacher, televangelist, and modernist Sufi Aa Gym (shortform for Abdullah Gymnastiar) has his share of dreams of the Prophet, bordering on the realm of exaggeration. Recounted in his autobiography with the subtitle, *Qolbugrafi* (Biography of the Heart), he recounted how his family dreamt of meeting the Prophet Muhammad. Here, the collective experience seemed more important than the personal. His dreams of the prophet were, however, far exceptional than the rest of the family. The Prophet instructed Aa Gym to call upon people to pray. This dream sanctioned his place as the leader of his congregation. It was the Prophet who asked him to lead his flock. In his second dream, he along with the four closest companions of the Prophet – Abu Bakar, Umar, Uthman, and Ali – prayed behind the prophet. Aa Gym narrates that he was standing next to Ali. Aa Gym gives the impression that even though he was not a part of the *ahlul bait* (family of the prophet), he had established such ties through his closeness with the prophet's noble son-in-law, Ali.

For Aa Gym, these dreams were reminders for him to strictly follow the path of the prophet. Dreams were motivations for constant self-improvement. The underlying message to his readers, however, is that he was the chosen one, a guide to the masses in fulfilment of the wishes of the prophet.[82] Aa Gym's dream encounters with the Prophet, as had those

---

[80] Faudzinaim Badaruddin and Muhammad Mahyuddin, "Autoriti Sanad Tarekat Dan Peranannya Dalam Ilmu Tasawuf," *International Journal of Islamic Thought* 20 (2021): 38.

[81] Patmawati and Elmansyah, *Sejarah Dan Eksistensi Tasawuf Di Kalimantan Barat* (Pontianak: IAIN Pontianak Press, 2019), 197.

[82] Abdullah Gymnastiar, *Aa Gym Apa Adanya: Sebuah Qolbugrafi* (Bandung: Khas MQ, 2006), 22–26.

that came before him, were "exemplary and prescriptive evocations."[83] Such dreams have certainly helped in the expansion of his popularity and the growth of his school, Pesantren Daarut Tauhid. Muslims persuaded by Sufi incredible tales conceive Aa Gym as a kyai with karamah endorsed by the prophet whose constant dream encounters with the prophet would guarantee their own salvation.[84]

CONCLUSION

Sanctified tombs and incredible tales are ways by which the Sufis in Southeast Asia monumentalized the idea of karamah generating memories of saints and their mystical experiences. These tombs and tales imbue power into benign spaces and ordinary personas. Through sanctified tombs and incredible tales, new meanings were infused into landmarks and new connotations were instilled into what would have been trivial stories. Tombs and tales challenged these imaginations of Muslims in Southeast Asia. Tombs and tales flouted accepted truths and orthodoxies.

Perhaps therein lies the continued fascination with Sufism as a dialogical tradition in Southeast Asia and the world. Sufis built their importance and sustained their relevance by straddling the borders of fact and fiction, real and surreal, myth and reality, intriguing the senses with things supra-rational and provoked questions about life and the afterlife. That way, Sufis established around them communities of ardent believers and sceptics, both of whom aired their views about sanctified tombs and contested the veracity of incredible claims.

In contemplating over the spirited dialogues between believers and sceptics spread across space and time in Southeast Asia, we get the sense that both recognize the importance and impact that Sufi tombs and tales have had in the local communities. Both are cognizant that sanctified tombs are "places of collective memory for the local communities, connecting them to their own history as well as to the sacred history of

---

[83] Shahzad Bashir, "Narrating Sight: Dreaming as Visual Training in Persianate Sufi Hagiography," in *Dreams and Visions in Islamic Societies,* eds. Özgen Felek and Alexander D. Knysh (Albany: State University of New York Press, 2012), 244.

[84] Dindin Solahudin, *The Workshop for Morality: The Islamic Creativity of Pesantren Daarat Tauhid in Bandung, Java* (Acton: ANU E Press, 2008).

Islam, and situating them in a sacred geography that transposes history, memory, and myth into space."[85]

Both realize that incredible tales revealed the anxieties of the common people. Stories were integral to attempts by the human beings to overcome everyday problems through sagas about extraordinary accomplishments. Although believers and sceptics would not agree on whether such tombs and tales should be upheld in the manner to how they have been, they would perhaps accede to the fact that idea of karamah has been monumentalized. Karamah has been so powerful that it would take more than the force of reason and logic to unravel its clasp on Muslim minds. Despite disagreements between believers and sceptics, karamah serves as a constituent in the dialogical tradition that defines Sufism in Southeast Asia.

---

[85] Daphna Ephrat, Ethel Sara Wolper, and Paula G. Pinto, "Introduction: History and Anthropology of Sainthood and Space in Islamic Contexts," in *Saintly Spheres and Islamic Landscapes: Emplacements of Spiritual Power across Time and Place, eds. Daphna Ephrat, Ethel Sara Wolper and Paulo G. Pinto* (Leiden: Brill, 2021), 11.

CHAPTER 3

Institutions

Sufis were master institutionalists. For over a millennium, they established *ribats* (outposts), guilds, lodges, learning hubs, mosques, and sanctified tombs. These institutions were usually grouped under the umbrella of *zawiya* or *khanqah* (large and integrated devotional complexes). Such complexes served various purposes: meeting places for the learned and seekers of knowledge, retreats for ascetics, storehouses of memories for pilgrims, and as centres by which politics and pieties intermingled. They produced and perpetuated the culture, doctrines, and practices of Sufism, entrenching tasawwuf into the physical, intellectual, and spiritual landscapes where they were created. Sufi institutions became formidable zones where transformations of selves, societies, and states were initiated. Waves of regime changes and colonial modernity greatly impacted these institutions. Many were downsized, some closed, and others reformed to fit colonial motives. Nevertheless, Sufi institutions developed an innate capacity of reform and renewal, strategically aligning with state funders and charitable sponsors committed to their longevity.[1]

Among the most influential and enduring Sufi institutions in Southeast Asia were those focused on inculcating three key elements of Islamic piety: *iman* (faith), *'ilm* (knowledge), and *amal* (praxis).[2] Known by various names, these educational centres also served as lodging

---

[1] Daphna Ephrat and Paula G. Pinto, "Sufi Places and Dwellings," in *Sufi Institutions*, ed. Alexandre Papas (Leiden: Brill, 2021), 105–144.
[2] Zailan Moris, *Revelation, Intellectual Intuition and Reason in the Philosophy of Mulla Sadra: An Analysis of the al-Hikmah al-'arshiyyah* (London: Routledge, 2013), 67.

Contemplating Sufism: Dialogue and Tradition Across Southeast Asia, First Edition. Khairudin Aljunied.
© 2025 John Wiley & Sons Ltd. Published 2025 by John Wiley & Sons Ltd.

houses for scholars and their students. In Java and other parts of Southeast Asia, they were called *pesantren* or *pondok pesantren*. In Aceh, they were known as *dayah* or *pesantren dayah*; in Minangkabau, *surau*. In Brunei, *sekolah Arab* (Arabic schools) is the term used to describe them, and in South Thailand and the Malay peninsula, they are popularly known as *pondok*. These institutions stressed the preservation of traditional Islamic learning and the development of righteous individuals. Operating on both full-time and part-time basis, students were taught a variety of Islamic sciences and related subjects towards inculcating and embodying the tenets of the faith. *Pesantren tarekat* and *pondok tarekat* referred to institutions linked to Sufi brotherhoods,[3] with curricula revolving around Sufi thought and practices.

Azmi bin Omar notes:

> It was rare to find that the pondok tok guru was simply a teacher and did not affiliate himself to any popular Sufi orders which he was supposed to receive from Sufi masters during his study time. It follows that the students consciously or unconsciously became associated with the spiritual practice of the teacher through the chanting of dhikr (the remembrance of God) and litanies repeated throughout the day. Thus, in a way the pondok can be considered the place of learning orthodox Islam in conjunction with Sufi piety.[4]

These institutions imposed stringent rules upon students, who were under the watchful eye of their teachers. Some scholars therefore construe pondok and pesantren as "total institutions," a concept developed by the anthropologist Erving Goffman. According to Goffman, a total institution is a place where the "mortifications of the self" occur. Pam Nilan extends this point through Michel Foucault's theory, explaining how various forms of power relations – juridical, pastoral, and bio-power – were at play in the creation of deferential, righteous, and highly disciplined students.[5] However, this analysis can be limiting as

---

[3] B. J. Boland, *The Struggle of Islam in Modern Indonesia* (Nijhoff: The Hague, 1971), 113; Manfred Ziemek, *Pesantren Dalam Perubahan Sosial* (trans. Butche B. Soendjojo) (Jakarta: Perhimpunan Pengembangan Pesantren dan Masyarakat, 1986), 99.

[4] Azmi bin Omar, "In Quest of An Islamic Ideal of Education: A Study of the Role of the Traditional Pondok Institution in Malaysia", 115, See also Muhammad Uthman El-Muhammady, "Pondok Education as Indigenous Education," *Jurnal Pendidikan Islam* 1, no. 1 (1984): 59.

[5] Pam Nilan, "The 'Spirit of Education' in Indonesian Pesantren," *British Journal of Sociology of Education* 30, no. 2 (2009): 219–232.

Institutions   **79**

it portrays power as top-down and contained within given institutions, without considering the dynamic relationships between masters and disciples and the currents of thought into and out of these institutions that spurred them to constantly reform and renew.

Alternatively, pondoks, pesantren, dayah, sekolah Arab, and madrasah of Sufi provenance (collectively referred as "Sufi seminaries") can be better understood not only as total institutions where many forms of power are played out but also as dynamic cosmoses where various actors, ideas, and things circulate. In other words, Sufi seminaries were "circulatory institutions." Like circuit boards, Sufi seminaries have functioned as conduits for a host of organic texts and pioneers of Muslim networks. Suffused with insights drawn from scholars affiliated with the Ash'arite, Shafi'ite, and Al-Ghazalian schools of thought, organic texts were furnished with fresh readings of Sufistic idioms. They were copied, taught, memorized, annotated, disseminated, explained, and discussed in a grammar suited for Southeast Asian realities. A system of 'ijazah linking teachers and students back to the *sanad* (lineage) of past scholars ensured that new readings of organic texts remained true to the spirit of the Sunni Sufi tradition. In providing new interpretations of age-old organic texts, these circulatory institutions kept alive what Mahmood Kooria describes as "textual cords" and "textual families," connecting Southeast Asian interpretive communities with the rest of the Muslim world.[6]

Sufi seminaries in Southeast Asia also housed spiritual mediators – founders, scholars, teachers, and mentors – who developed erudite, refined, and divine-oriented human beings. Known as *kiyai, tok guru, tuan guru, shaykh, ajengan,* and *buya* (all referring to "highly respected teachers"), they moulded these institutions into places for students desiring to seek knowledge, wisdom, and enlightenment. These spiritual mediators were itinerant scholars who travelled to prestigious universities and colleges within Southeast Asia and beyond, before settling into Sufi seminaries within their hometowns. They imbibed Sufi ethics and piety in their disciples using organic texts and everyday embodiment of Islamic precepts. Spiritual mediators beget spiritual mediators. Having achieved their pious and scholarly intents from a given Sufi seminary, religious-educated Muslims (often known as *santri, murid,* or *pelajar*) would move to other akin institutions to broaden their horizons of learning.

---

[6] Mahmood Kooria, *Islamic Law in Circulation: Shafi'i Texts across the Indian Ocean and Mediterranean* (Cambridge: Cambridge University Press, 2022), 5.

Many eventually returned to their alma mater, others established Sufi seminaries of their own. This constant movement and reproduction of spiritual mediators gave rise to a network of Sufi seminaries bound together by sanads, silsilahs, and shaykhs.[7]

Sufi seminaries can be called circulatory institutions because they accommodated devout communities who found solace, inspiration, and solutions to their tribulations. Devout communities consisted of people from both local and distant places who frequented specific Sufi seminaries. They believed in the capacities of spiritual mediators in resolving life's difficult questions. Their association and support for Sufi seminaries stemmed from their desire to share the karamah, barakah, and esoteric and worldly knowledge found in these places. Clifford Geertz colourfully characterizes spiritual mediators as advisors and guides for those with bodily and spiritual ailments. They assisted devout communities in addressing existential problems, making them more mindful of the incentives flowing from life's fortunes and misfortunes. They were also brokers of communal activities, from large feasts to pilgrimages to Makkah and other sacred sites, all supported by the active participation of devout communities.[8]

The triangular relationship between organic texts, spiritual mediators, and devout communities enabled circulatory institutions to enhance Sufism as a dialogical tradition in Southeast Asia. They fulfilled manifold purposes, ranging from the educational, relational, mystical, martial, and political. The circulation of people and ideas in Sufi seminaries through their extended networks helped them overcome challenges posed by empires and nation-states. Sufi seminaries amalgamated morality with modernity, tradition with technology, and spirituality with globality,[9] exhibiting diverse norms, cultures, rules, and management styles. Such diversity and polyvocality do not discount similar features between them and the constant interactions and competition among them.[10] Furthermore, these circulatory institutions are bounded by intersecting histories. To that we now turn to.

---

[7] Martin van Bruinessen, *Kitab Kuning: Pesantren Dan Tarekat* (Jakarta: Mizan Press, 1995), 15.

[8] Clifford Geertz, "The Javanese Kijaji: The Changing Role of a Cultural Broker," *Comparative Studies in Society and History* 2, no. 2 (1960): 231–234.

[9] Ronald Lukens-Bull, *A Peaceful Jihad: Negotiating Identity and Modernity in Muslim Java* (Basingstoke: Palgrave Macmillan, 2005), 6.

[10] Robert W. Hefner, "Introduction: The Culture, Politics, and Future of Muslim Education," in *Schooling Islam: The Culture and Politics of Modern Muslim Education,* eds. Robert W. Hefner and Muhammad Qasim Zaman (Princeton NJ: Princeton University Press, 2007), 2.

CIRCULATORY PASTS

The exact origins of the first Sufi seminary in Southeast Asia are uncertain. Some orientalists trace the origins of these institutions to Hindu-Buddhist monasteries that existed centuries before the arrival of Islam in the region. These monasteries were sites where budding scholar-mystics gathered around sages and priests to recite and internalize holy texts, living together for many years in tightly bound master-disciple relationships. According to this view, Sufi seminaries merely replicated and continued the existing Hindu-Buddhist tradition of teaching and learning in highly regulated settings. This interpretation, often promoted by Western scholars, downplays the novelty of Sufi seminaries as uniquely Islamic institutions and suggests that Southeast Asian Muslims never fully abandoned their earlier beliefs and practices, Islam being just an overlay on existing folk religious traditions.[11]

However, this viewpoint has been challenged by evidence pointing to a different historical trajectory of circulatory institutions in Southeast Asia. Most Sufi seminaries grew out of mosques, prayer places (*surau*), courts of kings, or homes of teachers, rather than full-time monasteries. These developments mirrored patterns seen in other parts of the Muslim world. Students and teachers gathered to read, memorize, and debate the Qur'an and other Islamic texts. Mosques, prayer places, palaces, and homes were expanded to include formal educational bodies.[12] The rapid growth of Sufi seminaries in Southeast Asia coincided with the spread of Islam throughout the region, and this soon eclipsed Hindu-Buddhist institutions. A local historian, Mahmud Yunus, argues in a rather tenuous way that pesantren were established as soon as Islam asserted its presence in Southeast Asia from the thirteenth century onwards,[13] dayahs in Aceh being particularly influential in the spread of Islam. The earliest dayah, Dayah Kan'an, was built by an Arabian scholar-trader, 'Abdallah Kan'an. Renowned Sufi scholars such as Abd al-Rauf al-Sinkili and Daud al-Jawi al-Rumi taught and wrote their famous treatises in these

---

[11] Andrea Acri and Verena Meyer, "Indic-Islamic Encounters in Javanese and Malay Mystical Literatures," *Indonesia and the Malay World* 47, no. 139 (2019): 279; Karel A. Steenbrink, *Pesantren, Madrasah, Sekolah, Pendidikan Islam Dalam Kurun Modern* (trans. Karel A. Steenbrink Dan Abdurrahman) (Jakarta: LP3ES, 1994), 20–21.

[12] George Makdisi, *The Rise of Colleges: Institutions of Learning in Islam and the West* (Edinburgh: Edinburgh University Press, 1981).

[13] Mahmud H. Yunus, *Sejarah Pendidikan Islam Di Indonesia* (Jakarta: Mutiara, 1979), 231.

A Quranic school in colonial Java: https://en.wikipedia.org/wiki/Pesantren#/media/File:COLLECTIE_TROPENMUSEUM_Een_Koranschool_op_Java_TMnr_10002385.jpg

circulatory institutions. In Java, Sufi seminaries developed in tandem with missionizing work of the Wali Songo.[14]

Most contemporary historians, however, date the origins of Sufi seminaries to the late sixteenth century. Prior to that era, Sufi seminaries were mostly informal and unstructured.[15] Regardless of the exact dating, Sufi seminaries became centres for would-be elites, educators, and entrepreneurs who acted as changemakers in Southeast Asia.[16] Until the seventeenth century, Southeast Asian Muslims received necessary grounding in language and Islamic sciences locally before pursuing higher studies in Makkah and other centres of Islamic learning.[17] Various factors could

---

[14] Asna Husin, "Leadership and Authority: Women Leading Dayah in Aceh," in *Gender and Power in Indonesian Islam Leaders, Feminists, Sufis and Pesantren Selves,* eds. Bianca J. Smith and Mark Woodward (London: Routledge, 2014), 49–51.

[15] Robert W. Hefner, "Introduction: The Politics and Cultures of Islamic Education in Southeast Asia," in *Making Modern Muslim: The Politics of Islamic Education in Southeast Asia,* ed. Robert W. Hefner (Hawai'i: University of Hawai'i Press, 2009), 17.

[16] Nancy K. Florida, *Writing the Past, Inscribing the Future: History as Prophesy in Colonial Java* (Durham, NC: Duke University Press, 1995), 345–348.

[17] S. Soebardi, "Santri Religious Elements as Reflected in the Serate Tjentini," *Bijdragen Tot de Taal-, Land-, En Volkenkunde* 127, no. 3 (1971): 331–349; Azyumardi Azra, *Surau: Pendidikan Islam Traditional Dalam Transisi Dan Modernisasi* (Jakarta: Logos, 2003).

explain for the flourishing of Sufi seminaries in the late eighteenth and early nineteenth centuries. Arguably, the most important was graduates trained in the Hijaz and India, and pilgrims who established schools throughout Southeast Asia. Their motivations were varied and overlapping. Khalifahs of tariqahs founded Sufi seminaries as a means to augment their followership. Of course, not all Sufi seminaries were directly linked to tariqahs. But it can be said that a large bulk of teachers in these circulatory institutions were tariqah members, mostly belonging to the Shattariyyah, Qadiriyyah, Naqshbandiyyah, Tijaniyyah, or the fusion and splinters of two or more of these brotherhoods. Sufis also founded seminaries as mediums to train a new breed of ulama and missionaries adept with local customs.[18] In Java, the growth of pesantrens was motivated by continuous defeats in wars fought against the Dutch and their adat allies. Chapter 4 delves into this theme. Sufis established schools in almost every village to recruit fighters in anticipation of another major war.[19]

Colonialism also boosted the creation of circulatory institutions. Sufis redoubled their efforts to resist the influence of colonial and Christian missionary institutions on their faith, values, and identities. This resistance intersected with the competition for converts. In Patani, the number of pondoks increased substantially since the 1820s in response to Siamese incursions into local politics and religious affairs. Students from Cambodia, the Malay peninsula, Kalimantan, and Sumatra attended these pondoks, and upon graduation, they returned home to form schools.[20] In Kelantan, Kedah, and Trengganu, prominent ulama established hundreds of pondoks inspired by the Patani model. The Kelantanese established hundreds of pondoks led by ulama such as Abdul Samad bin Muhammad Salih (or Tuan Tabal, d. 1891), Wan Ali Kutan (d. 1331), Awang Atas Banggul, Nik Daud bin Wan Sulaiman, and Tok Kenali. The established rites de passage of any student studying in Sufi seminaries in Kelantan was to further their studies in Patani, mostly in pondoks such as Pondok Berming, Pondok Semela, Pondok Dalo, Pondok Haji Mak Dagae, and Pondok Babayeh, and then to Makkah and following which return home to establish their own pondoks. In Trengganu, Hadrami-Arabs who migrated to Malay states in the twentieth century were most active in partnering with Patani-educated Malays to found authoritative

---

[18] Anthony H. Johns, "Islamization in Southeast Asia: Reflections and Reconsiderations with Special Reference to the Role of Sufism," *Journal of Southeast Asian Studies* 31, no. 1 (1993): 53–59.
[19] Endang Turmudi, *Struggling for the Umma: Changing Leadership Roles of Kiai in Jombang, East Java* (Canberra: ANU E Press, 2006); A. G. Muhaimin, *The Islamic Traditions of Cirebon: Ibadat and Adat among Javanese Muslims* (Canberra: ANU E Press, 2006).
[20] Philipp Bruckmayr, *Cambodia's Muslims and the Malay World: Malay Language, Jawi Script, and Islamic Factionalism from the 19th Century to the Present* (Leiden: Brill, 2019), 20–40.

Sufi seminaries.[21] Hadrami-Arab and Javanese merchants were also instrumental in the establishment of madrasahs of Sufi orientation.[22] At the beginning of the Second World War, pondoks and madrasahs were found in all parts of Southeast Asian island. Through their extensive networks, these Sufi seminaries eventually became staging grounds for political activities and anti-colonial struggles.[23]

The invention of steamship travel in the 1840s facilitated the development of Sufi seminaries. Students, teachers, missionaries, and activists from venerable Muslim universities and colleges in Makkah, Madinah, Hadramaut, Delhi, Damascus, Istanbul, and Cairo built similar institutions in Southeast Asia. These institutions were precursors to diploma and degree granting Muslim colleges such as the State Islamic Institutes (IAIN) and International Islamic Universities (IIU) inaugurated from the 1950s onwards.[24] The expansion of Sufi seminaries in Southeast Asia were also linked to the rise of Islamic reformism globally. New educational institutions such as the Madrasah Darul 'Ulum in Deoband, India produced many offshoots, one of which was the Madrasah Shaulatiyah which focussed on the study of hadith and Sufism. Teachers of this madrasah hailed and travelled regularly to Makkah. The madrasah attracted students from Southeast Asia. The curriculum of dayahs, pesantrens, and pondoks mirrored that of Madrasah Shaulatiyah and other similar institutions in South Asia.[25] In Aceh, a host of dayahs such as Dayah Krung Kale, Dayah Lam Diran, Dayah Meunasah Meucap, and Dayah Ujong Rimba took on modern curricula akin to the madrasah system.[26]

The introduction of the madrasah system was not a smooth process. Many conservative Sufis rebuffed attempts at modernizing their seminaries, even if the reformists were either Sufis or inclined to Sufism. Conservative Sufis labelled madrasahs as innovations of "westernized" and "anti-Islamic" forces. They opposed modern methods of teaching,

---

[21] Muhammad bin Abu Bakar, "Sayyid Muhammad Abdul Rahman Al-Idrus," in *Islam di Malaysia* (Kuala Lumpur: Persatuan Sejarah Malaysia, 1979), 34–51.

[22] Muhammad Abdul-Rauf, *A Brief History of Islam with Special Reference to Malaya* (Kuala Lumpur: Oxford University Press, 1964), 22.

[23] Hasan Madmarn, *The Pondok and Madrasah in Patani* (Bangi: UKM Press, 1999), 234.

[24] William R. Roff, "Pondoks, Madrasahs and the Production of 'Ulama' in Malaysia," *Studia Islamika* 11, no. 1 (2004): 1–21.

[25] Mahmud H. Yunus, *Sejarah Pendidikan Islam Di Indonesia*, 211–213.

[26] Asna Husin, "Leadership and Authority: Women Leading Dayah in Aceh," in *Gender and Power in Indonesian Islam Leaders, Feminists, Sufis and Pesantren Selves,* eds. Bianca J. Smith and Mark Woodward (London: Routledge, 2014), 49–51.

structured curriculums, examinations, and certifications, and above all, Western-style dress codes. The conservatives were particularly infuriated by the diminished sacred powers of the kiyais and tok gurus in many reformist madrasahs.[27] By the 1930s, however, a convergence between traditional pesantrens, pondoks, dayahs, and the modern madrasah ensued. Hybridized institutions known as "madrasah dayah," "pondok madrasah," and "madrasah pesantren" became popular. In Java, the leader of Nahdlatul Ulama (NU) and Indonesia's Minister of Religious Affairs, Abdul Wahid Hashim (1914–1953) spearheaded the adoption of madrasah system in pesantrens. Pesantren Tebuireng, Pesantren Krapyak, and Pesantren Tambak Beras were among the first NU-affiliated pesantrens to incorporate the madrasah system.[28] In East Aceh, the Bustanul Ulum dayah underwent similar reforms, introducing subjects such as mathematics, history, geography, and English. These reforms resulted in two types of Sufi seminaries: *salafi* and *khalafi*. Those that gave more emphasis on the memorization of organic texts were termed *salafi* (followers of predecessors) seminaries. The second type balanced traditional and modern subjects through an organized curriculum. They have been called *khalafi* (followers of later generations) seminaries.[29]

State patronage and regulations accelerated reforms within Sufi seminaries while also driving some towards radicalism and other forms of resistance. With support from Sultan Iskandar Shah (1878–1938), a foundation was established in the 1920s to overlook the modernization of all religious schools in Perak. The Sultan himself endowed a piece of land to build a new religious school named Al Madrasah Al-Idrisiah, at Kuala Kangsar.[30] In South Thailand, the exponential expansion of pondoks prompted the government to introduce a registration scheme in 1961. This scheme requires compliance with the Ministry of Education protocols in exchange for subsidies, scholarships, and other forms of assistance. However, it was negatively received by many Muslims and provoked the formation of separatist movements like the Patani United

---

[27] Azyumardi Azra, Dina Afrianty, and Robert W. Hefner, "Pesantren and Madrasa: Muslim Schools and National Ideals in Indonesia," in *Schooling Islam: The Culture and Politics of Modern Muslim Education,* eds. Robert W. Hefner and Muhammad Qasim Zaman (Princeton, NJ: Princeton University Press, 2007), 176.

[28] Zamakhsyari Dhofier, *Tradisi Pesantren: Studi Tentang Pandangan Hidup Kiyai* (Jakarta: LP3ES, 1980), 84–86.

[29] Baihaqi AK, *Ulama Dan Madrasah di Aceh* (Jakarta: Lembaga Ilmu Pengetahuan Indonesia, 1976).

[30] Badriyah Haji Salleh, *Kampung Haji Salleh Dan Madrasah Saadiah-Salihiah, 1914–1959* (Kuala Lumpur: Dewan Bahasa dan Pustaka, 1984), xxviii.

Liberation Movement (PULO) in 1968. By 1986, two hundred pondoks joined the scheme. Many pondok owners who refused to register were closed down and the founding of new pondoks was disallowed. These restrictions fumed many Sufi leaders who saw government-controlled pondoks as part of a conspiracy to secularize and nationalize Islam in Thailand.[31]

Despite the challenges, many Sufi seminaries accepted government funding to allow for infrastructural refurbishment and the inclusion of state-mandated subjects in their curricula. The Malaysian government divided religious schools into state-funded (*Sekolah Agama Negeri* (SAN) or State Religious Schools) and privately funded (*Sekolah Agama Rakyat* (SAR) or People's Religious Schools), both complying with national educational standards and receiving substantial governmental support.[32] Recent surveys indicate that close to fifteen to twenty-five per cent of Muslims in Malaysia, Indonesia, South Philippines, and Brunei Darussalam have attended Sufi seminaries either at some level, with figures as high as forty to sixty per cent in Patani, Aceh, and Cambodia. In Aceh alone, there were eight hundred dayahs in 2005, mostly affiliated to tariqahs, boasting hundreds of thousands of graduates who studied as either part-time or full-time students.[33]

Although segregated in terms of gender, girls were admitted to these circulatory institutions since a century ago. The rural–urban divide has also narrowed in that more rural students have been studying in urban-based Sufi seminaries and vice versa. Sufi seminaries included a mixture of students from different class backgrounds and nationalities. An increasing number of professionals have been sending their children to these circulatory institutions to expose them to the rudiments of Islamic sciences at an early age. By 2011, the Ministry of Religion in Indonesia listed 25,000 pesantrens in Indonesia. The more than three million students in these institutions make up thirteen per cent of students in the country.[34]

---

[31] Surin Pitsuwan, *Islam and Malay Nationalism: A Case Study of Malay-Muslims of Southern Thailand* (Bangkok: Thai Khadi Research Institute, Thammasat University, 1985), 2.

[32] Mohd. Shuhaimi bin Haji Ishak and Osman Chuah Abdullah, "Islamic Education in Malaysia: A Study of History and Development," *Religious Education* 108, no. 3 (2013): 302.

[33] Marzuki Abu Bakar, *Pesantren Di Aceh: Perubahan, Aktualisasi Dan Pengembangan* (Yogyakarta: Kaukaba Dipantara, 2015), 41.

[34] "Di Indonesia, Jumlah Santri Ponpes Mencapai 3,65 Juta," *Republika*, July 19, 2011.

ORGANIC TEXTS

Islam is a religion of texts, underlining the importance of the written word in the lives of Muslims. The Qur'an refers to itself as a book of divine guidance for all of creation. Memorized by believers since the time of the Prophet Muhammad, the Qur'an and the hadith were soon codified and canonized for posterity, creating an "oral-textual tradition" where texts were recited, remembered and, in turn, reinforced by writing. The intersection between the verbal and the written word became a hallmark of the Muslim civilization.

Seyyed Hossein Nasr describes the dynamics between orality and textuality in Islam:

> As a result of the influence of the Qur'anic revelation and also other factors related to the rise of the whole Islamic educational system, the significance of the oral tradition and memory as a vehicle for the transmission of knowledge came to complement the written word contained in books, especially those books which became central texts for the teaching of various schools of thought and which figured prominently in the relationship between the traditional master (*al-ustad*) and the students (*tullab*). Such books became more than simply the written text. Rather, they came to accompany and in a sense became immersed in the spoken word, through an oral teaching transmitted from master to student and stored in the memory of those destined to be the recipients of the knowledge in question. Such books were not exclusively written texts whose reality was exhausted by the words inscribed in ink upon parchment.[35]

Books and treatises in Islamic history are best described as "organic texts." In Sufi seminaries, these texts were organic in the sense that they were transmitted and interpreted by generations of masters and disciples. Sufi texts were also organic because the transmission process involved new exegeses, interpretations, and renderings. These texts structured the everyday practices of Muslims from all walks of life and have been referenced time and again by the learned in their bid to make sense of

---

[35] Seyyed Hossein Nasr, "Oral Transmission and the Book in Islamic Education," in *The Book in the Islamic World: The Written Word and Communication in the Middle East,* eds. George N. Atiyeh (State University of New York Press: Albany, 1995), 57.

what it means to be Muslim. For the Sufis, texts are deeply organic as they connect the souls with the divine. Incessantly recited, rehearsed, and reflected upon, texts chaperone a Sufi into the path of repentance, certainty, and higher truth. Texts transform society as vehicles for mobilization and social change.

Up until the twentieth century, organic texts used in Sufi seminaries included *kitab kuning* (yellow book), named after the yellow paper made from mulberry trees. Often written in Arabic script, these texts were divided into small sections of no more than twenty pages for ease of memorization. Kitab kuning were known as *kitab gundul* (bare books) due to the lack of diacritic symbols, and as *kitab jawi* when composed or translated into Malay but written in Arabic script. Most organic texts were authored by Arabs, Persians, and Indians, with a substantial number written by Southeast Asian ulama. If the authors of hikayats were mostly unknown, organic texts carried the names of the originators. Southeast Asian ulama often included their *laqab* (honorific) indicating their origins and sometimes their Sufi brotherhood. Hence, a scholar from Banten would put his pen name as "Nawawi al-Bantani (1813–1897), another from Patani referred to himself as "Daud Al-Fatani (1720–1879)," among many others. Such naming conventions are revealing of the fond connections the authors' had with their homelands, even if many did not return home after long sojourns in sprawling centres of religious learning. We can also interpret these naming conventions as the authors' and their attempts to reach out to Southeast Asian audiences who shared common visions and love for their land of origins. Names reflected bonds which the Sufi scholars had with their countrymen who were bounded by networks of brotherhoods linking Southeast Asia, South Asia, and the Arab-speaking world.[36]

Sufi seminaries in Southeast Asia taught a wide range of organic texts encompassing subjects such as *aqeedah* (theology), *tafsir* (Quranic exegesis), *hadith* (prophetic traditions), *fiqh* (Islamic jurisprudence), *usul al-din* (roots of faith), *usul al-fiqh* (bases of Islamic jurisprudence), *nahu* and *sharaf* (Arabic grammar), *mantiq* (logic), and tasawwuf. The selection of texts was geared towards inculcating the knowledge of *al-haqq*

---

[36] Anthony H. Johns, "Islam in the Malay World: An Exploratory Survey with Some Reference to Quranic Exegesis," in *Islam in Asia, Vol. II Southeast and East Asia,* eds. Raphael Israeli and Anthony H. Johns (Jerusalem: The Magnes Press, 1984), 131; Virginia Matheson and M. B. Hooker, "Jawi Literature in Patani: The Maintenance of an Islamic Tradition," *Journal of the Malaysian Branch of the Royal Asiatic Society* 61, no. 1 (254) (1988): 19.

Institutions

(the truth), *al-ʿadl* (justice), and *al-jamal* (beauty). As Mohammed Gamal Abdelnour has expertly shown, the three overlapping spheres of knowledge were derived from a well-known ḥadith of Gabriel (*hadith Jibril*) which influenced generations of Sufi and other Muslim seminaries and scholars in the Muslim world.[37]

Teachers in Sufi seminaries carefully selected the organic texts to be read and memorized, usually in line with the ijazahs they received from their masters. Rarely would each subject be tutored in great depth such that the students were qualified to be called ulama. Sufi seminaries often acted as preparatory launchpads for students to pursue higher studies outside Southeast Asia. Predictably, many students cut short their studies after memorizing several texts and learning various subjects with several teachers, often taking on other vocations such as *imam* (prayer leaders), *qadi* (judges), and *daʾi* (popular preachers). They led supplications and prayers during communal ceremonies.[38]

Sufi seminaries in Southeast Asia used different organic texts at different periods in response to changing intellectual landscapes and needs. L. W. C. van den Berg's study of pesantrens in Java in the 1880s noted the lack of tafsir and hadith texts in the curriculum.[39] Before the twentieth century, Sufi teachers and scholars in Javanese Sufi seminaries primarily focused on teaching and commenting on the works of great Sufis, emphasizing one's depth in mystical sciences. Many seminaries were also archives of veritable manuscripts of medieval Sufi texts.[40] This changed from the 1900s onwards, with books on Islamic jurisprudence and roots of faith becoming more prominent.[41] Influenced by the rise of Islamic reformism and ideas circulated by returning Southeast Asian students from the Hejaz and Cairo and deeply impacted by the Salafiyyah movement that called for the return to the spirit of pristine Islam, a new

---

[37] Mohammed Gamal Abdelnour, *The Higher Objectives of Islamic Theology* (New York: Oxford University Press, 2022), 57.

[38] Sabri Haji Said, *Madrasah Al-Ulum Al-Syariah Perak 1937–1977: Satu Kajian Pendidikan Islam* (Kuala Lumpur: Dewan Bahasa dan Pustaka, 1983), 20–21.

[39] L. W. C. van den Berg, "Het Mohammedaansche Godsdienstonderwijs Op Java En Madoera En de Daarbij Gebruikt Arabische Boeken," *Tijdschrift Voor In- Dische Taal-, Land-, En Volkenkunde* 31 (1886): 519–555.

[40] Michael F. Laffan, "A Sufi Century? The Modern Spread of the Sufi Orders in Southeast Asia," in *Global Muslims in the Age of Steam and Print,* eds. James L. Gelvin and Nile Green (Berkeley: University of California Press, 2013), 33.

[41] Virginia Matheson and M. B Hooker, "Jawi Literature in Patani: The Maintenance of an Islamic Tradition," *Journal of the Malaysian Branch of the Royal Asiatic Society* 61, no. 1 (254) (1988): 41.

breed of Sufi ulama sought to free Muslims from superstition, corrupted ideologies, and transgressions from the Qur'an and Sunnah.[42] Be that as it may, tasawwuf was not downplayed in the curriculum of these seminaries. It was infused into many subjects including the teaching of Arabic. In most Sufi seminaries, the work of the Spanish Sufi scholar Muhammad bin Abdullah bin Malik (1204–1274), *Alfiyya Ibn Malik*, was widely used. This book on Arabic grammar goes beyond the rules of language. The author covers themes which Sufis were conscientious about such as wasilah and iman.[43]

More than nine hundred titles have been used in the pesantrens. If all Sufi seminaries in Southeast Asia are considered over the last seven centuries, the number of titles used for teaching would probably exceed a thousand. Less than half of these organic texts were written by Southeast Asian ulama, with most written in Arabic. The texts used in Southeast Asia were similar to those assigned at the Al-Azhar University in Cairo.[44] Among the most notable texts, those authored by Arab and Persian Sufi scholars stood out. These included Abu Hamid Al-Ghazzali's *Ihya 'Ulum al-Din* (Revivification of the Religious Sciences), Ibn Ata Allah al-Iskandari's (1259–1310) *Kitab al-Hikam* (Book of Wisdom), and *Burhanuddin al-Zarnuji*'s (d. 1195) *Ta'lim Al-Muta'allim Thariq At-Ta'allum* (Instruction of the Student: The Method of Learning).

Some Sufi seminaries dedicated their curriculum solely to the teaching of Al-Ghazzali's works. In the learning and memorization of *hadith* (prophetic sayings), An-Nawawi's *Riyadhus Solihin* (Gardens of the Righteous) and his collection of forty hadiths were most popular, both books centring around living an ethical, virtuous, and pious life. The writings of Hadrami-Arab scholar, Abdallah 'Alawi al-Haddad (1634–1720), were staples for Sufi seminaries in Southeast Asia. Abdullah's *Risalat al-Mu'awana* (The Book of Assistance) and *An-Nasa'ih ad-Diniyya Wal Wasaya al-Imaniyyah* (Sincere Religious Advices and Counsels of Faith)

---

[42] Michael F. Laffan, "A Sufi Century? The Modern Spread of the Sufi Orders in Southeast Asia," in *Global Muslims in the Age of Steam and Print*, eds. James L. Gelvin and Nile Green (Berkeley: University of California Press, 2013), 28.

[43] For a brief commentary of this text, read: Sidney Glazer, "The Alfiyya of Ibn Malik," *The Muslim World* 31, no. 3 (1941): 274–279. See also: Muhammad bin Abdullah bin Malik, *Matan Alfiyah Ibnu Malik* (Maktabah Dar al-Arubah li Nashr wa Tawazi: Kuwait, 2006).

[44] Adhi Maftuhin, *Sanad Ulama Nusantara Transmisi Keilmuan Ulama Al-Azhar & Pesantren Disertai Biografi Penulis Kitab Kuning* (Bogor: Sahifa Publishing, 2018).

Institutions 91

being widely used, translated into several Malay-Indonesian dialects, and republished in many versions for use in circulatory institutions.[45]

Figures in the likes of Hamzah Fansuri, Shamsuddin al-Sumatrani, Nuruddin al-Raniri and Abdur-Ra'uf Singkel have been lauded as among the most profound Sufi writers in Southeast Asia, but their books have not been assigned as essential readings for Sufi seminaries. Highly philosophical works were rare in the curricula of Sufi seminaries, probably due to the difficulty in language, making them unsuited for pedagogical purposes for students below the advanced level of learning. Among the less philosophical and more practical texts were Abdul Samad al-Palimbani's *Sairus Salikin* (Progress of Travellers on the Sufi Path) and *Hidayatul Salikin* (Guidance of Travellers on the Sufi Path). They are renderings and commentaries of al-Ghazzali's works. Shaykh Ahmad Khatib al-Sambasi's *Fathul 'Arifin* (Victory of the Gnostics) was also a well-known book used in many Indonesian Sufi seminaries for many decades till this day. In the pondoks of South Thailand, Abd al-Qadir al-Mandili's *Penawar Bagi Hati* (Remedy for the Heart) was assigned a compulsory reading. Shaykh Daud Al-Fatani's (1769–1847) writings, blending Sufistic interpretations with theology, jurisprudence, and the refinement of character (*akhlaq*), have endured in Sufi seminaries in South Thailand and the Malay Peninsula for over two centuries. His *Kashf al-Ghummah* (Lifting the Hardship) and *Munyatul Musolli* (Hopes of Those Who Pray) have been must-read for anyone studying in pondoks in northern Malaysia and Patani.[46] The organic texts written by Southeast Asian Sufis may seem "unoriginal" to the Western eye as many of them were translations, redactions, or *sharh* (or *syarah* in Malay which means commentaries) of Arabic or Persian texts.[47] The claim to the lack of originality is unconvincing. Granted that many of these organic texts were adapted from other canonical writings, the process of selecting and the teasing out of relevant aspects of major works that uniquely inform local audiences about the universality of Islam demonstrate the inventiveness of many Southeast Asian Sufi ulama.

---

[45] Martin van Bruinessen, "Kitab Kuning; Books in Arabic Script Used in the Pesantren Milieu; Comments on a New Collection in the KITLV Library," *Bijdragen Tot de Taal-, Land- En Volkenkunde* 146, no. 2/3 (1990): 256–260. See: Abdullah Al-Haddad, *Nasihat Agama dan Wasiat Iman* (trans. Syed Ahmad Semait) (Singapore: Pustaka Nasional, 1989).

[46] Rajeswary Ampalavanar Brown Brown, *Islam in Modern Thailand: Faith, Philanthropy and Politics* (London: Routledge, 2014), 123.

[47] C. Snouck Hurgronje, *Mekka in the Latter Part of the 19th Century*, 258.

Centuries of teaching and learning these organic texts in circulatory institutions nourished the Jawi ecumene in Southeast Asia. The largest number of Islamic works written in Jawi script were produced in Patani, Java, and Aceh, making these sites hubs of Jawization.[48] The teachings of these texts entrenched a synthesis of Shafi'ite jurisprudence, Ghazalian ethics, and Ashari'ite theology. I will discuss this blending of Islamic thought in Southeast Asia in Chapter 5. I wish to underline here the inculcation of Ibn 'Arabi's doctrine of wahdat al-wujud through these texts. Many Sufis in Southeast Asia have elucidated their understandings of the wahdatul wujud doctrine through the concept of *martabat tujuh* (seven stages of being), foremost among them was Shaykh Fadhlullah al-Burhanpuri Al-Hindi. In his book *Al-Tuhfa al-Mursala ila Ruh al-Nabi* (The Gift Addressed to the Spirit of the Prophet) written in 1590, he asserts "the descent of Being [God] from absolute unity to the multiplicity of the phenomenal world."[49] The ideas discussed in al-Burhanpuri's treatise influenced many Sufi teachers in Southeast Asia, finding their way as well into Sufi seminaries.[50]

The ways in which these texts were taught further highlight their organic and circulatory nature. The pedagogical approach was both didactic and dialectic. Didactic, as students would sit in a small *halaqah* (study circle) or individually with a teacher reading a text aloud. Strong *adab* (manners) of learning is emphasized. Students were expected to listen attentively and display utmost respect towards teachers and fellow students, and repeat what the teacher had recited, one word at a time, in the *harfiyah* (word by word) approach. Such an approach was also dialectic because students' recitals and translations would be methodically corrected under the watchful ears of the teacher. The students were required to make notes based on the teachers' inputs. They were permitted to pose questions when allowed to. This dialectic method is known in Java as *bandongan* (to listen attentively and correct). In other parts of Southeast Asia particularly in the pondoks, it would be called *tadah kitab* or *buka kitab* which means "opening the book."[51] In both approaches to teaching organic texts, students would read selected texts cover to cover until the teacher was satisfied with their memorization and understanding. Senior students in the halaqah were assigned to assist the juniors. In many of

---

[48] Philipp Bruckmayr, *Cambodia's Muslims and the Malay World: Malay Language, Jawi Script, and Islamic Factionalism from the 19th Century to the Present* (Leiden: Brill, 2019), 20–40.

[49] Vladimir Braginsky, *The Heritage of Traditional Malay Literature: A Historical Survey of Genres, Writings and Literary Views* (Leiden: KITLV Press, 2004), 211.

[50] Muhammad ibn Fadl Allah Burhanpuri, *The Gift Addressed to the Spirit of the Prophet* (ed. and trans. Anthony H. Johns) (Australian National University, 1965).

[51] William R. Roff, "Pondoks, Madrasahs and the Production of 'Ulama in Malaysia," *Studia Islamika* 11, no. 1 (2004): 6–8.

Institutions   **93**

these Sufi seminaries, memorization was given as much emphasis as expounding and debating on what the students have learnt.

Another approach was *sorongan* (holding the text out), common in classes organized by the more senior students aiming to become kyais and tok gurus. Outside Java, this method is known as *muzakarah* or *munadharah*, involving lengthy debates and consensus building through questions posed by students or teachers on given texts and themes. Due to the intensity of this approach, muzakarah or munadarah was usually done individually, between student and teacher, but there were occasions when several students and teachers were engaged in cooperative learning.[52] Sufi seminaries were therefore not centres of rote learning, as some critics have it. Even if taqlid was emphasized, students were taught to reason out the texts they have memorized though within certain demarcated boundaries. These demarcated boundaries were not based on any curriculum design but on the premise that the teacher was the curriculum and that he was inviolable. Reformist Muslims critiqued some Sufi seminaries which were highly absolutist.

> The highly elevated and infallible position of the kyai or syekh created a system of education (in the pondok or surau) in which learning by heart rather than understanding was the main object. The student did not dare to express a different view from the kyai's. Teaching in the pesantren or surau was, and this was also true for advanced students, a one-way communication from teacher to student, not a discussion in which the students might have a chance to sharpen their minds and contribute to learning. The textbooks used were those used generations before, and the courses taught were purely religious. The pesantren or surau were not formally organized. There was no system of classes, no curriculum, no periodic assignment. Too much depended on the 'natural' progress made by the student without any guarantee as to what stage he could reach after a certain period of study. In addition, the continuance of the existence of pesantren depended to a large extent on the kyai personally; his death often resulted in its closing.[53]

Reading and memorizing texts demanded a lengthy period of commitment. Students spent an average of two years completing a text. Once several texts have been fully read and debated, students would

---

[52] Muhammad Rizal, *Pendidikan Dayah Dalam Bingkai Otonomi Khusus Aceh* (Lhokseumawe: Sefa Bumi Persada, 2016), 94–109.

[53] Deliar Noer, *The Modernist Muslim Movement in Indonesia, 1900–1942* (Singapore: Oxford University Press, 1973), 301.

then proceed to studying with another teacher in the same or some other seminaries. The total average duration of studies was between ten to fifteen years, subject to the teachers in the circulatory institutions and the abilities of the students. Moving from one seminary to another in search of deeper knowledge and mastery of texts was a long-standing tradition. Until modern reforms in the nineteenth century, students graduated from Sufi seminaries with simple *shahadah* (testimonials) permitting them to teach the texts they have mastered. These testimonials showcased the students' place within a matrix of sanads, silsilahs, and shaykhs, connecting their genealogies of knowledge back to the Prophet Muhammad.[54] A learned person's reputation was therefore judged by the number of texts she had studied, the number of circulatory institutions she had passed through, the time spent under the feet of learned teachers, as well as the inclusion of her name within the lineages of eminent scholars and saints across generations.[55]

One other reason why the texts taught and studied in Sufi seminaries should be styled as organic texts was because they were also put into practice and personified in the lives of the students and their teachers. Litanies and lessons from texts permeated all other activities in Sufi seminaries. Students participated in daily dhikr and communal prayers led by their teachers and seniors. They have to work together with other students in ensuring the upkeep of the institutions. In most Sufi seminaries, students cooked their own food.[56] While doing these multifarious activities, they correlated what they learnt from the organic texts. Organic texts became real and so did the pointers given by the teachers. Learning and experience were so closely tied together that it was not unusual to see students revising the texts they have memorized while doing their daily chores. Dawam Raharjo explains this in the most graphic terms:

> At certain specific times in the traditional pesantren, especially before the sunset prayers, there is the sound of a santri choir chanting tasauf (sufi/mystic) verses, a type of Illahi Las poem by the Sufi poet Abu Nuwus, or their prayers requesting God to increase, open their thoughts, and ease their efforts in pursuing their studies. On the anniversary of the Prophet Muhammad's birth a poem

---

[54] Martin van Bruinessen, "Traditionalist and Islamist Pesantrens in Contemporary Indonesia," in *The Madrasa in Asia Political Activism and Transnational Linkages*, Eds. Farish A. Noor, Yoginder Sikand & Martin van Bruinessen (Amsterdam: Amsterdam University Press, 2008), 220.

[55] Zamakhsyari Dhofier, "Traditional Islamic Education in the Malay Archipelago: Its Contribution to the Integration of the Malay World," *Indonesia Circle* 19, no. 53 (1990): 21.

[56] Ronald Lukens-Bull, *A Peaceful Jihad: Negotiating Identity and Modernity in Muslim Java* (Basingstoke: Palgrave Macmillan, 2005), 18.

Institutions

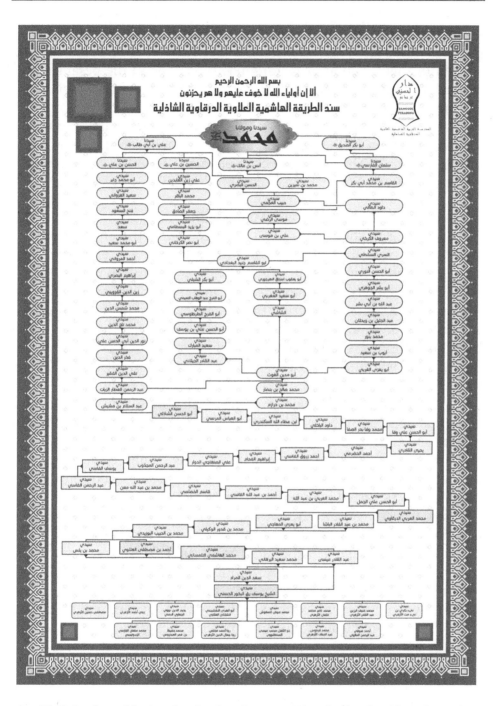

The Silsilah of Hashimiyyah-Alawiyyah-Darqawiyyah-Shazliyyah order.

of veneration or Barzanji and poems that retell the life of the Prophet are also performed. A more beautiful, first-rate presentation of this tradition of reading poetry is done in the pesantren such as the pesantren of Kaliwungu or Krapyek. A holy religious atmosphere of this kind is not found in pesantren like Gontor or Darul Falah. This beautiful religious atmosphere actually has a great function in the formation of noble character and humble Islamic souls. This is the superior element present in traditional pesantren which is lacking in pesantren that follow liberalism.[57]

Dawam's comparison between the "traditional" and "liberal" pesantren needs clarification. Up until the early twentieth century, there is a common saying that graduates from traditional Sufi seminaries specialized in the memorization of kitab kuning while those who studied in modernist madrasahs learnt *buku putih* (white books) which were mostly written romanized script. Both traditional and liberal institutions taught the Qur'an and hadith. The difference between them lies in the liberal institutions' stress on understanding and less on rote memorization. Liberal institutions provided new interpretations of classical texts to meet with the challenges of a modernizing world. From the 1930s onwards, a convergence between the two camps was conspicuous. Modernist madrasahs have incorporated the kitab kuning into their curriculum. Traditional Sufi seminaries began to adopt the romanized script and included subjects such as mathematics, geography, and science into their curriculums. The mastery of Arabic language and memorization of organic texts persisted in both institutions.[58]

I saw this convergence from the 1980s till the early 2000s during my part-time studies in Sufi-oriented madrasahs – Madrasah Aljunied and Madrasah Wak Tanjung – and later on in the modernist-reformist one run by the Muhammadiyah Association in Singapore. My two daughters, in turn, finished ten to twelve years of full-time education in madrasahs known for their Sufi leanings – Madrasah Al-Ma'arif and Madrasah Alsagoff. These circulatory institutions have incorporated modern curriculum and pedagogical methods. Students in both madrasahs have achieved excellent results in national exams and have graduated from mainstream as well as Islamic universities. Memorization of organic texts is still a core requirement for anyone wishing to study in these Sufi seminaries.

---

[57] M. Dawam Rahardjo. "The Life of Santri Youth: A View from the Pesantren Window at Pabelan." *Sojourn: Journal of Social Issues in Southeast Asia* 1, no. 1 (1986), 46.
[58] van Bruinessen, "Kitab Kuning", 227–228.

SPIRITUAL MEDIATORS

Organic texts on their own have no intrinsic value or consequence; they are merely objects. They come to life when people derive meanings from them, when interpretations speak to everyday experiences, and when elucidations generate social actions and the creation of more texts. Walter Ong reminds us, "no text can stand by itself independent of the extratextual world. Every text builds on pretext. For all texts have extratextual supports...the text has no meaning until someone reads it, and to make sense it must be interpreted, which is to say related to the reader's world."[59] Kiyais, tok gurus, shaykhs, and the ulama breathe life into these texts, imbuing them with meanings. These figures, best described as "spiritual mediators," operate within and between different Sufi seminaries. They assert their authority through their charisma, extensive knowledge, illustrious lineages, and the ijazahs they received from scholars and spiritual masters.

Their authority often reached a level of unquestioning obedience. Students of Sufi seminaries were expected to submit to their shaykhs completely and voluntarily. The dynamics in these seminaries were like those in tariqahs. Murids viewed themselves as corpses at the mercy of the corpse-washer, or empty vessels to be filled by the fountain of knowledge. The self was renounced, the ego denounced.[60] Nurcholish Madjid (1939–2005), a prominent Indonesian intellectual and product of Sufi seminaries, critiqued spiritual mediators for their paternalistic and autocratic tendencies. Their close-mindedness, resistance to modernity, and dictatorial management of circulatory institutions restricted the intellectual capacities and creative abilities of students.[61] Nurcholish was not wrong to argue that spiritual mediators generally endorsed the patriarchal and hierarchical nature of Sufi seminaries. Although there were female spiritual mediators, most Sufi seminaries were dominated by men. The male kiayi or tok guru would typically handed down leadership of Sufi seminaries to their sons or sons-in-law.

Women scholars who rose to leadership positions within these institutions were called *nyais* (senior ladies) in Java and *ustazahs* (female teachers) in other parts of the Malay world. Despite their significant roles, they were often disallowed from surpassing men in power, who were usually their husbands and regarded as de facto leaders of Sufi seminaries. Strict dress and behavioural conventions, coupled with gender

---

[59] Walter J. Ong, *Orality and Literacy* (New York: Routledge, 2002), 158.
[60] Seyyed Hossein Nasr, *Sufi Essays* (Albany: State University of New York Press, 1972), 62–63.
[61] Nurcholish Madjid, *Bilik-Bilik Pesantren: Sebuah Potret Perjalanan* (Jakarta: Paramadina, 1994), 6–7.

segregation, ensured that women were kept from overall leadership of Sufi seminaries. This does not, however, imply that women did not wield power; they often exercised subtle, informal influence over tok gurus, kiayis, and shaykhs. Women held paramount power behind the scenes in Southeast Asian societies and frequently exercised their cultural prerogative in Sufi seminaries.[62] Despite Nurcholish's criticisms and the patriarchal nature of Sufi seminaries, spiritual mediators have played crucial roles in Sufi seminaries and societies around them. Their roles can be described as connective, curative, and constructive. These roles required personal magnetism, extensive knowledge, and mythologies.

The first significant role spiritual mediators in Sufi seminaries played was connective. They connected students and communities in spirit and in knowledge as inscribed in organic texts. Through everyday lessons in Sufi seminaries, majlis ta'lim delivered at mosques, or dhikr sessions, spiritual mediators bound communities of learners and seekers. A spiritual mediator would teach certain texts to selected students and audiences, who would then teach others, creating a multi-level transmission of knowledge. A respected spiritual mediator was linked directly or indirectly to learners with different backgrounds and degrees of affiliation. It is still common to hear someone living far from a Sufi seminary to be a student of particular spiritual mediator, even if they rarely met. The connection between a learner and spiritual mediator could transcend circulatory institutions, bounded by knowledge, or membership within specific tariqahs. The connective roles of spiritual mediators were fortified by the allegiances and deference communities had towards them.[63]

Equipped with the strength of powerful ties with the communities around them, spiritual mediators also used their influence to mobilize their followers in times of war and peace. In Kelantan, tok gurus were often appointed as *penghulu*s (headmen) of villages surrounding the Sufi seminaries. They also employed villagers to manage their farms, plantations, and small businesses.[64] Until the 1960s, the connective roles these spiritual mediators played were made possible by the circulation of students coming from all corners of Southeast Asia who lived and studied

---

[62] Eka Srimulyani, *Women from Traditional Islamic Educational Institutions in Indonesia Negotiating Public Spaces* (Amsterdam: Amsterdam University Press, 2012), 27–29.

[63] Endang Turmudi, *Struggling for the Umma: Changing Leadership Roles of Kiai in Jombang, East Java* (Canberra: ANU E Press, 2006), 25–27.

[64] Robert L. Winzeler, "Traditional Schools in Kelantan," *Journal of the Malaysian Branch of the Royal Asiatic Society* 48, no. 1 (227) (1975): 96.

Institutions **99**

in Sufi seminaries for free. In return, students worked for their teachers, serving as *khaddam* (servants) or manual workers.[65]

Many NU-affiliated kyais have used their connective roles to garner mass political support, a topic that I will elaborate further in Chapter 6.[66] Parties such as Partai Bulan Bintang, Partai Sarikat Islam, and Partai Nahdlatul Ummah (PNU), among many others, were led and filled with former students, teachers, supporters, and sympathizers of Sufi seminaries.[67] Saifuddin Zuhri recalls his experience as a *santri* (student) eagerly listening to his teachers discuss resistance politics against the Dutch and their collaborators.[68] Another observer notes that "the wider influence and supra-village pattern of leadership of the *kiai* enables him access to private and government agencies. The *kiai* sometimes play a brokerage role in transmitting the government messages of development to the society, and the society can more easily accept any government's program when they are presented by the *kiai*."[69] Indeed, spiritual mediators addressed everyday piety and high politics, building and amplifying connections with the laity through kinship ties, alliance with political and business elites, and generations of students, thereby sustaining loyal power networks.[70]

Spiritual mediators also provided cures for many ailments, especially psycho-spiritual remedies. The curative powers of Sufi saints are well-documented. A noted scholar of Sufism explains:

> As for psychology, it must be remembered that Sufism contains a complete method of curing the illnesses of the soul and in fact succeeds where many modern psychiatric and psychoanalytical methods with all their extravagant claims, fail. That is because only the higher can know the lower; only the spirit can know the psyche and illuminate its dark corners and crevasses. Only he

---

[65] Fox James J. and Pradjarta Dirjosanjoto, "The Memories of Village Santri from Jombang in East Java," in *Observing Change in Asia*, eds. Ronald J. May and William J. O'Mallay (Bathurst: Crawford House Press, 1989), 94–110.

[66] Mawardi, *Practica Politika NU: Mendajung Ditengah Gelombang* (Jakarta: Jajasan Pendidikan Practica, 1967), 24.

[67] Other parties where Sufi mediators have played active roles are Partai Kebangkitan Ummat (PKU), Partai Keadilan Sejahtera, Partai Matahari Bangsa (PMB), and Partai Kebangkitan Nasional Ulama (PKNU). See: Isa Anshori, *Dinamika Pesantren Muhammadiyah & Nahdatul Ulama: Perspektif Sosial, Ideologi Dan Ekonomi* (Sidoarjo: Nizamia Learning Center, 2020), 64.

[68] Saifuddin Zuhri, *Guruku Orang-Orang Dari Pesantren* (Bandung: PT Alma'arif, 1974), 58–60.

[69] Endang Turmudi, *Struggling for the Umma: Changing Leadership Roles of Kiai in Jombang, East Java* (Canberra: ANU E Press, 2006), 23–24.

[70] Zamakhsyari Dhofier, "Kinship and Marriage among the Javanese Kyai," *Indonesia* 29 (1980): 53.

whose soul has become integrated and illuminated has the right and the wherewithal to cure the souls of others.[71]

In Southeast Asia, Sufis were known to be practicing physicians who managed institutions known as "Islamic healing clinics (*klinik rawatan Islam* or *klinik ruqyah*)." A widespread belief among Muslims in Southeast Asia is that spiritual mediators were gifted with powers to discern and receive inspiration from God and communicate with supernatural and paranormal beings. They have *'ilmu laduni* (direct knowledge from God), karamah, and barakah, acquired through birth or years of discipleship with Sufi masters. Exalted as doctors of the soul and heart with the ability to soothe the problems of the common man, spiritual mediators diagnosed and solved a broad range of sicknesses, from physical pain and black magic and to disturbances caused by evil spirits. Muslims from all walks of life sought their interpretations of dreams. Using their knowledge of Islam, folk medicine, and mysticism, spiritual mediators provided cures through Qur'anic verses, litanies (also known as the *ruqyah*), *ayer tawar* (healing water), *azimat* (amulets), and specialized surgeries.[72]

Many patients and visitors become students or supporters of Sufi seminaries. Spiritual mediators, from the perspective of people who consulted them, were multi-talented practitioners. They were psychologists, specialist doctors, counsellors, and foretellers, all in one.[73] State-religious authorities have, in the recent years, declared the belief in the curative powers of some spiritual mediators heretical because many of their practices contravened the teachings of Islam. Even so, by addressing the corporeal needs of the locals and giving solutions to the everyday trials and tribulations of ordinary people, the seeking of cures from Sufi mediators has remained unabated.[74]

Above all, spiritual mediators were constructive figures, shaping and reshaping the lives and personalities of their followers. Among the constructive functions was the reinforcement of gender norms. As mentioned earlier, Sufi seminaries were mostly patriarchal institutions

---

[71] Seyyed Hossein Nasr, *Sufi Essays* (Albany: State University of New York Press, 1972), 46–47.

[72] Robert L. Winzeler, "Traditional Schools in Kelantan," *Journal of the Malaysian Branch of the Royal Asiatic Society* 48, no. 1 (227) (1975): 99.

[73] Ziemek, *Pesantren Dalam Perubahan Sosial,* 134.

[74] Mahmud Saedon Awang Othman, *Ajaran Sesat Di Negara Brunei Darussalam: Satu Tinjauan* (Pusat Da'wah Islamiah: Brunei Darussalam, 2002), 68 and 137; Al-Attas, *Some Aspects of Sufism*, 48.

with strict men–women segregation. When women were admitted into Sufi seminaries, they were provided with lessons and skills that would prepare them to become good wives and mothers.[75] While there are sources pointing to women who rose up to high positions within selected tariqahs, we have no reliable evidence of them leading Sufi seminaries prior to the twentieth century. Omar Fathurrahman's study of female Sufis such as Ḥamidah binti Sulayman from Aceh and Ratu Raja Fatimah from Cirebon, Java, who featured importantly in local Sufi genealogies addresses the dearth of literature on female Sufis who acted as spiritual mediators.[76] In Pesantren Nahdlatul Wathan at Lombok, a spiritual mediator was said to have spiritual powers akin to her saintly father. She, along with other female leaders of nearby Sufi seminaries, were upheld as respected guides of their respective tariqas. They were visited by Muslims of all ages in their bid to overcome life's challenges. Even though revered, these female Sufis did not assume leadership of tariqahs.[77]

A shift occurred in the mid-twentieth century with women becoming more prominent in pesantrens and tariqahs. In Madura, Nyai Thobibah, Syarifah Fatimah, and Syarifah Nor attracted hundreds of followers from Madura, Western Kalimantan, and South Malang. They transmitted the ijazah of Naqshbandiyyah-Maẓhariyyah to women only.[78] Recently, there has been stronger push within pesantrens in Indonesia encouraging more gender parity. Sinta Nuryiah, the wife of the former president of Indonesia, Abdurrahman Wahid, founded a pesantren for women's empowerment. This movement advocates equality between the kyais and nyais. Together with other activists such as Kyai Hussein Muhammad, Siti Musdah Mulia, Lies Marcoes, and Lily Zakiyah Munir (d. 2011), these women pushed for the infusion of democratic values in pesantren and the respect for women.[79]

Through their constructive roles, spiritual mediators guided their students to become model Muslims of high ethics and fine character.

---

[75] Eka Srimulyani, "Muslim Women and Education in Indonesia: The Pondok Pesantren Experience," *Asia Pacific Journal of Education* 27, no. 1 (2007): 88–89.

[76] Oman Fathurahman, "Female Indonesian Sufis: Shattariya Murids in the 18th and 19th Centuries in Java," *Kyoto Bulletin of Islamic Area Studies* 11 (2018): 50–51.

[77] Eka Srimulyani, *Women from Traditional Islamic Educational Institutions in Indonesia Negotiating Public Spaces* (Amsterdam: Amsterdam University Press, 2012), 53–54.

[78] Martin van Bruinessen, *Tarekat Naqsyabandiyya Di Indonesia: Survei Historis, Geografis Dan Sosiologis* (Penerbit Mizan, 1992), 197–198.

[79] Ann Kull, "At the Forefront of a Post-Patriarchal Islamic Education: Female Teachers in Indonesia," *Journal of International Women's Studies* 11, no. 1 (2009): 25–39.

They placed high behavioural expectations on their students, who were expected to be obedient, disciplined, and submit fully to their teachers who would then construct their character, spirit, body, and mind.[80] They were made to sleep early, rise early, consume nutritious food, engage in sports, socialize respectfully with their peers, and participate in intellectual and spiritual activities. The process of nurturing a would-be spiritual mediator has been an integrative one. Every component of teaching and learning were interdependent as part of a meaningful and impactful experience.[81] Some Sufi seminaries require students to be initiated into tariqahs as part of their spiritual and personal development. But this has never been made obligatory.[82]

Upon graduation, students were equipped to become spiritual mediators and establish their Sufi seminaries that used similar systems and curricula. A web of connected circulatory institutions with their own hierarchies was created. As Zamakshari Dhofier explains:

> Being "centres of excellence," these big pesantren also train santri who become leaders of minor pesantren, which are culturally and intellectually dependent on major pesantren. There has been a process of interdependency between major and minor pesantren, in that major pesantren provide novice kyai to teach in the minor pesantren, which, in turn, provide santri with the elementary training necessary to continue their advanced studies in major pesantren. This relationship has also created an exclusive stratification system among the kyai: kyai of major pesantren form part of the national elite; kyai of secondary pesantren form part of the provincial elites; while kyai of minor pesantren form part of local district elites.[83]

---

[80] Marzuki Abu Bakar, *Pesantren Di Aceh: Perubahan, Aktualisasi Dan Pengembangan*, 45–46; Robin Bush, *Nahdlatul Ulama and the Struggle for Power within Islam and Politics in Indonesia* (Singapore: ISEAS Press, 2009), 30.

[81] Abdurrahman Wahid, "Principles of Pesantren Education," in *The Impact of Pesantren in Education*, eds. Manfred Oepen and Wolfgang Karcher (Jakarta: Friedrich-Naumann Stiftung, Technical University Berlin and P3M Jakarta, 1988).

[82] Michael F. Laffan, "From Alternative Medicine to National Cure: Another Voice for the Sufi Orders in the Indonesian Media," *Archives de Sciences Sociales des Religions* 51, no. 135 (2006): 93–94.

[83] Zamakhsyari Dhofier, "Kinship and Marriage among the Javanese Kyai," *Indonesia* 29 (1980): 49–50.

Institutions

103

DEVOUT COMMUNITIES

Circulatory institutions maintained their relevance not only through the agency of the spiritual mediators and their students but also through publics that frequented them and engaged in constant dialogue with them. These "devout communities" – both Muslims or non-Muslims – regarded Sufi seminaries as sites of transcendence and dependence. Sufi seminaries were spaces for social and religious networking, where stronger relationships with the divine could be forged and where sacred knowledge obtained. Many people saw Sufi seminaries as markers of their identities, similar to clubs and clan associations. They were also sanctuaries where devout communities found solace after work or during sabbaticals from years of labour. Drawing from Roy Oldenburg's concept, Sufi seminaries served "third places" for these communities accommodating them "when they are released from their responsibilities elsewhere...Those who have third places exhibit regularity in their visits to them, but it is not that punctual and unfailing kind shown in deference to the job or family. The timing is loose, days are missed, some visits are brief, etc. Viewed from the vantage point of the establishment, there is a fluidity in arrivals and departures and an inconsistency of membership at any given hour or day."[84]

A key differentiator between circulatory institutions and Oldenburg's "third places" was that activities in Sufi seminaries were mostly structured, organized, and planned. Devout communities adjust their schedules in accordance with the rhythms and regimes of teaching and learning in Sufi seminaries, achieving their respective objectives within that order of things. Most activities involving devout communities converged around the mosques within the Sufi seminary complex. These mosques have been the magnets for potential students, enthusiastic donors, energetic volunteers, and influential backers.[85]

Devout communities have contributed to the sustenance of circulatory institutions in several ways. Charitable acts were significant, with many Sufi seminaries funded by wealthy communities that donated money and land. *Zakah* (compulsory religious tax) and *sadaqah* (charity) in the form of cash, infrastructure, or foodstuffs were also directed

---

[84] Ray Oldenburg, *The Great Good Place: Cafes, Coffee Shops, Bookstores, Bars, Hair Salons, and Other Hangouts at the Heart of a Community* (New York: Marlowe & Company, 1999), 32.

[85] Redzuan Othman, "The Role of Makka-Educated Malays in the Development of Early Islamic Scholarship and Education in Malaya," *Journal of Islamic Studies* 9, no. 2 (1998): 146–157.

towards these institutions. Establishing *waqf* (endowments) for the construction of mosques, dormitories, classrooms, and other facilities was seen as fulfilling a great duty in the path of Allah.[86] In South Thailand and northern Malaysia, pondoks were closely linked to businesses, with entrepreneurs often endowing part of their earnings to Sufi seminaries, hoping for blessings on their undertakings and future generations.[87]

Devout communities gave life to circulatory institutions by sending their children to be nurtured there. Enrolling a child in Sufi seminaries meant sacrificing precious time with the child, as they typically studied under the guidance of spiritual mediators from ages seven to sixteen. Spiritual mediators became their foster parents, with some Sufi seminaries requiring students to use the terms such as "abuya" or "buya" (both meaning "father") when addressing their teachers. Sufi seminaries generally accepted two kinds of students: *santri mukim* or *pelajar sepenuh masa* (live-in students) and *santri kalong* (non-live-in student). The latter consisted of two types. First were those who only attended classes in Sufi seminaries. The second type were enrolled in secular schools and would proceed to Sufi seminaries after school hours or during weekends. These students were normally taught a watered-down version of the curriculum of full-time students. Many eventually obtained mastery of selected organic texts much like full-time students, depending on their intellectual aptitude. Subject to their parents' approval or wishes, some may eventually switch to become full-time students. Devout communities sending their children to Sufi seminaries on a part-time basis often saw it as a fulfilment of their duties towards Islam or in reverence of tok gurus and kiyais.[88]

Devout communities populate circulatory institutions frequently, making them dynamic. Frequency of attendance was a test of the depth of one's piety and love for the spiritual mediators and seminaries. Aside from pilgrimages to graves of spiritual mediators within Sufi seminaries, devout communities were actively involved in mass events such as mawlids, hauls, ratibs, communal prayers, Quran competitions, and mass lectures. These gatherings often centred around spiritual mediators or their students, whose sermons and updates were attentively listened

---

[86] Clifford Geertz, "The Javanese Kijaji: The Changing Role of a Cultural Broker," *Comparative Studies in Society and History* 2, no. 2 (1960): 231–234; Winzeler, "Traditional Schools in Kelantan".

[87] Hassan Madmarn, "Traditional Muslim Institutions in Southern Thailand: A Critical Study of Islamic Education and Arabic Influence in the Pondok and Madrasah Systems in Pattani", 37–49.

[88] Eka Srimulyani, "Muslim Women and Education in Indonesia: The Pondok Pesantren Experience," *Asia Pacific Journal of Education* 27, no. 1 (2007): 86.

Institutions

105

to and orders acted upon during crises. Devout communities were most active in Sufi seminaries during Ramadan, converging in mosques for communal prayers and *iftar* (the breaking of fast). Generosity was flaunted during such events, with food, clothing, and money presented to spiritual mediators, even by poor peasants hoping for blessings. These events received overwhelming support from the Malay royalty, the *kratons* (Javanese royalty), and other regional rulers.[89] In Lombok, for instance, the tuan gurus from the Sasak community commanded significant influence, making it compulsory for followers from whatever rank they may be in society to attend major gatherings. During these events, the clout of spiritual mediators and the obeisance of devout communities were visible. The tuan gurus had the power to punish those who transgressed legal, religious, and social norms, with ostracization serving as a form of social control and ensuring devout communities behaved according to shari'a and Sufi ethics.[90]

CONCLUSION

Sufi circulatory institutions can be likened to university towns, where texts, teachers, disciples, and devotees intersected, making Sufism a self-revitalizing entity in Southeast Asia.[91] While colonization and globalization transformed many Sufi seminaries into places where Islamic sciences, blended pedagogies, and latest technologies intersected, some persistent features remained for many centuries. Deep readings, faithful memorization, and dynamic dialogues over organic texts continue to be hallmarks of Sufi seminaries. Circulatory institutions continue to adapt their curricula by including modern subjects and approaches to balance traditional and contemporary education needs until now.

While such texts were updated from time to time in line with the vagaries of spiritual mediators, the general texture of works relating to Sufism rested mostly on the ideas of classical scholars in the likes of three key medieval Islamic scholars, Shafi'i, Ash'ari, and Al-Ghazzali. Since the coming of Islamic modernism and reformism in the nineteenth

---

[89] Hugh C. Clifford, "Report: Expedition to Trengganu and Kelantan," *Journal of the Malayan Branch of the Royal Asiatic Society* 34, no. 1 (1961): 68.

[90] Jeremy Kingsley, "Redrawing the Lines of Religious Authority in Lombok, Indonesia," *Asian Journal of Social Science* 42 (2014): 669.

[91] Azmi bin Omar, "In Quest of An Islamic Ideal of Education: A Study of the Role of the Traditional Pondok Institution in Malaysia", 122–123.

century, tasawwuf taught in these circulatory institutions tended to be more shari'a-oriented. The traces of philosophical Sufism expounded by Ibn 'Arabi were sidelined and his proteges discredited. And yet even with such changes, when viewed from the perspective of contemplative histories, the patterns of engagement between circulatory institutions and Southeast Asian societies over many centuries and across different spaces have remained relatively consistent.

The roles of spiritual mediators as a guide, counsellors, motivators, social glues, and paternal figures to their students and followers have sharpened over the years. The respect shown towards these persons remained even as reigning states and kingdoms changed. Their charismatic authority, mystical propensity, and revered genealogies provided them with the influence to command respect and loyalty from their communities. Spiritual mediators, both in life and in their after-lives, were consecrated by the communities that revered them.[92] These devoted men and women viewed Sufi seminaries as driving forces of their faith, supporting and sponsoring these hubs of learning and bonds, often sacrificing their time, children, and resources for the sake of their spiritual mentors and the seminaries they loved. This unbroken dialogical tradition linking organic texts, spiritual mediators, and devout communities propelled circulatory institutions into a "Cradle of Islam in Southeast Asia."[93]

---

[92] Eka Srimulyani, *Women from Traditional Islamic Educational Institutions in Indonesia Negotiating Public Spaces* (Amsterdam: Amsterdam University Press, 2012), 43–44.
[93] Saynee Mudmarn, "Language Use and Loyalty among the Muslim-Malays of Southern Thailand" (PhD Dissertation, State University of New York, 1988), 117.

CHAPTER 4

Struggles

The history of struggles in the Muslim world cannot be fully understood without considering the roles played by Sufis and their writings on the merits of such acts. Since the twelfth century, numerous treatises, hagiographies, and poetry extolling the valor of Sufis in the theatres of conflict and combat have been produced. Jihad was used as a mobilizing concept, justifying aggressive acts for self-defence and, at times, for offensive aims. Ibn 'Arabi, a venerated figure among generations of Sufis in Southeast Asia, commended *jihad fisabilillah* (struggling in the path of Allah) as "one of the sum total of good paths that bring one closer to God."[1] Shaykh Abdul Qadir al-Jilani summarized this neatly by dividing jihad into two: the outer and the inner.

> The inner is the jihad of the soul, the passion, the nature, and Satan. It involves repentance from rebelliousness and errors, being steadfast about it, and abandoning the forbidden passions. The outer is the jihad of the infidels who resist Him and His Messenger [Muhammad] and to be pitiless with their swords, their spears, and their arrows—killing and being killed. The inner jihad is more difficult than the outer jihad because it involves cutting the forbidden customs of the soul, and exiling them, so as to have as one's example the Divine commands and to

---

[1] Ibn 'Arabi, *Futuhat Al-Makkiyya, Vol. II* (Beirut: Dar al-Kutub al-'Ilmiyya, 1991), 275. The influence of "Ibn 'Arabi" in Southeast Asia has been discussed by Anthony H. Johns. See: "Sufism in Southeast Asia: Reflections and Reconsiderations," *Journal of Southeast Asian Studies* 26, no. 1 (1995): 169–183.

Contemplating Sufism: Dialogue and Tradition Across Southeast Asia, First Edition. Khairudin Aljunied.
© 2025 John Wiley & Sons Ltd. Published 2025 by John Wiley & Sons Ltd.

cease from what it forbids. Whoever takes God's command as his example with regard to the two types of jihad will gain a reward in this world and the next.[2]

Such texts inspired generations of Sufis to serve as legionnaires in the service of Muslim empires.[3] Sufi orders filled the ranks of warriors of the Qarakhanid Dynasty, which ruled in Transoxiana in Central Asia from 999 to 1211.[4] Sufis were also at the frontlines in the capture of Jerusalem (1187) and Constantinople (1453). They joined the invasion of the Deccan region in the fourteenth century, leading to the spread of Islam in the Indian subcontinent. In Islamic Africa, the most stubborn anti-colonial resistance was led by Sufis. Aware of their tenacity on the battlefields, the Ottomans dispatched Sufis from the Mevlevi brotherhood to fight the Allies in Syria and Palestine during the First World War. In the Caucasus and Afghanistan, brigades of Sufi citizen soldiers harassed the advancing Russian army.[5] The balance sheet of history reveals that Sufis were not just ascetics who preached peace and pacifism and who cowed in the face of oppression, exploitation, and dehumanization. They were hardened fighters for the causes of nations, polities, communities, solidarities, and the beliefs they deemed inviolable.

Although the Islamization of Southeast Asia through Sufis was predominantly peaceful, armed aggression was also used to protect and expand their faith. Recent works often portray Sufis in Southeast Asia as ambassadors of peace and preachers of tolerance, a meek image, to say the least.[6] However, historical and contemporary evidence shows that Sufis in the region were also aggressive and divisive, heavily involved and invested in many conflicts. They framed these clashes within the vocabularies of jihad and *perang sabil* (or *parrang sabbil*, holy war) or *perang kafir* (war against disbelievers).[7] Sufis played crucial roles in

---

[2] Quoted in David Cook, *Understanding Jihad* (Berkeley: University of California Press, 2005), 45. See also: Abd al-Qadir Al-Jilani, *al-Fath al-rabbani wa-l-fayd al-rahmani* (Cairo: Al-Maktabah al-Sya'biyyah, 1988), 83.

[3] Harry S. Neale, *Sufi Warrior Saints: Stories of Sufi Jihad from Muslim Hagiography* (London: I.B. Tauris, 2022).

[4] Jeff Eden, *Warrior Saints of the Silk Road* (Leiden: Brill, 2019).

[5] David Cook, "Sufism, the Army, and Holy War," in *Sufi Institutions,* ed. Alexandre Papas (Leiden: Brill, 2021), 315–321.

[6] For a critique of this thesis, see Mark Woodward et al., "Salafi Violence and Sufi Tolerance? Rethinking Conventional Wisdom," *Perspectives on Terrorism* 7, no. 6 (2013): 58–78.

[7] Iik A. Mansurnoor, "Muslims in Modern Southeast Asia: Radicalism in Historical Perspectives," *Taiwan Journal of Southeast Asian Studies* 2, no. 2 (2005): 6; Teuku Alfian Ibrahim, *Perang Di Jalan Allah: Perang Aceh, 1873–1912* (Jakarta: Pustaka Sinar Harapan, 1987), 20.

Struggles   **109**

struggles against rival states and in resisting the European encroachment in Muslim lands. Their engagements in violence are an elemental part of Southeast Asian history.[8]

In this chapter, I propose the concept "Sufi warriorism" as a heuristic device to analyse how Sufis in Southeast Asia struggled for their rights, resources, and religion. "Sufi warriorism" refers to a form of martiality through Islamic and social-cultural reasoning. It was a faith-based that conceived physical force as warranted or obligatory when faced with existential threats and violations of Islamic injunctions. Sufi scholars in Southeast Asia found support for this predisposition through an intensive dialogue with texts such as the Qur'an, hadith, works of classical Islamic scholars, millenarian beliefs, and folk prophecies. This fusion of Islamic and supra-Islamic ideas to justify militancy appeared in various guises, from stories of invulnerable saints to tales of the coming messianic figure, Imam Mahdi.[9] Such narratives rationalized the urgency of bodily sacrifice to preserve Islam's sanctity and to attain eternal bliss in the hereafter. Militancy was sanctioned against non-Muslims and fellow Muslims whom Sufis deemed heretics or traitors. In other words, Sufi warriorism entailed placing religion and community above the self. For Sufis in the region and globally, to engage in holy struggles was to embody one's true love of God.[10]

Sufi warriorism in Southeast Asia was driven by personal, social, and material considerations, as well as religious imperatives. Sufis condoned violence in times of social injustice, political instability, and denial of privileges once enjoyed by the religious class. These privileges included influential positions in state structures, land rights, institutional autonomy. A combination of faith-based and other factors provided essential catalysts for armed actions. Anticipating battles motivated by these considerations, most tariqahs in Southeast Asia encouraged members to undergo martial arts training alongside their spiritual instruction. They were taught specific chants and given *azimat* (amulets) believed to be

---

[8] Azyumardi Azra, "Sufism in Indonesian Islam: A Brief History and a New Typology," in *Knowledge, Tradition, and Civilization: Essays in Honour of Professor Osman Bakar,* ed. Khairudin Aljunied (Oldham: Beacon Press, 2022), 240.

[9] Sarit Helman, "The Javanese Conception of Order and Its Relationship to Millenarian Motifs and Imagery," *International Journal of Comparative Sociology* XXIX, no. 1–2 (1988): 126–138.

[10] Richard Maxwell Eaton, *The Sufis of Bijapur* (Princeton: Princeton University Press, 1978), 19; Carl Ernst, *Refractions of Islam in India: Situating Sufism and Yoga* (Thousand Oaks: Sage, 2016), 3–24; Harry S. Neale, *Jihad in Premodern Sufi Writings* (New York: Palgrave Macmillan, 2017), 123–132.

able to provide divine strength and protection during conflicts. These practices were sometimes linked to vernacular occultism.[11]

One common martial art practiced by Sufis in Southeast Asia was *silat* (Malay combative art), introduced in the region since the Hindu-Buddhist era, perhaps even earlier. With the arrival of Islam, Sufi elements were integrated into silat, creating a hybridized pugilistic tradition. Many Sufi shaykhs were also silat experts, blending Sufi mysticism with local shamanism and pre-Islamic totemism. Through the amalgamation of seemingly contradictory traditions, a devout Sufi trained in silat could achieve "magical results such as invulnerability, incredible speed, and 'superhuman' strength. In Sufi mysticism, which Sufi silat styles emulate, power is derived from the ability to manipulate time and space."[12]

I propose a typology of Sufi warriorism in Southeast Asia. The longue durée history of Islam in the region reveals three types of Sufi warriorism: protagonist, protectionist, and purist. The three types of Sufi warriorism will be analyzed separately, with a conscious view that they often overlapped. In the following pages, I bracket the period from the fifteenth century to the mid-twentieth century as the most active period of Sufi warriorism. These five centuries saw the expansion of Islam's influence in a predominantly Hindu-Buddhist terrain. Muslim and non-Muslim kingdoms frequently clashed for dominance. This was a time of passionate encounters with European powers imposing their ideas of civilizing mission, secular modernity, and muscular Christianity.[13] This was also a blossoming period of Sufism as a dialogical tradition in Southeast Asia.

By the seventeenth century, almost all Muslim kings in Southeast Asia patronized Sufi warriorism in their dominions. Sufis participated in expansionist wars launched by Muslim kingdoms against non-Muslim empires. They were present in the battles repulsing European colonizers. Most Muslim kingdoms in Southeast Asia subscribed to the ideology of jihad. Rulers were ardent followers or leaders of militant Sufi tariqahs. Sufi warriorism during this phase in Southeast Asian history was linked

---

[11] Sartono Kartodirdjo, *Ratu Adil* (Penerbit Sinar Harapan, 1984); Oman Fathurahman, "A New Light on the Sufi Network of Mindanao (Philippines)," *Indonesia and the Malay World* 47, no. 137 (2019): 108–124.

[12] Douglas S. Farrer, *Shadows of the Prophet Martial Arts and Sufi Mysticism* (New York: Springer, 2009), 53.

[13] Barbara Watson Andaya, "The Glocalization of Christianity in Early Modern Southeast Asia," in *Early Modern Southeast Asia, 1350–1800,* eds. Ooi Keat Gin and Hoang Anh Tuah (London: Routledge, 2015), 233–249.

to the global competition for religious converts.[14] Many Muslim revolts involved Sufi orders and were against Western intrusion into Muslim lands. A historian of global Islam, Nikki Keddie, divided these years into three phases: the pre-colonial (eighteenth century), early resistance to colonialism (beginning till late nineteenth century), and Islamic revivalism during the eve of colonial rule and thereafter (late nineteenth century to 1990s). Sufis led jihad movements in the first two phases.[15]

Extending Keddie's periodization, I show that Sufi warriorism in Southeast Asia began over three centuries earlier. Sufis commanded many violent conflicts during the rise of Muslim *kerajaans* (kingdoms). Advances in transportation and technology facilitated the rapid growth of these armed struggles. By the mid-nineteenth century, Sufism became a truly international force, with networks of scholars, students, missionaries, and warriors flowing from centres of learning in Hejaz, Cairo, Damascus, Hadramaut, and Delhi into Southeast Asia. The Indian Ocean was the zone within which Sufis travelled to expand their reach and forge spiritual, familial, and anti-colonial networks. Armed with the claims to prophetic lineages and leveraging their diasporic links, and oceanic Sufi connections, the Hadrami-Arabs incited Muslims to rise against European rule and trade dominance.[16] They used tariqahs for mobilization. The decline of Muslim-led domains further fuelled armed resistance. Messianic rhetoric and insurgencies unleashed by Sufis grew substantially during these turbulent decades.[17]

The three expressions of Sufi warriorism in Southeast Asia were centred around a few charismatic individuals. Consequently, resistance and other militant campaigns faltered quickly after the capture or demise of prominent figures, most of whom were regarded as *wali hidup* (living saints). Divisions within Sufi ranks over the legitimacy of European presence in Muslim domains further weakened the efforts to sustain

---

[14] Jeyamalar Kathirithamby-Wells., "Ahmad Shah Ibn Iskandar and the Late 17th Century 'Holy War' in Indonesia," *Journal of the Malayan Branch of the Royal Asiatic Society* 43, no. 1 (217) (1970): 48–72; Barbara Watson Andaya, "Islam and Christianity in South-East Asia 1600–1700," in *Christian-Muslim Relations. A Bibliographical History Volume 11 South and East Asia, Africa and the Americas (1600–1700)*, eds. David Thomas and John A. Chesworth (Leiden: Brill, 2017), 15–27.

[15] Nikki Keddie, "The Revolt of Islam, 1700 to 1993: Comparative Considerations and Relations to Imperialism," *Comparative Studies in Society and History* 36, no. 3 (1994): 463–487.

[16] Engseng Ho, "Empire through Diasporic Eyes: A View from the Other Boat," *Comparative Study of Society and History* 46, no. 2 (2004): 210–246.

[17] Michael F. Laffan, *Under Empire: Muslim Lives and Loyalties Across the Indian Ocean World, 1775–1945* (New York: Columbia University Press, 2022); Anne Bang, *Sufis and Scholars of the Sea: Family Networks in East Africa, 1860–1925* (London: Routledge, 2003).

a long-drawn resistance. Personality-centred, poorly armed, internally divided, and often haphazardly organized, Sufi warriorism in Southeast Asia struggled to overcome European colonialism. Additionally, Sufi warriorism was bound by the idea of jihad as "the gateway to a millennium in which society would be governed by Islamic values once and for all."[18] Sufi warriors developed their ideological bases from the works of prominent scholars both within the region and globally. Revolutionary ideas among Sufis in Southeast Asia were borne out of affiliations and solidarity with local Sufi ideologues and those from the wider Muslim world. Jawi scholars based in the holy land of Makkah were also part of the Sufi warriorism complex, spreading their ideas on jihad to students and hajjis. This circulation of ideas underscores Islam's trans-civilizational connectedness, amplified by global reconfigurations brought about by Western modernity. Sufi networks dilated Islam's international reach and augmented its anti-colonial potential. Sufis capitalized on these networks to rally fellow Muslims, even those not favouring Sufism, to join their ranks in battling Western colonialism through both armed and literary jihad.[19]

Three Sufi scholars were most authoritative in shaping the minds of their brethren in Southeast Asia regarding jihad and perang sabil. They were Nuruddin Al-Raniri, Shaykh Daud al-Fatani, and 'Abdul Samad Al-Palimbani (1704–1789). Al-Raniri's treatise, *al-Fawa'id al-Bahiyyah fi al-Ahadith al-Nabawiyyah* (The Beautiful Benefits of Prophetic Sayings), included a section eulogizing the virtues of holy war and the ills that would befall the Muslims when armed struggle was shunned. He cited several Quranic verses and ahadith highlighting the superiority of martyrs and the highest rewards they stood to gain in dying for Islam.[20] Dubbed a keen scholarly advocate of holy war, Al-Palimbani's book became a standard reference for centuries of holy war literature produced in Southeast Asia.[21] The title of his canonical text, *Nasihat al-Muslimin wa-tadhkirat al-mu'minin fada'il al-jihad fi sabil Allah wa-karamat al-mujahidin fi sabil Allah* (Advice for Muslims and an admonition for believers on the virtue of jihad in the way of God and honouring those who wage

---

[18] Sartono Kartodirdjo, "Agrarian Radicalism in Java: Its Setting and Development," in *Culture and Politics in Indonesia,* ed. Claire Holt (Jakarta: Equinox Publishing Ltd, 2007), 91.

[19] Zachary Valentine Wright, *Realizing Islam: The Tijaniyya in North Africa and the Eighteenth-Century Muslim World* (Chapel Hill: University of North Carolina Press, 2020), 18–52.

[20] Nuruddin Al-Raniri, *Al-Fawa'id Al-Bahiyyah Fi Al-Ahadith Al-Nabawiyyah* (trans. and ed. Mohd Muhiden Abd. Rahman) (Kuala Lumpur: Dewan Bahasa dan Pustaka, 2009).

[21] G. W. J. Drewes, "Further Data Concerning Abd Al-Samad al-Palimbani," *Bijdragen Tot de Taal-, Land- En Volkenkunde* 132, no. 2/3 (1976): 267–292.

Struggles   **113**

jihad in the way of God), was telling enough.[22] Written in Arabic to rally Muslims globally in support of their co-religionists in Southeast Asia, Al-Palimbani argued for armed struggle to undo injustices. He agreed with Al-Raniri that armed jihad must be conceptualized strictly within the ambit of the shari'a. Going further than Al-Raniri, Al-Palimbani encouraged Sufis to learn martial arts and to be in constant preparation for war in response to European colonization of Muslim lands. His treatise included dhikr to be read for self-protection during wars. He wrote letters to Muslim rulers in Southeast Asia, urging them to take up arms against the antagonistic disbelievers.[23]

Al-Palimbani's writings emerged as canonical texts, inspiring subsequent Sufi authors to produce poems, tracts, and manifestos of urging Sufis to embody jihad. One such work was by al-Fatani, who declared it *fard al-'ayn* (obligatory) for all Muslims, including women and slaves, to take up arms in defense of their homelands.[24] *Wasiat Abrar, Peringatan Akhyar* (Pious Bequest, Excellent Reminders) may at first seem like a mere compilation of Islamic litanies and sagely advice from a Sufi master to his students. However, on closer reading, it becomes clear that he was urging his readers to stand up for justice and use force when necessary.

> The worst of acts are the prohibited and spending on sinful things. The worst of humankind are those complicit with oppressors and who scorned the oppressed.... Help your oppressed kin or anyone who are suffering from any kind of oppression, because Allah Almighty does not love those who do not love humankind. War in the path of Allah is the most superior and humbling act for the learned...the best form of jihad is to speak truth to an oppressive ruler.[25]

---

[22] Two versions of this texts have been published by Hasanuddin Yusof (ed.), *Karya Jihad Ulung Syeikh Abdul Samad Al-Palimbani: Nasihat al-Muslimin Wa Tazkirat al-Mukminin* (Seremban: Dr. Mohd Hasanuddin Mohd Yusof, 2023).

[23] Merle C. Ricklefs, *Jogjakarta under Sultan Mangkubumi, 1749–1792: A History of the Division of Java* (London: Oxford University Press, 1974); Peter G. Riddell, "'Abd Al-Samad All-Palimbani," in *Christian-Muslim Relations: A Bibliographical History, Vol 12, Asia, Africa, and the Americas,* eds. David Thomas and John Chesworth (Leiden: Brill, 2018), 614–620.

[24] Mohd. Nor bin Ngah, *Kitab Jawi: Islamic Thought of the Malay Muslim Scholars* (Singapore: ISEAS Press, 1983), 43–44; Wan Mohd Shaghir Abdullah, *Syeikh Daud Bin Abdullah Al-Fatani: Ulama' Dan Pengarang Terulung Asia Tenggara* (Selangor: Hizbi, 1990), 97.

[25] Syeikh Daud Al-Fatani, *Wasiat Abrar, Peringatan Akhyar.* ed. H.W.M. Saghir Abdullah (Shah Alam: Penerbit Hizbi, 1992).

The works of these Sufi scholars generated commentaries and more treatises inciting holy wars, notably the *Hikayat Prang Sabi* in Aceh and the *Parang Sabil Kissa* in Mindanao. Spanning a few centuries and emerging from different temporalities in Southeast Asia, these works formed a cumulative corpus of jihad narratives written by Sufi authors. Such jihad narratives were memorized and read before every confrontation between Muslims and Dutch combatants.[26]

PROTAGONIST SUFI WARRIORISM

Within Islamic law, the use of force is permissible only in specific and highly restrictive situations. Force is justifiable for self-defence, to liberate the oppressed, to restore peace within a given realm, and in cases when treaties were breached.[27] In embodying holy struggles, Sufi warriors did not always abide by these stipulations. Jihad in Southeast Asia was not always defensive. Sufis were protagonists of offensive campaigns. They interpreted jihad from a triumphalist perspective, viewing it as an "Islamic duty to conquer non-Muslim territories wherein cause/case for war (*casus belli*) is to establish political, not necessarily religious, supremacy of Muslims over others."[28] Hence, the term "protagonist Sufi warriorism" points to struggles instigated by Sufis to achieve imperial ends. The overriding objective was to subdue as many non-Muslim powers in the region under the flag of Islam. Along with the conquests came control of resources, trade, and commerce, as well as the conversion of defeated populations. This tendency was most visible during the populist phase of Islamization in Southeast Asia (thirteenth to eighteenth centuries), as Muslims emerged from being a minority to becoming an influential majority.[29] During this phase, Sufi scholars served as confidants of Muslim rulers, providing ideological validations for empire building and other worldly gains, a topic discussed in the next chapter.[30]

---

[26] Teuku Alfian Ibrahim, *Sastra Perang: Sebuah Pembicaraan Mengenai Hikayat Perang Sabil* (Jakarta: Balai Pustaka, 1992), 18.

[27] Niaz A. Shah, "The Use of Force under Islamic Law," *European Journal of International Law* 24, no. 1 (2013): 343–365; Mohammad Z. Sabuj, *The Legitimacy of Use of Force in Public and Islamic International Law* (Basingstoke: Palgrave Macmillan, 2021).

[28] Emin Poljarevic, "Jihad," in *Encyclopedia of Indian Religions,* eds. Zayn R. Kassam, Yudit Kornberg Greenberg and Jehan Bagli (New York: Springer, 2018), 392.

[29] Khairudin Aljunied, *Islam in Malaysia: An Entwined History* (Oxford University Press, 2019), 61–106.

[30] Martin van Bruinessen, *Mullas, Sufis, and Heretics: The Role of Religion in Kurdish Society: Collected Articles* (New Jersey: Gorgias Press, 2011), 231–240.

Struggles   **115**

The scarcity of documented sources on Sufi combatants during the populist Islamization phase in Southeast Asia meant that we can never fully uncover the lives of those involved in such battles. However, it is certain that these holy struggles and displays of religious martiality were extensions of practices in Muslim empires elsewhere. The conquerors of India, Mahmud of Ghazni (971–1030) and Shihab al-Din Ghuri (1144–1206), received spiritual and intellectual support from the shaykhs of the Chistiyyah tariqah during their jihad against the Hindu princely states. The Chisti Sufis provided manpower and encouraged Mughal kings to consolidate their power through armed conquests.[31] The Ottoman king, Mehmet II, was advised and tutored by the founder of the Shamsiyyah-Bayramiyyah Sufi order. Muhammad Shamsuddin bin Hamzah (Turkish: Aksemseddin, 1389–1459) was a pivotal figure who exhorted the emperor to hold fast to prophecies about his eventual victory. Without Shamsuddin's inducement, Mehmet II might have withdrawn the siege of Constantinople.[32]

Protagonist Sufi warriorism in Southeast Asia was undoubtedly induced by these Muslim conquerors and their narratives of conquests. In Demak on the island of Java, the tariqahs joined fierce battles against the Majapahit kingdom when the Hindu-Buddhist polity obstructed their Islamizing agenda. Raden Patah (1455–1518), the ruler of the Demak Sultanate and son-in-law of one of the Wali Songo, dispatched Sufis to fight against Majapahit rulers. Raden had blood relations with Majapahit rulers but refused to accept the dominance of disbelievers on Java. He launched a military campaign in 1478, laying waste to much of Majapahit's army. In 1527, one of Java's revered saints, Sunan Kudus (d. 1550), invaded Majapahit's capital and brought a death knell to the Hindu-Buddhist kingdom.[33] To mobilize Muslims during such battles, Sufi authors used the hikayats and babads. Vladimir Braginsky maintains that the hikayats were not just sentimentalized chronicles of noble feats and great battles fought by Muslim rulers in world history. They were affective texts that enchanted rasa and invigorated the spirit of struggle among listeners. The hikayats were mostly written since

---

[31] Muzaffar Alam, *The Mughals and the Sufis: Islam and Political Imagination in India, 1500–1750* (Albany: State University of New York Press, 2021), 115 and 392.

[32] Hüseyin Yilmaz, *Caliphate Redefined: The Mystical Turn in Ottoman Political Thought* (New Jersey: Princeton University Press, 2018), 134.

[33] Slamet Muljana, *Runtuhnya Kerajaan Hindu-Jawa Dan Timbulnya Negara-Negara Islam Di Jawa* (Yogyakarta: LKiS, 2005), 88–95; Theodore Gauthier Th. Pigeaud, *Islamic States in Java 1500–1700: Eight Dutch Books and Articles by H. J. de Graaf as Summarized by Theodore G. Th. Pigeaud* (The Hague: Nijhoff, 1976), 8.

the fifteenth century, an epoch saturated with jihad and perang sabil launched by Sufi rulers in Southeast Asia.[34]

Similar expressions of protagonist Sufi warriorism could be seen in North Sumatra. Hubs of Sufistic thought and the arts in Southeast Asia, the kingdom of Samudera Pasai (1267–1521) and its successor, the Acehnese Sultanate (1496–1903), were imperialistic. They hastened the decline of neighbouring non-Muslim kingdoms such as Srivijaya.[35] The sultans of Aceh, Ali Mughayat Syah (d. 1530), Alauddin al-Kahar (d. 1571), and Ali Riayat Shah (d. 1579), were promoters of Sufism and zealous militarists. They forged alliances with Muslim kingdoms in India and the Ottomans to heighten support for the invasion of non-Muslim states and Muslim rivals. Periodic battles were fought against the Portuguese and the Muslim kingdom of Johor. Though the campaigns against the Portuguese were mostly repulsed, the Acehnese dominated the Straits of Malacca for much of the seventeenth century. Sufi missionaries and orders from North Sumatra spread their wings into Southeast Asia as Acehnese armies maintained their commanding presence in the Malay peninsula.[36]

Not all Sufi rulers were protagonists of conflicts against competing states. Some maintained neutrality and paid tributes to more powerful Muslim and non-Muslim polities. Still, jihad and perang sabil featured strongly in the ruling ideology of most kingdoms. Preparations were made for every able man to be conscripted for holy wars. The legal digests enacted by the rulers, such as during the reign of Sultan of Pahang from 1592 to 1614, included directives like:

> For Holy War, one must be a male adult sane Muslim in good health, courageous and strong. Captured infidels may be enslaved along with women and children, or adult males may be slain, enslaved, released, or let go after seizure of their property. Whoever embraces Islam before capture, should have his goods and children preserved.[37]

---

[34] Vladimir I. Braginsky, *The Turkic-Turkish Theme in Traditional Malay Literature: Imagining the Other to Empower the Self* (Leiden: Brill, 2015).

[35] Howard M. Federspiel, *Sultans, Shamans, and Saints: Islam and Muslims in Southeast Asia* (University of Hawai'i Press, 2007), 36.

[36] Anthony Reid, *An Indonesian Frontier: Acehnese and Other Histories of Sumatra* (Singapore: NUS Press, 2005), 69–94; Leonard Y. Andaya, *Leaves of the Same Tree: Trade and Ethnicity in the Straits of Melaka* (Honolulu: University of Hawai'i Press, 2008), 125–129.

[37] Anon., "A Malay Legal Digest Compiled for 'Abd al-Ghafur Muhaiyu'd-Din Shah Sultan of Pahang 1592–1614 A.D. (ed. John E. Kempe and Richard O. Winstedt)," *Journal of the Malayan Branch of the Royal Asiatic Society* 21, no. 1 (144) (1948): 18–19.

Struggles   **117**

Textualized in such state-commissioned texts and institutionalized as policies of Islamic polities, protagonist Sufi warriorism bridged imperial ambitions, material aspirations, and pietistical intentions of Muslim rulers and their Sufi supporters. The convergence of motives was personified in the life of Sultan Agung, the third ruler of the Mataram kingdom in Central Java. A devout Sufi, a votary of Javanese mysticism (*kejawen*), and a gifted war strategist, Agung expanded his kingdom to the furthest reaches of Java. He developed his penchant for jihad through his relationships with other Sufi-oriented kingdoms in Aceh and Patani.[38] In a poem attributed to him, *Suluk Garwa Kancana*, explicit references were made to his inclination towards armed struggle and his celebration of the virtues of jihad. Agung's ultimate aim was to remove the Dutch from Java. His lifetime ambition was never realized. Towards the end of his reign, Agung was faced with rebellions from Sufi orders who were opposed to his policies. Even so, his fusion of local and Islamic ideas for the cause of holy war made him a legendary and iconic Sufi warrior-king who was feared, respected, and adulated by Muslims and non-Muslims alike.[39]

Martin Van Bruinessen observes that due to the instrumentalist use of Sufism by power elites, Sufism did not have a wide appeal in Southeast Asia until much later in the nineteenth century. "The *tarekat* [i.e., *tariqa*] was perceived as a source of spiritual power, at once legitimating and supporting the ruler's position. It was obviously not in the rulers' interest to make the same supernatural power available to all their subjects."[40] While I agree that rulers kept their mystical powers exclusive, I remain unconvinced that Sufism had little appeal among the common people before the nineteenth century. Despite the scarcity of sources to generalize the extent of Sufi influence on the masses, it is hard to imagine rulers mobilizing thousands to fight and die on battlefields without a unifying creed. Sufism undoubtedly provided one of the ideological fuels needed to realize the conquering visions of kings. Further, Muslim rulers in Southeast Asia during the populist phase of Islamization were not immune to assassinations by family members and closest aides. As Sultan Agung's case demonstrates, rebellions by fellow Sufis were common. The idea of a king with supernatural powers whose orders must be obeyed can only detail one aspect of the ideology used to wage wars.

---

[38] Merle C. Ricklefs, *Mystic Synthesis in Java* (Norwalk: Signature Books, 2006).

[39] Hermanus Johannes de Graaf, *De Regering van Sultan Agung, Vorst van Mataram (1613–1645) En Die van Zijn Voorganger Panembahan Séda-Ing-Krapjak (1601–1613)* (Leiden: Brill, 1958).

[40] Martin van Bruinessen, "The Origins and Development of Sufi Orders (Tarekat) in Southeast Asia," *Studia Islamika: Indonesian Journal for Islamic Studies* 1, no. 1 (1994): 1–23.

The promise of paradise along with the belief in invulnerability from Sufi cosmology and local mysticism, as the next section illustrates, is another compelling reason why thousands were ready to sacrifice their lives in battles against rival kingdoms.

PROTECTIONIST SUFI WARRIORISM

If protagonist Sufi warriorism was prompted by territorial ambitions, protectionist Sufi warriorism aimed to preserve an existing status quo or a way of life threatened by new systems infiltrating into the heart of Muslim societies. While protagonist and protectionist Sufi warriorism sometimes overlapped, protectionist warriorism was reactive, especially when regimes progressively violated Sufi domains of influence.[41] Martial expressions were precipitated by regime instability, threats from contending groups, failing alliances between Sufis and powerbrokers, or disenchantment with despotic and treacherous authorities. Loss of positions, privileges, and platforms for propagating teachings prompted Sufis to use force to restore the old order. As one study indicates, "Sufi orders (*tariqat*) can be politically active and even contentious" during uncertain times.[42]

Protectionist Sufi warriorism was often provoked by political fragmentation, religious polarization, and economic dislocation in Muslim societies. In Java, for example, Sufi resistance was "inseparable from violent hatred against foreign rulers and against prijaji officials who were alleged to have dishonoured their religion by cooperating with the infidel."[43] The point made by the Indonesian historian, Sartono Kartodirdjo, can be extrapolated to the rest of Southeast Asia and beyond. European colonialism was the chief factor triggering protectionist Sufi warriorism. Structural transformations brought by European presence fumed Sufis,[44] similar to their counterparts in North Africa who framed battles as wars against inhumane colonial states "that behaved, even by European standards, with remarkable cruelty and ruthlessness."[45]

---

[41] Alexander Knysh, *Islamic Mysticism: A Short History* (Leiden: Brill, 2000), 300.

[42] Raphaël Lefèvre, *Jihad in the City: Militant Islam and Contentious Politics in Tripoli* (Cambridge: Cambridge University Press, 2021), 166.

[43] Sartono Kartodirdjo, "Agrarian Radicalism in Java: Its Setting and Development," in *Culture and Politics in Indonesia,* ed. Claire Holt (Jakarta: Equinox Publishing Ltd, 2007), 100.

[44] Nile Green, *Sufism: A Global History* (Oxford: Wiley-Blackwell, 2012), 187–239.

[45] Michael Gilsenan, "On Conflict and Violence," in *Exotic No More: Anthropology on the Front Lines,* ed. Jeremy MacClancy (Chicago: Chicago University Press, 2002), 105.

Struggles   **119**

These seismic transformations generated a genre of Muslim writings depicting colonial powers as cosmic enemies. Such texts had a tone of urgency and audacity: Muslim power must be instated through violent struggles.[46] The *Hikayat Prang Sabi* was one of them. Widely circulated in Aceh from the second half of the nineteenth century, Hikayat Prang Sabi was a collection of sermons written in a melodious way to appeal to the rasa of lay Muslims. The style of writing reveals the influence of Sufi sha'irs. The text openly exhorted holy war. It adulates the merits of annihilating the warring disbelievers, promising manifold rewards that come with martyrdom. With death in the path of Allah came everlasting happiness with beautiful maidens in heaven. For the Acehnese warriors, the hikayat was an indispensable companion. It was read with passion before every violent confrontation.[47]

The first case of protectionist Sufi warriorism considered here occurred in east Sumatra. From 1686 to 1695, Ahmad Shah ibn Iskandar staged a rebellion causing trepidation for the Dutch and their collaborators. Ahmad was affiliated with the Shattariyah tariqah led by Abdul Rauf al-Singkili (1620–1693 AD), an Acehnese who lived most of his life in Makkah, embracing shari'a-oriented Sufism. Abdul Rauf's students hailed from many corners of Southeast Asia and many eventually became scholars, advisors to kings, and warriors on battlefields.[48] Ahmad's rebellion must be understood within the context of his Sufi affiliations and awareness of contemporaneous uprisings in nearby kingdoms, such as in Banten (1670–1683). Shaykh Yusuf Al-Makassari, a Shattari Sufi master in Banten, fought alongside Sultan Ageng against his son, Sultan Haji, who received Dutch support. This fratricide led to the militarization of Shattari Sufis throughout the Indonesian archipelago. Ahmad was one of many tariqah leaders who espoused the view that jihad against European colonizers was just.[49]

---

[46] Rijali, *Historie van Hitu. Een Ambonse Geschiedenis Uit de Zeventiende Eeuw* (trans. Hans Straver, Chris van Fraassen and Jan van Der Putten) (Utrecht: LSEM (Landelijk Steunpunt Educatie Molukkers), 2004); Entji' Amin, *Syair Perang Mengkasar: The Rhymed Chronicle of the Macassar War* (ed. and trans. Cyril Skinner) (The Hague, 1963).

[47] Imran T. Abdullah, "Ulama Dan Hikayat Perang Sabil Dalam Perang Belanda Di Aceh," *Humaniora* 12, no. 3 (2000): 243.

[48] Nancy K. Florida, "Shattariya Sufi Scents: The Literary World of the Surakarta Palace in Nineteenth-Century Java," in *Buddhist and Islamic Orders in Southern Asia: Comparative Perspectives,* eds. R. Michael Feener and Anne M. Blackburn (Honolulu: University of Hawai'i Press, 2019), 157.

[49] Abu Hamid, *Syeikh Yusuf: Seorang Ulama, Sufi, Dan Pejuang* (Jakarta: Yayasan Obor Indonesia, 1994), 5.

Ahmad's revulsion centred on colonial lackeys. Claiming royal lineages and using local mythologies to rouse the masses, Ahmad positioned himself as a prince from the Minangkabau kingdom and a descendant of Alexander the Great. He also used Hindu-Buddhist and Islamic rhetoric to stake his claim as a saint, gathering thousands of militias from Sumatra and north Java to fight a holy war against the kafir and their local allies. Although he did not achieve his ultimate goal, Ahmad left behind dozens of colonial soldiers and local chiefs dead. Throughout his decade-long rebellion, "he fired the imagination of the leaders of the late seventeenth century anti-kafir movement as a symbol of indigenous unity."[50]

These short-lived outbreaks of protectionist Sufi warriorism differed from the sustained resistance found in South Philippines. There, Muslim rulers and religious leaders defied Spanish colonialism well until the second half of the nineteenth century, only to reignite such struggles against American colonizers (1898–1946) and successive postcolonial governments. Among Muslims in Mindanao and the Sulu Zone (also called "Moros"), the language of warriorism was framed by the concept of *parrang sabbil* (Malay for perang sabil). For them, self-sacrifice during battles was honourable. Young and well-trained Muslim warriors would charge into colonial settlements and army posts, killing as many enemies as possible before succumbing to violent reprisals.[51] These ferocious acts of self-sacrifice were termed *juramentado* by Spaniards. Cesar Adib Majul describes juramentado graphically, indicating Sufi traces found in this self-sacrificing act:

On the eve of the day set for the performance of the duty, the mujahid (one who does the jihad) was completely shaved off his hair and eyebrows. He then went through a complete ritual bathing as a symbol of purification followed by dressing completely in white. Sometimes he wore a small white turban. The colour here is that of mourning and the clothing signified the burial shroud. The mujahid would spend the evening in prayer in the company of panditas who would not only recite Qur'anic verses but probably local prayers not entirely devoid of pre-Islamic elements. The work Parang Sabil-ullah (Fighting in the Way of Allah) with its exhortations and description of Paradise was read to him to encourage him in his decision. He would also carry with him a

---

[50] Kathirithamby-Wells, "Ahmad Shah Ibn Iskandar and the Late 17th Century 'Holy War' in Indonesia," 63.

[51] Thomas M. Kiefer, "Parrang Sabbil: Ritual Suicide among the Tausug of Jolo," *Bijdragen Tot de Taal-, Land- En Volkenkunde* 129, no. 1 (1973): 108–109.

Struggles   **121**

few amulets some of which would normally contain inscriptions of a few Qur'anic verses.[52]

Although there is no direct evidence of tariqahs participating in such wars, Sufi elements were evident in the preparatory rituals before self-sacrifice. Combatants donned white robes and turbans and read certain dhikr commonly used by Sufi communities.[53] It is challenging, according to Howard Federspiel, to separate the Moros from the Sufi tradition given the pervasive influence of that strand of Islam throughout Southeast Asia. Arrayed in Sufi idioms, juramentado was used against "an enemy who was a threat to the political integrity of a Muslim state or its ruler, but such blessed warfare was used in other situations as well."[54]

If Sufis in the Mindanao and Sulu Zone had to contend with external powers, Sufis in South Thailand faced a juggernaut in their backyard. The seventeenth and twentieth centuries were the bloodiest chapters in the history of the Muslims living in the provinces of Pattani, Yala, and Narathiwat, all of whom are styled as "*Orang Melayu Patani* (Patani Malays)."[55] Siamese troops serving the Ayutthaya and Chakri kingdoms, as well as subsequent postcolonial regimes, unleashed many armed campaigns to keep the Muslim provinces within their grip. Generations of Patani Malay Sufi orders and scholars took part in the fight against the Siamese. The fiercest resistance came from the pondoks.[56] Among them was Shaykh Abdur Rahman Pauh Bok (d. 1780), whose descendants kept alive Sufi warriorism in Patani. His pondok produced generations of spiritual mediators known for their organic texts and networks of scholarly communities in Makkah, Madinah, and other Muslim cities. Many returned to serve as teachers and Sufi shaykhs, maintaining familial and spiritual ties with Patani Sufi scholars and warriors abroad. Graduates of these pondoks sustained battles against non-Muslim interference in South Thailand for over a century, with jihad against the Siamese, and later, Thailand included the use of magic spells and mystical ceremonies.[57]

---

[52] Cesar Adib Majul, *Muslims in the Philippines* (University of the Philippines Press, 1999), 356.

[53] Vic Hurley, *Swish of the Kris: The Story of the Moros* (Seattle: Cerberus Books, 2010), 126–131.

[54] Howard M. Federspiel, "Islam and Muslims in the Southern Territories of the Philippine Islands during the American Colonial Period (1898 to 1946)," *Journal of Southeast Asian Studies* 29, no. 2 (1998): 353–354.

[55] Ibrahim Syukri, *Sejarah Kerajaan Melayu Patani* (Bangi: Universiti Kebangsaan Malaysia, 2002), 74, 84 and 122.

[56] Christopher Mark Joll, *Muslim Merit-Making in Thailand's Far-South* (New York: Springer, 2012), 41.

[57] Duncan McCargo, *Tearing Apart the Land: Islam and Legitimacy in Southern Thailand* (Ithaca, NY: Cornell University Press, 2008), 19 and 138–139.

Protectionist Sufi warriorism directed against fellow Muslims was as rancorous as against non-Muslims. Sufis in Southeast Asia waged battles to outdo fellow Sufis, sometimes involving members of the same tariqah. In the late seventeenth to early eighteenth centuries, the *kraton* (Javanese royalty) and the *kauman* (religious community) were locked in bloody tussles for supremacy in the kingdom of Mataram. Panembahan Rama, the overlord of the Kajoran religious dynasty in the Klaten area of Surakarta, launched major rebellions with the help of the Madurese. They were quickly defeated by Mataram and Dutch forces. These long wars widened the rift between different Sufi groups. Java was a powder keg, that exploded in the first quarter of the nineteenth century.[58]

Fighting between Diponegoro's forces and the Dutch colonial forces in Gawok (1900 drawing): https://en.wikipedia.org/wiki/Diponegoro#/media/File:Aanval_van_de_colonne_Le_Bron_de_Vexela_op_Dipo_Negoro_nabij_Gawok.jpg

---

[58] Anon., *Babad Tanah Jawi: The Chronicle of Java* (ed. and trans. Willem Remmelin) (Leiden: Leiden University Press, 2022), 163–164; Soemarsaid Moertono, *State and Statecraft in Old Java: A Study of the Later Mataram Period, 16th to 19th Century* (Singapore: Equinox Publishing Ltd, 2009), 43–44.

Struggles   **123**

From 1825 to 1830, the great war of Java broke out with the Sufi prince of the Yogyakartan court, Diponegoro (or Dipanagara, 1785–1855) at its helm. Supported by Sufi teachers and scholars, many were Hadrami-Arabs affiliated with the Shattariyah tariqah. They were skilled in war tactics, charms, and amulets, as well as modern and traditional weapons. Interestingly, the war saw the involvement of janissaries sent by the Ottoman emperor to serve as Diponegoro's bodyguards. Women like Nyai Ageng Serang and Raden Ayu Yudakusuma also led troops. Both were mystics with large followings. Captured by the Dutch with a fully shaven head in 1828, Raden Ayu stated that her outer appearance was "a sign of her dedication to the holy war against the kafir Dutch and their apostate Javanese allies."[59]

The use of mystical tropes and the idea of defending their estranged homeland from the disbelievers were major factors encouraging Sufi men and women in Java to fight against the odds. Diponegoro was hailed by Muslims as a living saint capable of predicting the future and performing miracles. Perceived as invulnerable, his declaration of perang sabil against the Dutch and their Javanese allies received mass support from ulama and santris. A contemporaneous Javanese source documents this story of Sufi protectionist warriorism: "Their weapons were various according to their personal tastes, some (carried) dwarflike short spears, other pointed bamboos, staves and slings. The approximate number of Dipanagara's men was five hundred. All had been given invulnerability, (and) had been guaranteed that bullets could not strike; the shots would (fall) short, or (go) too far."[60] Like the juramentado combatants in the Philippines, these Sufis went into battles donning turbans and white robes and chanting dhikr with the hope that God would grant victory to Muslims. Diponegoro's army was defeated and he was sent to exile at Makassar.[61]

In British-occupied Malaya and Borneo, the cycle of Sufi protectionist warriorism began in late nineteenth century and endured into the 1940s. Names such as Tok Ku Paloh al-Naqshbandi, Haji Abdul Rahman

---

[59] Peter Carey, *The Power of Prophecy: Dipanagara and the End of an Old Order in Java, 1785–1855* (Leiden: KITLV, 2008), 613–615.

[60] Anon., *Babad Dipanagara: A Surakarta Court Poet's Account of the Outbreak of the Java War (1825–30)* (ed. and trans. Peter Carey) (Kuala Lumpur: Malaysian Branch of the Royal Asiatic Society, 2019), 87.

[61] Oman Fathurahman, "Female Indonesian Sufis: Shattariya Murids in the 18th and 19th Centuries in Java," *Kyoto Bulletin of Islamic Area Studies* 11 (2018): 55.

Limbong, Mat Kilau, Dato' Bahaman, Mat Salleh, Tok Janggut, Tok Gajah, and Kiai Salleh were members or leaders of tariqahs, remembered as Sufi warrior-saints who valiantly stood against foreign rule.[62] However, none of these conflicts reached the scale of the Java war, with some lasting no more than a few days. The difference in scale may be linked to partnerships the British developed with local rulers, who wielded Sufi support. State-linked Sufis, appointed as muftis and village headmen, refused collaborations with rebel groups, branding them treasonous. One incident of failed Sufi rebellion in Malaya occurred on 20 May 1928, when more than two thousand armed men gathered under the leadership of Abdul Rahman Abdul Hamid (known as Lebai Deraman or Tok Janggut Telemong) at Kuala Telemong in Trengganu. They protested the colonial state's disregard of shari'a and customary laws. Abdul Rahman was a known pugilist and Sufi with karamah. But "in spite of his vaunted invulnerability," writes a colonial report, he "fell to a single bullet."[63] Eleven rebels died of gunshot wounds, a dozen ringleaders were imprisoned within a week after the violent dissent. Cognizant of his influence in the local community, the British exiled Abdul Rahman to Makkah with a monthly pension of fifty pounds. He died over a year later in November 1929.

Perhaps the most massive sample of Sufi protectionist warriorism that Southeast Asia was during the Indonesian revolution from August 1945 to December 1949. In this bloody struggle, Sufis gained the upper hand and emerged victorious alongside other revolutionaries despite heavy losses. One collective that left an imprint in the revolution's history was the Laskar Hizbullah. Founded by the Japanese during the closing stages of the Second World War to resist incoming Allied troops, Christened as *Kaikyo Seinen Teishintai* (Japanese for "Islamic Youth Corps," in short, Hizbullah or Laskar Hizbullah), the militant group was led by scholars from various Islamic movements in Indonesia, with the Sufis from the Nahdlatul Ulama forming the core group.[64]

After the Second World War, this armed group remained active as a guerrilla force without a central coordinating body. Spread across Indonesia, Hizbullah recruited women warriors who inflicted severe damage

---

[62] Khairudin Aljunied, *Radicals: Resistance and Protest in Colonial Malaya* (Dekalb: Northern Illinois University Press, 2015), 21.

[63] Sturrock, *Annual Report of British Adviser, Trengganu for the Years A.H. 1346 to 1347* (Singapore: Government Printing Office, 1929), 12.

[64] Latief M Hasyim, *Laskar Hizbullah: Berjuang Menegakkan Negara RI* (Surabaya: Lajnah Ta'lif wan Nasyr, 1995).

on the Dutch war machinery. Islamic revolutionaries eradicated remnants of public fear towards the old feudal order, supercharging the pursuit of *merdeka* (independence). Fatwas, religious manifestoes, amulets, magic, and trances were used to wage fierce resistance. According to Saifuddin Zuhri, a leader of Hizbullah in Java, the tariqahs most active in sending troops were the Shadhiliyyah, Qadiriyyah wa Naqshbandiyyah, and Khalidiyyah-Naqshbandiyyah.[65] Armed with machetes and light firearms, shaykhs and murids charged tanks and automated guns, believing no harm would befall them.[66] While most previous episodes of Muslim resistance against colonial rule extended European control in Southeast Asia, the four years of war against the Dutch had the opposite outcome. Indonesia was granted unconditional sovereignty by the United Nations on 27 December 1949.

PURIST SUFI WARRIORISM

The third expression of Sufi warriorism was motivated by the aspiration to purify Muslim societies of all forms of heterodoxies, inequalities, and iniquities. I term this "purist Sufi warriorism." Although some scholars use the term "orthodox Sufis," I find it inapplicable because not all historical actors were against bid'ah or focused on implementing shari'a.[67] Purist Sufis insisted on complete adherence to traditional rules and customary structures, demanding a restoration of authentic belief systems, and a Muslim way of life obliterated by modern influences. They envisaged a society where personal piety and public morality aligned with Islamic precepts. They were driven by a sense of nostalgia and utopia framed in activist terms.

Restoring neglected Islamic mores, manners, moralities, and mentalities in societies required coercion or violence. Jihad and perang sabil were waged to radically change Muslim norms. A conspicuous dimension of purist Sufi warriorism was to invalidate the menacing effects of social inequalities and economic injustice caused by colonialism. Armed

---

[65] Zuhri Saifuddin, *Berangkat Dari Pesantren* (Yogyakarta: LKiS, 2013), 269.

[66] Kevin W. Fogg, *Indonesia's Islamic Revolution* (Cambridge: Cambridge University Press, 2020), 47–91.

[67] For examples of the use of the term "orthodox Sufis", see: Annemarie Schimmel, *Mystical Dimensions of Islam* (Chapel Hill: University of North Carolina Press, 1978), 147; Michael F. Laffan, *The Makings of Indonesian Islam: Orientalism and the Narration of a Sufi Past* (Princeton University Press, 2011), 131.

struggle was deemed necessary to dismantle repressive policies and alleviate the suffering and frustrations of the common people. Militancy, dressed in the language of purification, was seen as the antidote to systemic tyranny. Purist Sufis in Southeast Asia were similar to protectionist Sufis and their counterparts in North Africa, who positioned themselves as "saviours from injustice" in reaction to the excessive anguish towards exploitative states.[68] Thus, purist Sufi warriorism must be understood as a corollary of the nexus between pious motivations, social alienation, status deprivation, and economic frustration, all of which were interdependent variables engendering violence.

The Padri war (or the Minangkabau war) in 1803 to 1837 is an illustrative sample of purist Sufi warriorism in Southeast Asia. Historical literature often describes the Padris as men who returned from Makkah with the zeal of implementing Wahabism, envisioning a society free from bid'ah and shirk. They strictly enforced shari'a laws and critiqued local customs that contravened Islamic beliefs. Alcohol, betel

Portrait of Tuanku Imam Bonjol (1772–1864): https://en.wikipedia.org/wiki/Tuanku_Imam_Bonjol#/media/File:Portret_van_Tuanku_Imam_Bonjol.jpg

---

[68] Julia A. Clancy-Smith, *Rebel and Saint: Muslim Notables, Populist Protest, Colonial Encounters (Algeria and Tunisia, 1800–1904)* (Berkeley: University of California Press, 1997), 67.

Struggles **127**

nut, tobacco, opium, gambling, cockfighting, wearing of silk, and adorning gold were forbidden. Women were made to cover their heads when in public and men were made to grow beards. Violators were severely punished, sometimes mortally. However, a closer look at the backgrounds of the Padri leaders such as Tuanku Rao (1790–1833), Imam Bonjol (1772–1864), Tuanku Nan Tuo (1723–1830), and Tuanku Nan Renceh (1762–1832) reveals a different picture. They were Sufis from the Shattariyah tariqah, carrying *tasbih* (rosary) and embracing practices shunned by the Wahabis.[69] Harsh towards Muslim shrine worshippers, they did not desecrate saints' tomb or condemn the idea of karamah. Although impacted by some aspects of Wahabi creed, the Padris were rooted in Sufi thought and tradition.[70]

The Padri puritanical war was linked to the economic injustices ushered in by colonial rule and local exploitation. Padris hunted down robbers and slave traders, releasing captives and returning stolen goods. They inveighed Dutch-imposed cash economy and forced labour, attacking adat elites for collaborating with the Dutch in coffee cultivation monopolies. The Padri war was the longest lasting instance of Sufi purist warriorism in nineteenth-century Sumatra, ending with the killing and exile of movement leaders. A truce and a compromise were soon reached between Sufis and adat elites, harmonizing Islamic law and local customs and ensuring Muslim share in the colonial economy.[71]

The expansion of colonial rule and quashing of Sufi purist warriorism in Sumatra only increased the prevalence of such revolts in Southeast Asia. One caveat should, however, be made. Until the 1940s, with the advent of the Darul Islam movement, none of the subsequent episodes of Sufi purist warriorism in Southeast Asia shared the same degree of intransigence towards Islamic laws as the Padris. If Marshall Hodgson's concept is relevant here, then purist Sufis and the Padris in the later years were less "shari'a minded."[72] The Padris' imposition of the shari'a in everyday life and ridding much of what they saw as wayward customs through violent means were never revived. Sufi purist warriorism in the ensuing decades utilized

---

[69] Christine Dobbin, *Islamic Revivalism in a Changing Peasant Economy: Central Sumatra, 1784–1847* (London: Curzon Press, 1983), 127.

[70] Rex S. O'Fahey, "Small World: Neo-Sufi Interconnexions between the Maghrib, the Hijaz and Southeast Asia," in *The Transmission of Learning in Islamic Africa,* ed. Scott Reese (Leiden: Brill, 2004), 282.

[71] Jeffrey Hadler, *Muslims and Matriarchs: Cultural Resilience in Indonesia through Jihad and Colonialism* (Ithaca: Cornell University Press, 2008), 29.

[72] The term shari'a-minded was introduced by Hodgson in his classic, *The Venture of Islam: Conscience and History in a World Civilization, Vol. 1,* 403.

pre-Islamic myths as mediums to legitimize protest. Despite criticizing native cultures and beliefs, they did so usually in reaction to some unjust practices, and rarely envisaged complete abolition of the adat.

The peasant revolt in Cilegon, Banten in 1888, diverged from the shari'a-minded approach of the Padris. Banten was struck by a volcanic eruption, epidemic, and famine that claimed thousands of human lives, including livestock. Exacerbating social suffering was Dutch imposition of new regulations prohibiting the loud dhikr and prayers in mosques and forbidding the reconstruction of an old minaret. The stage was set for conflict. Leaders of the Naqshbandiyyah and Qadiriyyah tariqahs utilized their networks to recruit combatants and planned attacks against the Dutch. They wielded support from returning hajjis and Hejazi students exposed Islamic revivalism, pan-Islamism, millenarianism, and holy war. Xenophobia grew as new institutions threatened Muslim livelihood and beliefs. Sufi leaders expected mass support given the frustrations of Muslims at the time, leveraging discipline and loyalties forged within tariqahs, mosques, and Sufi seminaries.[73]

One such leader was Kiai Wasyid bin Muhammad Abbas (or Ki Wasyid, 1843–1888), who issued fatwas against idolatry shamanism and tree worship. Consequently, he was fined, whipped, and jailed. Upon release, he gathered tariqah leaders and hajjis to train their disciples in silat, weapon training, and the use of azimat for jihad against the kafir. They believed in their *sakti* (magical powers) and charisma, attracting devoted followers in villages and pesantren.[74] On 9 July 1888, hundreds of men led by Sufis set out to attack Dutch officials, local loyalists, and a prison where some Sufis were detained. The three-week melee forced the Dutch to dispatch a battalion of soldiers from Batavia to quell the uprising. Ki Wasyid and other key leaders were killed, with survivors fleeing to Makkah and distant villages. Those captured alive were exiled to distant provinces.[75]

European colonial rule also provoked violent reactions from Sufis in South Kalimantan in the late nineteenth and early twentieth centuries. Sufis and hajjis, who were also traders and political brokers connected with the Banjarmasin sultanate, were disturbed by the presence of Christian missionaries, viewing it as part of the colonial strategy to erode Muslim faith. There was a grain of truth in this conspiracy.

---

[73] C. Snouck Hurgronje, *Kumpulan Karangan Snouck Hurgronje* (Jakarta: INIS, 1993), 178.

[74] Sartono Kartodirdjo, *Protest Movements in Rural Java: A Study of Agrarian Unrest in the Nineteenth and Early Twentieth Centuries.* (Singapore: Oxford University Press, 1973), 59–60.

[75] Ibid., 59–60.

Struggles **129**

Dutch interference in court politics was visible when a puppet ruler was installed as the Sultan in 1852. This move provoked supporters of the crown prince Pangeran Hidayatullah (1822–1904). Assisted by Dayak tribes, ulama, hajjis, Sufis, royal loyalists, Hidayatullah's faction attacked Dutch and usurpers.[76]

Two Sufi-oriented collectives headed most of the battles. The first was called Gerakan Muning. Their spiritual leader was Panambahan Muda Datu Aling. A blind man from peasant background, his daughter was married into the royal family. Aling was viewed by his followers as a saint and a messianic figure sent by God to rout the disbelievers.[77] The second collective was known as *beratib beramal* (chanting and practicing). They splintered from the Sammaniyyah and Naqshbandi-yah tariqahs and invented special rituals in preparation for war. Some Sufi scholars in Kalimantan branded this group as heterodox with Sufi-inflected mysticism.[78] Needless to say, both groups rallied peasants to join the holy war. Using spears and daggers, they believed that victory was guaranteed in anticipation of the coming of the messiah and Imam Mahdi. This revolt lasted for a few years, but it had, in effect, shepherded the end of the Banjarese Sultanate after the killing of one of the competitors to the throne, Sultan Muhammad Seman (1862–1905).[79]

The Darul Islam rebellion in West Java, Aceh, South Kalimantan, and South Sulawesi that broke out from 1945 to 1962 is another momentous case of Sufi purist warriorism. Similar to insurgencies in South Thailand and South Philippines, leaders envisaged an Islamic state governed by the shari'a and God as the supreme source of political authority. As Wael Hallaq aptly explains, the vision of an Islamic state captivated many anti-colonial Muslim activists, thinkers, rebels, and politicians seeking an alternative to the modern state. However, such projects were chimerical. "The 'Islamic state,' judged by any standard definition of what the modern state represents, is both an impossibility and a contradiction in terms.... modernity and its state could not and cannot accept the

---

[76] Helius Sjamsuddin, *Pegustian Dan Temenggung Akar Sosial, Politik, Etnis Dan Dinasti Perlawanan Di Kalimantan Selatan Dan Kalimantan Tengah 1859–1906* (Jakarta: Balai Pustaka, 2001), 271–273.

[77] M. Idwar Saleh and Sri Sutjiatiningsih, *Pangeran Antasari* (Jakarta: Departemen Pendidikan dan Kebudayaan, 1993), 31–41.

[78] Pieter Johannes Veth, "Het Beratip Beamal in Bandjermasin," *Tijdschrift Voor Nederlandsch-Indië* 3, no. 2 (1870 1869): 197–202.

[79] Sjamsuddin, Helius, "Islam and Resistance in South and Central Kalimantan in the Nineteenth and Early Twentieth Centuries," in *Islam in the Indonesian Social Context,* ed. Merle C. Ricklefs (Melbourne: Centre of Southeast Asian Studies, Monash University, 1991), 7–17.

Shari'a on its own terms because these terms are profoundly moral and egalitarian, whereas the state and the world that produced it relegated the moral to a subsidiary domain."[80] Indeed, the Darul Islam ideologues were faced with acute tensions with modernist Muslims who lived within a Western-defined secular government and accepted religions as important constituents of the nation-state. Yet, they were unwilling to embrace a revolutionary Islamic polity. Furthermore, Darul Islam's categorical approaches generated scepticism among Muslims who preferred gradualism and evolutionary shift from the colonial order of things to a more Islamic form of statehood.[81]

The progenitor of the Darul Islam movement, Soekarmadji Maridja Kartosuwiryo (1905–1962), believed in realizing an Islamic state. A staunch adherent of Sufi teachings who became radicalized during the revolutionary struggle for Indonesian independence (1945–1949), he was expelled from Dutch medical school for possessing communist books. Kartosuwiryo delved into Islamic activism, first with Jong Isla-mieten Bond (JIB) before joining Partai Syarikat Islam (PSI). At PSI, he studied with traditional Islamic scholars and was initiated into the Qadi-riyyah order.[82] Sufism was a medium for recruiting and training young men and women for political mobilization. He achieved this through the establishment of the Suffah Institute in 1940. Its members became his loyal soldiers. In 1946, Kartosuwiryo declared at a gathering with Muslim activists that repulsing all forms of colonialism, including those imposed by countrymen. To achieve freedom and liberty, Muslims were obligated to "struggle in the path of Allah, or in other words engage in *qital* or *ghazwah* (militant campaigns) and sacrifice our possessions and lives towards that noble path."[83] He styled himself as the *imam* (leader) of a new Islamic state, *ad-Daulatul Islamiyyah* (or Darul Islam), and in 1949, Kartosuwiryo proclaimed the founding of *Negara Islam Indonesia* (NII, the Islamic State of Indonesia) in West Java.[84]

---

[80] Wael B. Hallaq, *The Impossible State: Islam, Politics, and Modernity's Moral Predicament* (Columbia University Press, 2013), 1 and 167–168.

[81] For a new history of the Darul Islam movement and its failed visions, see: Chiara Formichi, *Islam and the Making of the Nation: S.M. Kartosuwiryo and Political Islam in 20th Century Indonesia* (Leiden: KITLV Press, 2012).

[82] Solahudin, *The Roots of Terrorism in Indonesia: From Darul Islam to Jema'ah Islamiyah* (Ithaca, NY: Cornell University Press, 2013), 30.

[83] S. M. Kartosoewirjo, *Haloen Politik Islam* (Malangbong: Dewan Penerangan Masjoemi Daerah Priangan, 1946), 18.

[84] Cornelius Van Dijk, *Rebellion under the Banner of Islam: The Darul Islam in Indonesia* (The Hague: Martinus Nijhoff, 1981), 3.

Struggles **131**

Darul Islam's ideology aimed to purify society of Islam's enemies to establish an Islamic state. Sufi ideas and Javanese mysticism were visible in the spiritual training of its members. Following Sufi practices, members pledged bay'ah with Kartosuwiryo, whom they regarded as murshid and a wali directly communicating with God. He was said to have supernatural powers of vanishing and appearing in different places.[85] Protected by spirits, no weapons could harm him. An element of fear was also instilled in the Darul Islam fighters. Desertion and disobedience would lead to divine catastrophes. Some deserters, including Kartosuwiryo's former teachers, exposed his gambits. But anyone hostile to Darul Islam was excommunicated and declared heretic, often assassinated by former comrades. Mutilated bodies of objectors were publicly displayed.[86]

Darul Islam's terror claimed more than thirteen thousand civilian and combatant lives, destroying thousands of houses, mosques, and schools in Java, Aceh, South Kalimantan, and South Sulawesi. Common people's fury, including Sufi groups aiding the Indonesian army, subdued the rebels. By May 1962, Darul Islam in Aceh was crushed. The Sulawesi branch led by Kahar Muzakar in Sulawesi broke ranks, and other offshoots lost ground in the battle for the hearts and minds of Muslims. On 4 June 1962, Kartosuwiryo surrendered. Most Darul Islam members were granted amnesty by the Indonesian government as a strategic bargain to end the years of violence. Kartosuwiryo was executed by a firing squad. His demise marked the failure of purist Sufi warriorism in postcolonial Indonesia, an era of emasculation of most Sufi groups under the Sukarno and Suharto regimes.[87]

CONCLUSION

The following contemplative histories unsettle commonplace portrayals of Sufism as a pacifist strand in Southeast Asia. Utilized by states in their ideological battle against religious extremism, such one-sided portrayal of the "peaceful and tolerant Sufi" does not accurately represent the historical trajectories of Sufism in that region or elsewhere in

---

[85] S. Soebardi, "Kartosuwiryo and the Darul Islam Rebellion in Indonesia," *Journal of Southeast Asian Studies* 14, no. 1 (1983): 109–133.

[86] Van Dijk, *Rebellion under the Banner of Islam*, 122.

[87] Hiroko Horikoshi, "The Dar Ul-Islam Movement in West Java (1948062): An Experience in the History Process," *Indonesia* 20 (1975): 58–96.

the Muslim world.[88] A notable segment of Sufis in Southeast Asia were warriors, using Sufism as a legitimating and mobilizing tool for conflicts. As protagonists seeking to acquire territories, protectionists desiring the return of past mandates, or purists wanting to expunge heterodoxies and institutionalize moral leviathans, Sufis used the concepts of jihad and perang sabil to amass support for their armed struggles. Sufi warriorism was a vital mainstay of the dialogical tradition.

Several factors motivated Sufis towards jihad and perang sabil, all associated with the dialogues with their faith, traditions, communities, states, and opposing forces. Millenarianism, the expectation that a messiah would restore Islam, and a looming Armageddon, motivated Sufis towards the path of self-sacrifice. Martyrdom was regarded as noble for manifold rewards in the afterlife. Local mysticism and folk beliefs also justified aggression. These ideational factors interacted with material and personal concerns, creating an atmosphere for violent struggle. Gripes over the loss of status, new laws, and alien political-economic arrangements in Southeast Asia added to Sufi wrath. European colonialism supercharged the growth of Sufi warriorism, making battles in the name of jihad and perang sabil recur for many decades. To borrow Jacques Waardenburg's perceptive reflections, Sufi warriorism, like most cases of Muslim protest, was "concerned with concrete social and cultural realities but endowed with a profound symbolic dimension expressed in Islamic terms whose true meanings are difficult for an outsider to unravel."[89]

Due to the sporadic nature of their mobilization and the lack of majority support, all three expressions of warriorism were mostly detrimental for Sufis. Since the seventeenth century, Sufis were overpowered by the forces they opposed. Stories of valour in defeat, however, lived on in oral narratives and didactic texts. This may explain why Sufi warriorism in Southeast Asia persevered for centuries.[90] Knut S. Vikør is incorrect in viewing colonial rule and modern nation-states as a final blow for Sufi warriorism, as "none of the Sufi orders that were most active in resistance grew from the efforts; most declined or

---

[88] Fait Muedini, *Sponsoring Sufism How Governments Promote "Mystical Islam" in Their Domestic and Foreign Policies* (Basingstoke: Palgrave Macmillan, 2015).

[89] Jacques Waardenburg, "Islam as a Vehicle of Protest," in *Islamic Dilemmas: Reformers, Nationalists and Industrialization in the Southern Shore of the Mediterranean,* ed. Ernest Gellner (Amsterdam: Mouton Publishers, 1985), 40.

[90] Ahmad Fauzi Abdul Hamid, "Malay Anti-Colonialism in British Malaya: A Re-Appraisal of Independence Fighters of Peninsular Malaysia," *Journal of Asian and African Studies* 42, no. 5 (2007): 374–376.

faded away."[91] In Southeast Asia, Sufi warriorism survived retaliatory violence, inspiring new outbreaks and forming a cycle of protest. Although ephemeral, Sufi rage against injustices smouldered, waiting to reignite. To end, the notion that Sufis were mostly quietists and seldom aggressive, as I have shown, is a historiographical flaw. Sufis in Southeast Asia embodied holy struggles. For that, they were feared, yet respected, and memorialized.

---

[91] Knut S. Vikør, "Sufism and Colonialism," in *The Cambridge Companion to Sufism,* ed. Lloyd Ridgeon (Cambridge: Cambridge University Press, 2015), 231.

CHAPTER 5

Politics

More than just scholars, saints, and sages, Sufis have contributed immensely to shaping politics. While it is true that for centuries Sufis viewed rulers and political figures with suspicion and were driven by a sense of disenchantment with worldly power and excessive materialism, they also engaged in state-making and in establishing regimes. As both convivial or conflictual forces in politics, Sufis navigated the halls of power and networks of activists, thus becoming influencers who shaped the decisions of elites and laypersons alike.[1] The formation and survival of *kerajaans* (kingdoms) in Southeast Asia would not have been possible without Sufis as legitimating ideologues and skilled networkers. Through their networks, Sufis also acted as restraining forces, advising kings and even leading rebellions against rulers when peaceful protest was impossible.

Under colonial rule, Sufis asserted their place in politics and contributed greatly in the struggles for national liberation. In Indonesia, the world's largest Muslim country, Sufis have been kingmakers, swinging votes during elections, and backing both authoritarian and democratic leaders.[2] Paul Heck corrects the mistaken view of Sufis as apolitical: "Sufism has been involved in all that we think of as politics: conceptions of authority and power, legitimacy and contestation of rule, formation

---

[1] Tanvir Anjum, "Sufism in History and Its Relationship with Power," *Islamic Studies* 45, no. 2 (2006): 257.

[2] Martin van Bruinessen, "The Origins and Development of Sufi Orders (Tarekat) in Southeast Asia," *Studia Islamika: Indonesian Journal for Islamic Studies* 1, no. 1 (1994): 1–23; Geoffrey C. Gunn, *History Without Borders: The Making of an Asian World Region* (Hong Kong: Hong Kong University Press, 2011), 45–81.

Contemplating Sufism: Dialogue and Tradition Across Southeast Asia, First Edition. Khairudin Aljunied.
© 2025 John Wiley & Sons Ltd. Published 2025 by John Wiley & Sons Ltd.

of the socio-moral order of a community of nation, competition for patronage, prestige, and control of society's wealth, the mobilization of people and resources in support of or against the status quo."[3]

This chapter explores Sufi contributions to the development of politics in Southeast Asia. Here, politics is understood in the broadest sense to include all forms of discourses, actions, contestations, claims, and practices that enhance a person's or a group's influence within a given time and space. Traditional view of politics as mere struggles for material power falls short of comprehending Muslim struggles for position, privilege, and place in their societies. Contemporary social science often separates secular politics from spiritual goals, failing to capture the unique blend of piety and politics practiced and perceived by Muslims.[4] I align closely with Dale Eickelman and James Piscatori's interpretation of "Muslim politics" that integrates interpretations of sacred texts and spiritual aspirations with Muslim responses to specific contexts:

> Muslim politics involves the competition and contest over both the interpretation of symbols and control of the institutions, formal and informal, that produce and sustain them. The interpretation of symbols is played out against the background of an underlying framework that, while subject to contextualized nuances, is common to Muslims throughout the world...The distinctiveness of Muslim politics may be said to lie rather in the specific, if evolving, values, symbols, ideas, and traditions that constitute "Islam." These include notions of social justice and communal solidarity that have been inspired by the founding texts of Islam such as the Qur'an and the sayings (*hadiths*) of the Prophet. They may also include a sense of obligation to authority that has been informed as much by social practice as by Qur'anic injunction, the practices of mystical orders (*tariqas*), and the established schools (*madhhabs*) of Islamic law.[5]

This definition structures my exploration of the dynamics between Sufis and politics. To extend Eickelman and James Piscatori's insights,

---

[3] Paul L. Heck, "Introduction," in *Sufism and Politics: The Power of Spirituality*, ed. Paul L. Heck (Princeton: Markus Wiener Publishers, 2007), 1–2.

[4] Saba Mahmood, *The Politics of Piety: The Islamic Revival and the Feminist Subject* (Princeton, NJ: Princeton University Press, 2004), xxiii.

[5] Dale F. Eickelman and James Piscatori, *Muslim Politics* (Princeton: Princeton University Press, 2004), 7–14.

I divide Muslim politics in Southeast Asia into three dialogical realms: conversion politics, reformist politics, and royalist and democratic politics. First, I explore how Sufis disseminated Islam in the region, employing various strategies to eclipse the prevalence of animism, Hinduism, and Buddhism. In examining conversion politics, I show how Sufis refashioned the contours of piety in Southeast Asia, shifting belief-systems from the worship of spirits and a pantheon of gods to a Tawheedic cosmology. This process involved negotiations and sometimes resistance from potential converts.

Then, I examine how Sufis pushed the boundaries of reformist politics by promoting ideas of *islah* (reform) and *tajdid* (renewal) in response to secularism and modernism in Southeast Asia. In the concluding section, I delve into the involvement of Sufis in both monarchical and democratic political realms. Throughout history, from the era of Muslim sultanates to modern times, many Sufis served as advisors to rulers. With the onset of Western colonialism, others emerged as leaders in political movements. Regardless of their changing roles, they were key players in the dynamics of power politics.

From a conceptual standpoint, it is crucial to echo Anthony Milner's caution regarding the term "politics." The word, used to denote power struggles, was absent in the Southeast Asian lexicon until the early twentieth century when the concept of *politik*, stemming from the English "politics," began to rapidly gain prominence. The term *siasah* (*siyasa* in Arabic) was more commonly used by Malay-Indonesian communities to refer to statecraft, governance, and management of public affairs. This does not, however, preclude the presence of politics in Southeast Asia. I use the term politics here in the broadest sense to incorporate premodern Southeast Asian notions of siasah and modern understandings of politics.[6]

Southeast Asian Sufis shared two commonalities in their approach to politics. Most sought the support and membership of power elites to ensure the vitality and expansion of their activities and collectives. Many rulers, ministers, headmen, and warriors claimed to be Sufis and were initiated into tariqahs. The rajas patronized Sufi murshids and scholars, financing Sufi seminaries, as discussed in Chapter 4.[7] The relationship between Sufis and powerbrokers in Southeast Asia mirrored that of their

---

[6] Anthony C. Milner, *The Invention of Politics in Colonial Malaya: Contesting Nationalism and the Expansion of the Public Sphere* (Cambridge: Cambridge University Press, 1995), 267.

[7] Mohd Faizal Harun, *Tasawuf dan Tarekat Sejarah Perkembangan dan Alirannya di Malaysia* (Kedah: UUM Press, 2017), 157–265.

Politics · 137

brethren globally. Alexander Papas observes: "In spite of the repeated warnings by Ṣufis about the dangers of political power and those who wield it, a continual relationship has existed between spiritual authorities and worldly powers; in fact, Sufism has been so useful to rulers that the institutionalisation of Islamic mysticism may appear to be the creation of rulers and states, and Sufism itself has eventually acquired its own hierarchical organisations and structures of power."[8]

The second commonality is linked to the first. While engaging in high or low politics, Sufis in Southeast Asia asserted their liberty to interpret Islam, autonomously managing their estates and followers, and seeking freedom to express their spirituality. This assertion of independence often results in conflict with states and religious authorities. Maintaining self-determination and authenticity in politics have generated both positive and negative outcomes for Sufis in Southeast Asia. While many became influential shapers of the parties and policies, others were proscribed and vanquished by the forces they opposed.

CONVERSION POLITICS

Religious conversion is not a sheer leap of faith. It is imbued with the politics of persuasion, advocacy, and even coercion and manipulation. Religious conversion involves employing various strategies to appeal intended audiences. Winning over would-be converts entails dynamism, creativity, innovation, deep knowledge of lifestyles, languages, cultures, and a high degree of astuteness in the path to overcome and circumvent obstacles and imperatives that may hinder preaching the faith. Conversion strategies are themselves contentious, often entangled with projects of domination and hegemony, as seen in conversion of Filipinos to Catholicism under Spanish rule.[9] And since religious conversion involves a shift in identities and allegiances to ideologies, places, enterprises, communities, and polities, all efforts at changing the faith of groups of people would be met by resistance. In the long history of religious conversion factors such as geography, the appeal of the faith, diplomacy, marriages, high birth rates, and the economic prowess of Muslims

---

[8] Alexandre Papas, "Sufism and Worldly Powers," in *Sufi Institutions,* ed. Alexandre Papas (Leiden: Brill, 2021), 255.

[9] Vincente L. Raphael, *Contracting Colonialism: Translation and Christian Conversion in Tagalog Society Under Early Spanish Rule* (Durham, NC: Duke University Press, 1993).

have made Islam fastest growing religion in the world. The histories of conversion to Islam are as complex as any other religion and are "not amenable to any one simple and universal explanatory paradigm."[10]

Sufis hold a prominent place in the history of religious conversion in Southeast Asia. They arrived in the region recognizing the influence of Indic religions on the worldview, habits, customs, and religious practices of the locals. Southeast Asian rulers were defenders and promoters of these faiths and beliefs, and the metaphysical and the political were already fused when the Sufis arrived. Most polities were Hindu-Buddhist in orientation, a belief system that permeated the language and everyday practices of both the elites and masses. The idea of the divine king further cemented the relationship of the syncretic faith with the lives of people, where obedience to the ruler was equated with obedience to gods. In fact, rulers were seen as gods in human form.[11]

However, Hinduism and Buddhism were not organized faiths or "isms," as understood today. Southeast Asians selected and appropriated aspects of the two belief systems, melding them with age-old primordial beliefs. They took what was relevant to enhance and enrich the indigenous essences. External sources of belief did not radically change local customs passed down from the animistic era. Brahman priests and Buddhist monks – scholars in their own right – tolerated the fusion of divine philosophies, embracing and facilitating the Malay inclinations towards religious and cultural synthesis. Hence, it is more than accurate to describe Southeast Asian worldview and religious praxis before the coming of Islam, "Hindu-Buddhist."[12]

From the stories found in the hikayats, babads, and other foreign sources, we can discern a few conversion strategies utilized by the Sufis over many centuries: conversion of the elites followed by mass conversion; conversion through marriage; conversion via trade pacts; conversion through direct preaching in circulatory and cognate institutions such as mosques, suraus, and community halls; and conversion through language. The last strategy focuses on imbuing Islamic concepts and terms into Southeast Asian languages, changing names of months

---

[10] Marcia Hermansen, "Conversion to Islam in Theological and Historical Perspectives," in *The Oxford Handbook of Religious Conversion*, eds. Lewis R. Rambo and Charles E. Farhadian (New York: Oxford University Press, 2014), 623–666.

[11] Kenneth R. Hall, *A History of Early Southeast Asia: Maritime Trade and Cultural Development, 100–1500* (Lanham, MD: Rowman & Littlefield, 2011), 255.

[12] George Coedès, *Indianized States of Southeast Asia* (trans. Sue Brown Cowing) (Honolulu: University of Hawai'i Press, 1996), xvii.

and days to reflect the Hijri calendar, and incorporating Arabic and Persian vocabularies into texts relating to medicine, the environment, spirituality, statecraft, ethics, and law.[13]

These innovative and undying conversion strategies can be termed *populist da'wa* (preaching of Islam). Highly sensitive to and adaptive towards local beliefs, practices, and temperaments, the Sufis commingled local practices with Islamic rituals. They combined local myths with Muslim stories, interlacing local beliefs with Qur'anic and Prophetic injunctions. To transform the established Hindu-Buddhist belief systems, Sufis heralded what Merle Ricklefs describes as "mystic synthesis," allowing them to bypass the contentious politics of conversion. Ricklefs further notes: "One can say with some confidence that there were Javanese in the court city [of Majapahit] – evidently including members of the courtly elite – who saw no problem in being both Javanese and Muslim. They proclaimed their Javaneseness in their use of the local pre-Muslim dating system and numerals, their elite status in the sunburst medallion on the gravestones, and their faith in pious Arabic phrases and Quranic quotations."[14]

This mystic synthesis is well alive in Java today. It is found in the conduct of ceremonies, in pugilistic arts, and healing practices. Sufis manifested this mystic synthesis by serving in various vocations, thus shaping the landscape of conversion politics. According to Niels Mulder, Sufis and other Sufi-inflected mystics filled many occupations, from white-collar professionals to blue collar labourers. "Often they are markedly extrovert, and virtually all of them show the self-confidence of persons who are in close contact with higher reality. Most are convinced of their mission and the uniqueness of their teachings; in spite of their secular activities, they tend to explain worldly events, especially politics and personal experiences, from a cosmological and symbolic perspective."[15]

To further expand their influence among the populace, many Sufis vernacularized Sufism with folk mysticism, founding new and pseudo-Islamic versions of spirituality. Many *kebatinan* (the search for inner truth) movements in Indonesia and Malaysia incorporated aspects of *kejawen* (Javanism) and *adat nenek moyong* (ancestral customs) into their credos. The kebatinan movements advocated cleansing the *kejiwaan* (inner soul), viewing themselves as an *aliran kepercayaan* (stream of

---

[13] Khairi O. Al-Zubaidi, "The Main Characteristics of Arabic Borrowed Words in Bahasa Melayu," *AWEJ for Translation & Literary Studies* 2, no. 4 (2018): 232–260.

[14] Merle C. Ricklefs, *Mystic Synthesis in Java* (Norwalk: Signature Books, 2006).

[15] Niels Mulder, *Mysticism in Java: Ideology in Indonesia* (Amsterdam: The Pepin Press, 1998), 50.

thought) within the fold of Islam.[16] Within these kebatinan teachings were also claims that their Sufi shaykhs were the long-awaited Al-Mahdi, a prophesized messianic hero who has appeared during the end of times. The doctrine of Al-Mahdi has been a central feature of Sufi beliefs for centuries, in reaction to injustices Sufis faced under cruel regimes. Al-Mahdi served as a consolatory symbol to oppressed Sufis, calling for their continued existence and justifying their actions in anticipation of an impending victory of Islam led by a mystical and martial figure. This powerful and galvanizing ideology spurred many Sufi tariqahs towards socio-political activism.[17] In Malaysia, Sufis who espoused the Al-Mahdi doctrine reinterpreted Islamic teachings, claiming union with God, prescribing dhikrs purported to have been taught by the Prophet in dream visions, and flaunting the shari'a as they believed they had reached the highest maqam of tasawwuf.[18]

Sufis also employed the arts to subtly convert locals. Drawing from Qur'anic verses, stories from Muslim histories, and local prose works, these Sufi-inflected groups appealed to Southeast Asians predisposed to traditional beliefs and pre-Islamic provenance. The Wali Songo and their disciples pioneered the use of performance and musical ensembles as tools of populist da'wa. They "held that when people do not feel challenged in their old habits, the elements of Islamic doctrine can seep in slowly and surely."[19] This approach proved successful. Islamicized versions of wayang kulit soon mushroomed in other parts of Southeast Asia including Malaysia. Sufis also capitalized on a Malay traditional artform, the *dikir barat* (choral sung in groups). They transformed its contents while maintaining much of the form to transmit Islamic values and beliefs. This lyrical performing art, originating from Patani and nearby provinces, was performed during times of harvest in the Hindu-Buddhist period. In Kelantan and northern Malaysia, Islam flourished partly due to the dissemination of Islamic teachings through dikir barat. More recently, an incarnation of this populist da'wa among the Sufis

---

[16] Paul Stange, "Legitimate Mysticism in Indonesia," *Review of Indonesian and Malaysian Affairs* 22, no. 2 (1986): 76–117; Suwardi Endaswara, *Mistik Kejawen: Sinkrestime, Simbolisme Dan Sufisme Dalam Budaya Spiritual Jawa* (Yogyakarta: Penerbit Narasi, 2006).

[17] Hugh Beattie, "The Mahdi and the End-Times in Islam," in *Prophecy in the New Millennium When Prophecies Persist,* eds. Suzanne Newcombe and Sarah Harvey (London: Routledge, 2013), 89–104.

[18] John Bousfield, "Adventures and Misadventures of the New Sufis: Islamic Spiritual Groups in Contemporary Malaysia," *Sojourn: Journal of Social Issues in Southeast Asia* 8, no. 2 (1993): 328–344.

[19] Anna Gade M., "Sunan Ampel of the Javanese Wali Songo," in *Tales of God's Friends: Islamic Hagiography in Translation,* ed. John Renard (Berkeley: University of California Press, 2009), 356.

has taken the form of nasyids, rock bands, and hip-hop groups whose songs made explicit references to Sufi visions of Islam. The trailblazer of the Sufi song industry was the Nada Murni Group. Since 1987, they have released twenty albums and more than two hundred songs, most of which became hits for decades across Southeast Asia. This recording company had effectively made nasyids produced in Southeast Asia a global sensation, popularized by bands such as Raihan, Rabbani, Hijjaz, Inteam, and Snada, as well as solo artists in the likes of Mawi, Sabyan, and Syakir Daulay.[20]

Solawatul Burdah by Raihan viewed by 882k views: https://www.youtube.com/watch?v=7NvYDCUaFwE

---

[20] Joel S. Kahn, "The Inner Lives of Javanese Muslims: Modern Sufi Visions in Indonesian Islam," *Social Imaginaries* 3, no. 2 (2017): 15–36.

Sufis also employed magic and divination as part of their populist da'wa, using their abilities to subdue invisible beings and cure psycho-spiritual illnesses. They produced many healing texts filled with Qur'anic concepts, talismanic magic squares, divinatory compass diagrams, hemerological tables, and grids of symbols, numbers, letters, or words.[21] Sultan Agung was known for his occult powers. One of the Wali Songo, Sunan Bayat, was reported to have converted a Hindu-Buddhist mystic simply by displaying the superiority of his magical skills.[22] In the Philippines, such epiphenomenal powers and myths proved equally effective for conversion ends. In tarsilas and oral histories, it is said that seven *makhdumin* (teachers) with extraordinary powers brought Islam to the islands of Jolo, Sibutu, and Lugus.

One of the most formidable saints in the Philippines was Tuan Sharif Awliya' (Master of Saints) or Karim Al-Makhdum, whose tomb still exists at Tandu Banak. A peripatetic missionary of Arab origins, he and several Chinese Muslim preachers attracted elites and masses on the Filipino islands to Islam partly through a display of their supernatural powers. These hybrid group of proselytizers married the daughters of rulers and *datu* (chiefs) while engaging in commercial activities with locals. As a result, Islam grew in the archipelago, reaching present-day Manila. These magical stories have been viewed with much scepticism by Sufi scholars, who argued that the sincerity and commitment of devout preachers of Islam, rather than incredible feats of soothsayers and magicians, were the main drivers of religious conversion.[23]

To further the point, Sufis in Southeast Asia were known to have been expert traders. The relationship between Sufi trade guilds and the Islamization of Southeast Asia is well-documented. The Indian Ocean, the Silk Road, and the South China Sea were trading concourses where Sufis traded with local merchants, exporting and importing goods from Southeast Asia to the wider Muslim world and back. Trade provided platforms for sharing of beliefs between Muslims and non-Muslims.[24] One highly successful Sufi missionary-business movement was Darul Arqam. At its height in the 1990s, the Darul Arqam owned a long list

---

[21] Farouk Yahya, *Magic and Divination in Malay Illustrated Manuscripts* (Leiden: Brill, 2016).

[22] Douwe A. Rinkes, *Nine Saints of Java* (trans. H.M. Froger, ed. Alijah Gordon, Intro. GWJ Drewes) (Kuala Lumpur: Malaysian Sociological Research Institute, 1996).

[23] Cesar Adib Majul, "Islamic and Arab Cultural Influences in the South of the Philippines," *Journal of Southeast Asian History* 7, no. 2 (1966): 61–73.

[24] Anthony H. Johns, "The Role of Sufism in the Spread of Islam to Malaya and Indonesia," *Journal of the Pakistan Historical Society* 9, no. 3 (1961): 143–160.

Politics

of businesses selling groceries, poultry, traditional Islamic fashionwear, educational books, and other media items.[25] These multimillion-dollar business networks were avenues to recruit potential members and sympathizers to the movement and to convert the non-Muslims. Functioning like a transnational tariqah with branches in Southeast Asia, the Arab World, China, Uzbekistan, Australia, and the United States, Darul Arqam's populist appeal hinged upon total obedience to their murshid, Ashaari Muhammad. The members led highly disciplined and entrepreneurial lives. They donned kohl eyeliner, robes, turbans, *niqab* (face veils), and carried prayer beads. Most members practiced polygamy. In Malaysia, the members of this Sufi group lived in privately owned communes. They engaged in street da'wa, enjoining Muslims and non-Muslims to steer away from immorality and cupidity.[26]

Populist da'wa were not without its hazards. Because such conversion strategy may challenge dominant ideas of religiosity, Sufis in Southeast Asia have been proscribed and persecuted, sometimes by fellow Sufis. The fusion of folk beliefs with Islamic ones and the introduction of unconventional methods of conveying Islam invited negative and even violent responses from the religious orthodoxy. With followers and ideas hailing from both Muslim and non-Muslim roots in search of inner knowledge, many Sufis have been arrested and punished by death. Their teachings were banned, their properties confiscated, and they were branded heretical by shari'a-minded Sufis for mixing Islamic practices with pre-Islamic devotions.

Due to the lack of documented sources, we can only safely trace the earliest evidence of the persecution of Sufis engaging in populist da'wa to the fifteenth century. Previously endorsed by Sultan Alauddin Riayat Syah (1588–1604) and Sultan Iskandar Muda (1583–1636), the poetic cum monist writings of Hamzah Fansuri, Shamsuddin Al-Sumatra'i, and their Wujudiyyah followers saw a turn of fortunes upon the installation of Nuruddin Al-Raniri as the *Shaykh Al-Islam* (Chief Judge) of the Acehnese kingdom in 1637. A shari'a-minded Sufi scholar supported by Sultan Iskandar Tsani (1610–1641), Al-Raniri, branded the Wujudiyyah a heretical sect. He issued fatwas sentencing their followers to death and imprisonment should they refuse to renounce their beliefs. He ordered their writings to be burnt and, neutralizing opposition against Iskandar

---

[25] Rahman Arifai and Ishak Saat, "Al-Arqam: Pioneer of Nasyid Art in Malaysia, 1975–1997," *International Journal of Academic Research in Business and Social Sciences* 11, no. 4 (2021): 685–694.
[26] Judith A. Nagata, "Alternative Models of Islamic Governance in Southeast Asia: Neo-Sufism and the Arqam Experiment in Malaysia," *Global Change, Peace & Security* 16, no. 2 (2004): 99–114.

Tsani's rule festering among the Wujudiyyah fraternity. The punishment meted out against the Wujudiyyah was based on religious grounds in as much as it was closely tied to political struggles between opposing Sufi groups intending to convert the masses to their versions of Sufism.[27] In the twentieth century, the Arab-Hadrami Sufi scholar and former Mufti of Johor, Alwi bin Thahir Al-Haddad (1884–1962), reiterated Al-Raniri's views that any Muslim who believed in wahdatul wujud and other concepts such as *ittihad* (union with Allah) and *hulul* (incarnation) as understood by Ibn 'Arabi must be considered *murtad* (apostates).[28]

Another instance of conversion politics playing out between Sufis can be seen in the case of Shaykh Siti Jenar (also known as Shaykh Lemah Abang) in early fifteenth-century Java. Dubbed as the Mansur Al-Hallaj (858–922) of the Malay world, Siti Jenar's teachings emulated the Wujudiyyah. He preached a mystical union between man and God, termed as *manunggaling kawula gusti*, and saw obligatory acts in Islam no longer applicable to mystics of his maqam. His popularity grew throughout the Jepara region as Hindu-Buddhists found Siti Jenar's philosophy of life and the divine congruent with their own. These pantheistic ideas irked the Wali Songo. The long-standing political rivalries between Siti Jenar's hometown, Pengging, and that of Demak, where the Wali Songo had a large following worsened the conflict.[29] In a trial conducted by the Wali Songo, Siti Jenar affirmed that Friday prayers were not compulsory and mosques do not exist since nothing in the world exists except God. He and others who fused Javanese mythologies with Sufi mysticism were sentenced to death. As a later source, the Serat Cabolek recounts: "The one punished in the city of Giri was Shaykh Siti Jenar who was sentenced to death by the sword. In the past during the period of Demak, it was Pengeran Pangun who was sentenced to death by fire. As for the period of Pajan, Ki Bebeluk was drowned; fire and water had the same effect."[30] The killing of Siti Jenar, like Al-Hallaj, did not drown populist da'wa of the Sufis. It became stronger and bolder. While travelling in Java in the early sixteenth century, Tomé Pires (1465–1540) encountered

---

[27] Ahmad Daudy, *Allah Dan Manusia Dalam Konsep Nuruddin Al-Raniri* (Jakarta: Rajawali Press, 1983), 201–239.

[28] Sayyid Alwi bin Tahir Al-Haddad, *Fatwa-Fatwa Mufti Kerajaan Johor, Vol.2* (Johor Bharu: Jabatan Agama Johor, 1981), 319–322.

[29] Douwe A. Rinkes, *Nine Saints of Java* (trans. H.M. Froger, ed. Alijah Gordon, Intro. GWJ Drewes) (Malaysian Sociological Research Institute, 1996), 42.

[30] S. Soebardi, *The Book of Cabolèk: A Critical Edition with Introduction, Translation and Notes* (Dordrecht: Springer, 1975), 104.

Politics **145**

many nomadic mystics who "are also worshipped by the Moors, and they believe in them greatly...they say they are sacred."[31]

The persecution of Sufis in Southeast Asia for their unorthodox populist da'wa reached the ears of esteemed masters of tasawwuf in Makkah, who too passed rulings against "wayward Sufis." One of them was a Kurdish Sufi master and murshid of some tariqahs, Ibrahim al-Kurani (1615–1690). He wrote in his *Ithaf al-Dhaki bi Sharh al-Tuhfa al-Mursala ila Ruh al-Nabi* (The bestowal addressed to one of discriminating intelligence in explanation of the gift addressed to the spirit of the Prophet) on how some Southeast Asian Sufis were susceptible to heresy:

> We have been reliably informed by a group (*jama'a*) of Jawiyyin that some books on *Haqiqa* (Divine Realities) and esoteric knowledge (*'ulum al-asrar*) have spread among the population of the lands of Jawa being passed from hand to hand by those endowed with knowledge based on their studies and the teaching of others, but who have neither understanding of the *'ilm al-shari'a* (knowledge of the Islamic jurisprudence) of the Prophet, the Chosen, the Elect of God, peace be upon him, nor the *'ilm al-haqa'iq* (knowledge of truth) conferred on those who follow the path of God the Exalted, those who are close to Him, those admirable ones, or those who have set their foot on any path of their paths based on the Koran and the Sunna through perfect obedience both outwardly (*al-zahir*) and inwardly (*al-batin*), as rendered by the devout and pure. This is the reason why many of them (the Jawiyyin) have deviated from the right path and why impure belief has arisen; in fact they have entered into the crooked camp of atheism (*al-zandaqa*) and heresy (*al-ilhad*).[32]

Capital punishments against Sufi tariqahs and personalities were relatively rare. Most states and Sufi scholars in Southeast Asia preferred to conduct surveillance and investigations of suspected deviant Sufi groups based on public reports before taking tough actions. Numerous tracts guiding the people to the Sufi path in line with the shari'a have been written. An eighteenth-century work by Shihabuddin Palembang, for example,

---

[31] Tomé Pires, *The Suma Oriental of Tomé Pires* (ed. and trans. Armando Cortesao) (Hakluyt Society, 1994), 177.

[32] Quoted in Azyumardi Azra, "Controversy and Opposition to Wahdat Al-Wujud: Discourse of Sufism in the Malay-Indonesian World in the 17th and 18th Centuries," in *Measuring the Effect of Iranian Mysticism on Southeast Asia*, ed. Imtiyaz Yusuf (Bangkok: Cultural Centre, 2004), 103.

warned the masses about the dangers of the wahdatul wujud and martabat tujuh doctrines. Shihabuddin did not spare his words against the Sufis who taught such doctrines, calling them "*Dajjals* (deceitful messiahs) in human shape; in their mouths [are] words [of] unbelief, while they are not conscious of their sinning against God nor of the fact that their being confused by the devil who is at the bottom of their rejection of the sacred law of the Prophet."[33] Other reformist Sufis saw the martabat tujuh doctrine as bid'ah. Muhammad Arshad Al-Banjari (1710–1812) and Sayyid 'Uthman bin Yahya attacked the corrupting influence of the martabat tujuh and issued fatwas against these teachings. In South Kalimantan, some proponents of martabat tujuh who refused to retract their beliefs after undergoing religious counselling were executed.[34]

The rooting of Sunni orthodoxy into the Southeast Asian religious landscape by states and Sufi scholars meant that all other alternative Sufi teachings and Sufi-inflected mysticism were deemed heterodox. Throughout Southeast Asia, Muslim kingdoms and majority Muslim postcolonial states have imposed strict measures on any Sufi group construed to be outside the fold of *Ahlus Sunnah wal Jama'ah* (The People of the Sunnah and the Majority) or by implication against anyone who espoused views in opposition to the Qur'an and Hadith collections of Sunni scholars. In Brunei, for example, a few transnational tariqahs have been outlawed since the establishment of the modern kingdom, including the Naqshbandiyyah and Mufarridiyyah which were regarded as extreme sects. Upon crackdown by the *Bahagian Kawalan Aqidah* (Creed Regulator Section), members of these Sufi orders were made to undergo rehabilitation sessions to return them to the state-defined interpretation of Islam.[35] Another locally founded Sufi group, the Abdul Razak Tarekat, began life in the 1970s as an offshoot of the Ahmadiyyah tariqah. Things came to a head when the murshid by the name of Abdul Razak bin Haji Muhammad flaunted his karamah. A healer of many serious ailments, he was reported to have called upon spirits of the dead to enter the bodies of his students (*tahdir al-arwah*). Abdul Razak's followers were convinced of their leader's powers and ability to have direct

---

[33] Shihabuddin Palembang, "A Risalah", in GWJ Drewes, *Directions for Travellers on the Mystics Path* (The Hague: Martinus NIjhoff, 1977), 101.

[34] Ian Chalmers, "The Islamization of Southern Kalimantan: Sufi Spiritualism, Ethnic Identity, Political Activism," *Studia Islamika - Indonesian Journal for Islamic Studies* 14, no. 3 (2007): 391; Nico N. J. Kaptein, *Islam, Colonialism and the Modern Age in the Netherlands East Indies: A Biography of Sayyid 'Uthman (1822–1914)* (Leiden: Brill, 2014), 122.

[35] Mahmud Saedon Awang Othman, *Ajaran Sesat Di Negara Brunei Darussalam: Satu Tinjauan* (Pusat Da'wah Islamiah: Brunei Darussalam, 2002).

communication with the Prophet Muhammad and Shaykh Abdul Qadir al-Jailani through dream visions. Men and women under his tutelage were permitted to shake hands, and he was said to have had intimate relations with some women in his congregation. On 25 April 1995, the Home Affairs Ministry declared "the society or association known as the jemaah of the followers of the teachings of Abdul Razak bin Haji Mohamad to be an unlawful society."[36]

The Darul Arqam movement discussed above was the largest transnational Sufi group in Southeast Asia to be clamped down. It illustrates how the dialogues between populist da'wa, contending Sufi groups, and state politics could lead to disastrous consequences for a Sufi tariqah. With branches firmly established across Southeast Asia, Darul Arqam movement attracted many members of other tariqahs into its fold, making it a powerful competitor within the expanding Sufi terrain at the height of Islamic revivalism in Southeast Asia in the 1990s. A highly hierarchical movement with leaders appointed by way of *shura* (consultation), Darul Arqam was akin to a state within a state, which once held the prospect of providing a Sufi-inspired model of Islamic governance in Malaysia. Darul Arqam's meteoric rise caused its downfall. Messianic claims made by Ashaari Muhammad along with reports of a military unit in Thailand linked to the organization, alarmed the governments in the region. Ashaari's avowal about being the future global leader of the Muslim world threatened Prime Minister Mahathir Mohammad's strongman politics in Malaysia. In mid-1994, Ashaari and his followers were sentenced to two-year imprisonment by Malaysian authorities. Darul Arqam's activities and communes were eventually dissolved by all Muslim majority states in Southeast Asia. Upon their release from prison, Darul Arqam leaders founded the Rufaqa Corporation and later, Global Ikhwan, that continued the work of preaching Islam through businesses. However, their influence had plummeted, making their impact on potential converts negligible.[37]

---

[36] Haji Matussein bin Haji Jumat and Wan Zailan Kamaruddin Wan Ali, "Tarekat Abdul Razak: Analisis Intipati Pengharamannya Di Brunei Darussalam," *Borneo Research Journal* 10 (2016): 51. For a list of Sufi and other groups that have been outlawed, see: https://www.mora.gov.bn/SitePages/Ajaran-Ajaran%20Sesat%20Yang%20Telah%20Difatwakan.aspx, accessed 6 March 2023.

[37] Ahmad Fauzi Abdul Hamid, "From Darul Arqam to the Rufaqa' Corporation: Change and Continuity in a Sufi Movement in Malaysia," in *Islamic Thought in Southeast Asia: New Interpretations and Movements,* eds. Kamaruzzaman Bustamam-Ahmad and Patrick Jory (Kuala Lumpur: University of Malaya Press, 2013), 45–65.

Amidst such proscriptions, Sufi populist da'wa has prevailed and is still defining the terrain of conversion politics. Julia Howell documents the revitalization of Sufism in Southeast Asia since the late twentieth century which has produced "a particular modern, Sufi-coloured Islamic habitus."[38] An interesting dimension of this Sufi revitalization is the decoupling of Sufism from Sufi orders. Some modern and influential Sufis emphasized individualized piety and the use of the latest media technologies to reach out to the deepest reaches of society. Such rebranding of Sufism appealed to the needs of the urbanized population who were in search of solace amidst the hustle and bustle of city life. Conversely, another aspect of this revitalization was the revival of the "habaib phenomenon." Arab-Hadrami Sufi scholars and celebrity preachers adorning turbans and robes attracted mass audiences. Among them were non-Muslims who embraced Islam through interactions with these Sufis. Many converts were from Chinese backgrounds who soon became noted preachers and purveyors of Islamic spirituality.[39]

All in all, through their involvement in the conversion efforts and in navigating through political circuits, Sufis achieved gradual transformations in Southeast Asia without upsetting the harmony and balance in local societies. The Southeast Asian habit of consuming alcohol, for example, was not openly prohibited until two centuries or so after arrival of Islam. Up until the seventeenth century, foreign travellers to Sumatra noted that the Muslims they encountered were still fond of distilling and drinking alcohol despite knowing its prohibition in Islam.[40] Writing in the nineteenth century, the Scottish orientalist, John Crawfurd, praised the Sufis and other missionaries, stating they "acquired their language–followed their manners–intermarried with them–and melting into the mass of the people, did not on the one hand give rise to a privileged race nor on the other to a degraded caste."[41] This gradualism can be seen in

---

[38] Julia D. Howell, "Revitalised Sufism and the New Piety Movements in Islamic Southeast Asia," in *Routledge Handbook of Religions in Asia,* eds. Bryan S. Turner and Oscar Salemink (London: Routledge, 2015), 278.

[39] Ismail Fajrie Alatas, *What Is Religious Authority?: Cultivating Islamic Communities in Indonesia* (Princeton, NJ: Princeton University Press, 2021); Wai-Weng Hew, "Expressing Chineseness, Marketing Islam: The Hybrid Performance of Chinese Muslim Preachers," in *Chinese Indonesians Reassessed: History, Religion and Belonging*. eds. Siew-Min Sai and Chang-Yau Hoon (London: Routledge, 2012), 178–199.

[40] Gérald R. Tibbets, *A Study of the Arabic Texts Containing Material on South-East Asia* (Brill, 1979), 211.

[41] John Crawfurd, *History of the Indian Archipelago, Vol. II* (Edinburgh: A. Constable, 1820), 276.

the pervasive wearing of hijabs by women, which only became wide-spread and more socially enforced from the 1960s onwards. This slow but sure method of transforming lifestyles and habits ensured respect and preservation of Southeast Asian cultures while Islamic beliefs were subtly and progressively imbued.

REFORMIST POLITICS

"Popular Islam" is an expression of Muslim religiosity devoid of strict conformity with the religious orthodoxy and adapted to suit local customs and beliefs.[42] Despite its pervasiveness, such manifestations of Islam do not resonate with many Sufi scholars, whose compliance with scriptural injunctions moved them to brand fellow Sufis and other Muslims as deviants. For most ulama, as John Voll notes, popular Islam "is often defined in negative terms as Islamic experience that has been 'diluted' by non-Islamic practices."[43] The ulama engaged in reformist activities to correct the excesses of popular Islam. In Southeast Asia, reformist pulses stretched way back to the sixteenth century, as Sufism was making a headway into the region. Networks of Sufi scholars and missionaries from Makkah, Cairo, Delhi, and Istanbul promulgated the rise of "neo-Sufism." Despite their diverse backgrounds, their common aim was to harmonize shari'a and tasawwuf towards a radical reconstruction of the moral–religious universe of Muslims.[44]

However, Sufi reformism was not confined to scholarly contests. Intellectual engagements were often entwined with imposition of authority and defiance towards it. I describe the opposition between Sufi scholars and popular Islam as "reformist politics." The reform project entailed utilizing power, whether governmental, social, or discursive. Scholars used their influence and appealed to the powerful to address and remedy deviations among laity. The laity too mustered support from other religious forces to defend their beliefs and practices. The diatribes between the shari'a-oriented and popular Sufism were

---

[42] For an illuminating discussion on popular Islam, see: Patrick D. Gaffney, "Popular Islam," *The Annals of the American Academy of Political and Social Science* 524 (1992): 38–51.

[43] John O. Voll, *Islam: Continuity and Change in the Modern World* (Syracuse University Press, 1994), 20.

[44] Azyumardi Azra, *The Origins of Islamic Reformism in Southeast Asia* (Honolulu: University of Hawai'i Press, 2004), 3.

documented in the works of many prominent Southeast Asian Sufi authors.[45] Through their writings, these scholars strove to "reconstitute authentic Sufism (*mengembalikan tasauf kepada pangkalnya*)."[46] Brutal and frank in their criticisms, their words were populated with caustic labels to describe what were, to them, errant Sufis and tariqahs. "Enemies of Islam," "ignoramus," "frauds," "extremists," "corrupt," "devilish," and "deviant" were the common terms they used against their rivals. One of the leaders of the Sammaniyyah tariqah in Perak, Muhammad Samman Kati (1922–1995), sums up centuries of Sufi reformist critiques against pseudo-Sufis as follows:

> (Beware) of late of rumours of people practising Sufism [within their] brotherhoods. They chant in many different melodies. They claim genealogies that are traced back to the Prophet of Allah, but barely showed any commitment to the study of obliga-tory matters such as tawheed, fiqh, tasawwuf, arguing instead that these are *ilmu kulit* (surface knowledge). They desired something deeper. These sects have isolated themselves from the community; [they are] avoiding prayer places, shying away from mosques. They are the odd ones, strangers. Their teachings are devilish because the devil ignores the laws of Allah.[47]

In their enthusiasm to reform societies from the ills of popular Sufism, Sufi scholars clashed, accusing each other as promoters of the wrong version of Sufism. Some of these clashes went beyond the con-cern for reform and were highly personal and vindictive. In Cirebon from 1928 to 1930, the shaykhs of the Tijaniyyah, Naqshbandiyyah, and Qadiriyyah engaged in highly emotive debates expressed in sermons and pamphlets. The context was the Tijaniyyah's growing popularity among the locals. Seeing a rapid loss of followership, Naqshbandiyyah and Qadiriyyah scholars accused the Tijaniyyah of being part of a wider "Wahabi conspiracy." Tijani scholars were labelled as heretical for professing their ascendancy over all other tariqahs and that they were guaranteed paradise. The Tijani scholars responded by appealing for

---

[45] Among which were Abdul Rauf al-Sinkili (1615–1693), Yusuf al-Maqassari, Abdul Samad al-Palimbani, Daud al-Fatani, Muhammad Arshad al-Banjari, Muhammad Nafis al-Banjari, Muhammad al-Nawawi al-Bantani, Shaykh Isma'il Minangkabawi, Shaykh Ahmad Khatib, Kiai Shaleh Darat, H. Abdul Kadir, Kiyai Haji Hasyim Asy'ari, Hamka, and To' Kenali (1868–1933).

[46] Hamka, *Mengembalikan Tasawuf Ke Pangkalnya* (Jakarta: Pustaka Panjimas, 1973).

[47] Muhammad Samman Kati, *Kitab Tasawwuf* (Kuala Lumpur: Akademi Jawi Malaysia, 2018), 66.

Politics

mediation by the prominent Nahdlatul Ulama (NU). The passionate exchanges were put to rest, a clear testimony of the interplay between competition for power and manpower on the one hand, and Sufi reformist politics on the other. The dialogue between them led to dire outcomes for Sufis.[48]

To be sure, Sufi scholars were barely cohesive; disagreements abounded. Sufi reformist politics revolved around recurrent issues. Foremost was theological matters. Sufi scholars combatted ascriptions of divinity to Sufi leaders and battled against Muslims assigning supernatural powers to themselves or others. They were sensitive to the fallacies of khurafat and shirk. Fully committed to the Ashari'ite theology, Sufi scholars had different interpretations on some finer matters. One such matter was the theory of Nur Muhammad (*al-Nur al-Muhammadi,* or Light of Muhammad) or *Haqiqah al-Muhammadiyah* (The Truth of Muhammad). Derived mostly from Persian Shi'ite traditions enmeshed with Neoplatonic and Biblical ideas of prophethood, this theory posits that God first created light from which other essential elements of the universe emerged. Such beliefs found its way into Sunnism when Muslim empires expanded. Sufis were exposed to many of these non-Muslim beliefs and philosophies.[49]

Nur Muhammad was introduced into Southeast Asia as early as the thirteenth century by an Acehnese Sufi writer, Shaykh 'Abdullah Arif, in his book *Bahr Al-Lahut* (Sea of Divinity). The theory pervaded many hikayats, babad, serats, mawlid texts, and other scholarly works.[50] Fierce controversies have been waged over whether Nur Muhammad was valid. Ahmad Khatib Al-Minangkabawi, a respected Southeast Asian Sufi scholar based in nineteenth-century Makkah, saw the Nur Muhammad theory as weak, lacking support from Qur'anic verse or hadith. To him, the *qalam* (pen) was God's first creation. Other Sufi scholars were more caustic, viewing the Nur Muhammad theory as based on Jewish fables and traditions attributed to the Prophet Muhammad.[51]

---

[48] Martin van Bruinessen, "Controversies and Polemics Involving the Sufi Orders in Twentieth-Century Indonesia," in *Measuring the Effect of Iranian Mysticism on Southeast Asia*, ed. Imtiyaz Yusuf (Bangkok: Cultural Centre, 2004), 129–162.

[49] Uri Rubin, "Pre-Existence and Light—Aspects of the Concept of Nūr Muhammad," *Israel Oriental Studies* 5 (1975): 62–119; Khalil Andani, "Metaphysics of Muhammad The Nur Muhammad from Imam Ja'far al-Sadiq (d. 148/765) to Nasir al-Din al-Tusi (d. 672/1274)," *Journal of Sufi Studies* 8 (2019): 99–175.

[50] Shaykh 'Abdullah Arif, *Bahr Al-Lahut* (Johor Bahru: Jahabersa, 2022); Anon., *Inilah Hikayat Nur Muhammad Dan Nabi Bercukur Dan Nabi Wafat* (Pulau Pinang: Dar al-Maarif, n.d.).

[51] Mohd. Nor bin Ngah, *Kitab Jawi: Islamic Thought of the Malay Muslim Scholars* (Singapore: ISEAS Press, 1983), 14.

However, until the advent of modernist reformism in the late nineteenth century, none of the prominent Southeast Asian Sufi scholars and movements were against the notion of the ruler as the "Shadow of Allah on Earth (*Zilullah fil-ardh*)," which had parallels with the Nur Muhammad theory in that some form of divinity was ascribed to human beings. A residue from the pre-Islamic idea of divine kingship and the Persianate concept of the cosmic ruler endorsing kings as God's shadow meant that they must be obeyed even if they transgressed the shari'a. Granted many Southeast Asian Sufis led rebellions and wars, yet few Sufi scholars legitimized disobedience against Muslim rulers or condemned immoral rulers in their fatwas, treatises, or essays as did modernist reformers such as the Al-Imam collective. Works by Sufi scholars on the state and governance emphasized rulers' virtues and vices, underlining positive and negative lessons from past Muslim rulers outside Southeast Asia. This included Al-Raniri's *Bustanul Al-Salatin* (The Garden of Rulers) and Bukhari Al-Jauhari's *Tajus Salatin* (The Crown of the Ruler).[52] Seen in that light, Sufi reformist politics in Southeast Asia during the precolonial period was modulated by the belief that rulers could do no wrong or that their errors ought to be overlooked as long as they protected the faith and welfare of the masses.[53]

In their bid to reform public understanding of tawheed from any forms of corrupting influences, Sufi scholars and movements in Southeast Asia have flagged the teachings of syncretic cults. In Indonesia, many kebatinan and aliran kepercayaan groups were censured by Sufi scholars, the most vocal among them being the NU. These movements drew from many traditions to propagate ideas such as the unity of and similarity between all religions. They conceived murshids as living embodiments of God. They used Sufi texts and tariqahs as vehicles of recruitment. To stop the spread of these cults, since the 1950s, NU developed its own list of legitimate Sufi brotherhoods. NU collaborated with its critic and competitor, the Muhammadiyah along with other reformist NGOs (non-governmental organizations), to support the *Pengawas Aliran Kepercayaan Masyarakat* (PAKEM or "Coordinating Board for Monitoring Mystical Beliefs in Society") established in 1954. Under the Ministry of Religious Affairs, PAKEM recommended outlawing syncretic sects claiming to be Sufi groups and obstructing kebatinan groups

---

[52] Jelani Harun, "Bustan Al-Salatin, 'the Garden of Kings': A Universal History and Adab Work from Seventeenth-century Aceh," *Indonesia and the Malay World* 32, no. 92 (2004): 21–52.
[53] Milner, *The Invention of Politics in Colonial Malaya*, 146–153.

Politics

153

from declaring themselves as new religions. It is a powerful body that steered Indonesian Sufism and other offshoots of Islam towards stronger regulation and shari'atisation.[54]

Another theme that Sufi reformist scholars indulged in was Islamic law and jurisprudence. Through alliances with rulers, Sufi scholars codified and institutionalized the Shafi'ite jurisprudence. Other schools of jurisprudence were allowed to co-exist but were not recognized as the official *madhab* (school of Islamic jurisprudence) to be adhered to by the majority population. There has been no recorded instance of persecutions against other schools of jurisprudences in Southeast Asia, contrasting with what took place in the Arab world and South Asia. Many Indians and Chinese immigrants who were Hanafis lived peacefully with other Muslims. Sufi tolerance of all schools of Islamic jurisprudence may have prompted some followers of the Hanafite madhab to convert to Shafi'ism. The "Javanese Books of Tales" recorded the story of Sunan Ngampel Denta of Surabaya, who switched from the Hanafite to the Shafi'ite school in the mid-fifteenth century. Of Chinese background, he was the oldest among Wali Songo and taught Islamic precepts using Javanese loanwords.[55]

Alexander Knysh is right to state that as "any successful religious movement, Sufism has generated a large amount of rule books. Sufi rules of good manners and proper conduct (adab) fall into two major categories: (a) how one should behave oneself toward God; (b) how one should deal with various categories of people both inside and outside one's Sufi community. Definitions abound."[56] I would add that in Southeast Asia such rule books were used by Sufi scholars for law and order and to forge social contracts between the state and the masses. The *Hukum Kanun Pahang* (Pahang Digest), *Batu Bersurat Terengganu* (Terengganu Inscription), and *Undang-undang Sembilan Puluh Sembilan Perak* (Ninety-Nine Laws of Perak), among others, were Shafi'ite legal codes used by rulers and scholars to enforce Islamic laws in

---

[54] Herman Beck, "The Contested State of Sufism in Islamic Modernism: The Case of the Muhammadiyah Movement in Twentieth-Century Indonesia," *Journal of Sufi Studies* 3 (2014): 183–219; Syafiq Hasyim, *The Politics of the Council of Indonesian Ulama (Majelis Ulama Indonesia, MUI)* (Leiden: Brill, 2022), 281–282.

[55] Hermanus Johannes de Graaf and Theodore G.Th. Pigeaud, *Chinese Muslims in Java in the 15th and 16th Centuries: The Malay Annals of Semarang and Cerbon* (Melbourne: Monash University, 1984).

[56] Alexander Knysh, *Sufism: A New History of Islamic Mysticism* (New Jersey: Princeton University Press, 2017), 139.

154   CONTEMPLATING SUFISM

Malay states. Maritime laws outlined rules governing trade, commerce, port operations, and fair dealings with Muslims and non-Muslims.[57]

These texts suggest that the shari'a in Southeast Asia was a mixture of Shafi'ite jurisprudence, Sufi ethics, and customary laws. In the Philippines, as in the rest of the region, drafting and codifying legal codes were carried out in the spirit of shura between rulers and other elites, including scholars.[58] Through these legal texts, Sufis scholars reformed public morality, beliefs, and rituals. Voluminous works explicated on *fardhu 'ain* (obligatory duties) connected to ritual purity, prayers, fasting, zakat, hajj, *munakahat* (marriage and family building), and consumption of prohibited items. These topics were regarded as the highest priority before property, governance, trade and commerce, order, and rules of war. Such prioritization persisted until the nineteenth century when colonial powers limited the shari'a to cover only family and property laws.

Nor is this all. Shafi'ite-based legal writings in Southeast Asia were syarah, *mukhtasar* (abridgements), or *hasyiyah* (glosses) of Shafi'i fiqh, as expounded in the writings of Abu Zakaria Mohiuddin Yahya al-Nawawi (1233–1277), Jalal ad-Din al-Maḥalli (1389–1440), Zakariyya al-Ansari (1420–1520), Ibn Hajar al-Haytami (1503–1566), and Abu Bakr Muhammad Syata al-Dimyati (1849–1893), among others. A productive scholar based in Makkah, Al-Dimyati's protéges and intellectual descendants included prominent Southeast Asian Sufi reformist scholars such as Hasyim Asy'ari, Manfuzh at-Tarmasi (1868–1920), and Habib Ali bin Abdurrahman Al Habsyi (Habib Kwitang, 1870–1968). Al-Nawawi's *Minhaj Al-Talibin* (Way of the Seekers) provided the intellectual frame for most Southeast Asian Sufi works on Shafi'ite jurisprudence. It is not excessive to argue that the laws subscribed to by Southeast Asians then and now have been more Nawawi'ite in content and mediated by local cultures than Shafi'ite in the strictest sense.[59] The texts can be viewed as reformulations and redactions of Imam Shafi'i's ideas. Mostly in Arabic or Jawi, the texts written by Southeast Asian Sufi scholars were not necessarily formalistic in tone. They also came in poetry, prose, or imagined conversions between two interlocutors that resembled Socratic

---

[57] To be included are *Undang-Undang Melaka* (Melakan Laws), *Hukum Kanun Kedah* (Kedah Digest), *Hukum Kanun Johor* (Johor Digest), and the Sungei Ujong Digest. See: Ahmad Ibrahim and Ahilemah Joned, *The Malaysian Legal System* (Dewan Bahasa dan Pustaka, 1987), 16–17.

[58] Cesar Adib Majul, "The General Nature of Islamic Law and Its Application in the Philippines," *Philippine Law Journal* 52 (1977), 381.

[59] Mahmood Zuhdi Haji Abd. Majid, "Mazhab Syafi'i di Malaysia: Sejarah, Realiti Dan Prospek Masa Depan," *Jurnal Fiqh* 4 (2007): 1–38.

Politics **155**

dialogical style. The point of writing in these different styles was to ease understanding for both young and old learners.[60] Reforming public knowledge on Islamic laws demanded creative presentations of highly complex subjects.

One example of such works was by the Sufi scholar and poet, Raja Ali Haji (1808–1873). A prolific writer, prominent murid of the Naqshbandi-yyah tariqah, and promoter of Shafi'ism in Riau Islands, he explained Islamic laws through beautifully written sha'irs. One such sha'ir was *Syair Suluh Pegawai* (Poem of the Torch for Officials, also known as *Syair Kitab Al-Nikah* [Poem of the Book of Marriage]) comprising 325 stanzas. This poem should be read against the distress felt by many Muslim scholars in the nineteenth century regarding rampant divorce, especially among the Malays.[61] Raja Ali Haji's sha'ir underscored the need for intervention and reform of established customs and societal views about marriage life. He interlaced legal obligations with social practices, showing how both could be reconciled. The poem heartfully advises choosing a spouse and leading a harmonious and lasting marriage. In one stanza, Raja Ali writes:

> This is addressed to the honourable one
> On marriage laws I humbly present
> For all officials to fathom
> As hindrance from the immoral.
>
> Let it be known to you oh kindred
> The laws of marriage are diverse
> Discern them in their full significance
> As an avoidance from harm.[62]

Sufi reformist politics in the wake of Raja Ali included efforts to undo extremist tendencies within the Muslim community. Extremism among Southeast Asian Muslims ranged from groups that promoted an overly legalist interpretation of Islam to interpretations of

---

[60] Syed Salim Syed Shamsuddin et. al, "Kitab Turath Fiqh Syafie Jawi Sebagai Medium Penyampaian Ilmu Fardu Ain Di Malaysia: Analisis Metodologi Penulisan Kitab Hidayat Al-Sibyan Fi Ma'rifat Al-Islam Wa Al-Iman" (International Seminar on Islam and Science 2020 (SAIS 2020), Malaysia: Universiti Sains Islam Malaysia, 2020), 752–774.

[61] John Michael Gullick, *Malay Society in the Late Nineteenth Century: The Beginnings of Change* (Singapore: Oxford University Press, 1987), 52 and 217.

[62] Abu Hassan Sham, *Puisi-Puisi Raja Ali Haji* (Kuala Lumpur: Dewan Bahasa dan Pustaka, 1993), 307.

mysticism that flaunted legal injunctions and public welfare. Through his privately funded university, the Paramadina, the modernist Muslim scholar Nurcholish Madjid (1939–2005) introduced a new movement called "neo-Sufism" in the 1990s to address Muslim extremism. Inspired by Hamka and the latter's notion of *Tasauf Moderen* (Modern Sufism), Madjid and his group of intellectuals critiqued fanaticism of all colours in their lectures and publications. They provided contextualized interpretations of Sufi ethics, encouraging Muslims to lead highly productive and socially engaged lives.[63] Nurcholish's ideas and programmes paralleled other Sufi reformers. Hussein Shahab, Haidar Bagir, Agus Affendi, Nasaruddin Umar, and Komaruddin Hidayat took on a more intellectual approach to modernizing Sufism, intending to make Sufis more attuned to contemporary developments.[64]

Another group used Sufi ideas to propound motivational messages to the public. The leitmotif of this group is to marry Sufism with Muslim quest for material success. Ary Ginanjar Agustian called it "Emotional Spiritual Quotient (ESQ)" while Erbe Sentanu packaged his reformed Sufism as "*Quantum Ikhlas.*" Both attracted thousands of followers across Southeast Asia and have gained endearing reputations as motivational gurus. Their workshops, lectures, books, and courses have been used by governmental bodies, corporations, and Sufi seminaries in the region. Combining pop psychology, life coaching, human resource management, and spiritual therapy, these figures have structured the reformist politics of Muslims in Southeast Asia to embrace selected aspects of neo-liberalism and capitalism without necessarily diluting the fundamentals of the shari'a and Sufi ethics.[65]

ROYALIST AND DEMOCRATIC POLITICS

Sufis have been heavily involved in the royalist politics of kingdoms in Southeast Asia for many centuries. In the precolonial period, they laid the ideological foundations of Muslim polities and advanced state power over the masses.[66] The hikayats and other local texts inform us of Sufis

---

[63] Triyoga A. Kuswanto, *Jalan Sufi Nurcholish Madjid: Neo Sufisme* (Yogyakarta: Pilar Media, 2007).

[64] Sukardi (ed.), *Kuliah-Kuliah Tasawwuf* (Bandung: Pustaka Hidayah, 2000).

[65] Daromir Rudnyckyj, *Spiritual Economies: Islam, Globalization, and the Afterlife of Development* (Cornell University Press, 2010).

[66] Anthony C. Milner, "Islam and Malay Kingship," *Journal of the Royal Asiatic Society of Great Britain and Ireland* 1 (1981): 46–70.

Politics   **157**

acting as trusted guides and healers in the courts of rulers. They advised rajas and sultans to be compassionate towards their subjects while displaying piety, chivalry, wisdom, and generosity to ensure the prosperity of their kingdoms. By making their presence felt in the lives of rulers and by painting the image of rulers as representatives of God, Sufis made Islam an official, martial, and missionizing faith in Southeast Asia.[67] As Anthony Johns observes:

> It appears probable, moreover, that the first significant Islamic communities were important functional groups within the city or state, which eventually gained sufficient power to overthrow a 'pagan' king. A ruler, on the other hand, might accept Islam, either because a wandering derwish presented it to him with a charismatic conviction, or because of its emergence as a power among his people. There is little reason to suppose that the rulers accepted Islam to associate themselves with a higher civilization, or that the people became Muslims merely to follow the example of their kings. It is likewise possible to exaggerate the importance of political considerations, such as the need to secure an ally, in an analysis of the factors leading to the spread of Islam, although this may have been an important consideration in the conversion of Malacca from Pasai.[68]

Although Johns changed some of his views on crucial roles Sufis played in the Islamisation of Southeast Asia, the above observation is evidenced most vividly in the accounts given by a prominent Malay court text, the *Hikayat Merong Mahawangsa*, which influenced generations of courtly literature. Shaykh Abdullah, a Sufi mystic of Arab Hadrami background, travelled from Baghdad to Kedah. Like many Sufi missionaries who traversed the circulatory routes linking the Arab world and Southeast Asia, he found an audience with Hindu-Buddhist king, Phra Ong Mahawangsa. The sovereign was informed about Islam, the true religion that nullifies all others before it. Fascinated by the expanding faith and allured by the empires grown from it, the king quipped: "If that is so, it is hoped that your kind self would help us here to teach the

---

[67] Ibid., 46–70.
[68] Anthony H. Johns, "The Role of Sufism in the Spread of Islam to Malaya and Indonesia," *Journal of the Pakistan Historical Society* 9, no. 3 (1961): 143–160.

true religion of Islam."[69] Shaykh Abdullah proceeded to destroy all idols in the kingdom, and wine was banned from the palace. This conversion story showed the strategic alliance formed between Sufis and rulers, a partnership kept intact in the centuries to come.[70]

Southeast Asian Muslim kings trusted Sufis and inducted them into their inner circles, privileging with the highest positions in their polities. In 1602, a British East India Company's representative, James Lancaster, arrived at the court of Sultan Alauddin Ri'ayat Shah in Aceh to discuss the terms of a trade treaty. He expected a military chief or minister to broker the deal but was welcomed by the Sultan's spiritual guide and chief judge, Shamsuddin al-Sumatra'i. Lancaster described Al-Sumatra'i as "the chief bishop" and the most authoritative person in the kingdom.[71] So authoritative were the Sufis that they influenced the naming of important places in the Acehnese kingdom. Forts were called "The Abode of Purity (*Darul Safa*)." There were also sites known as the "Town of Seclusion (*Kota Khalwat*)," "Island of Mercy'(*Pulau Rahmat*)," "Plain of Imagination (*Medan Khayyali*)," and "The Bay of the Threshold of Love (*Teluk 'Ishqidar*)," all revealing the influence of Sufism at that time.[72] In Riau, the ruler and the murshid were the same person. Raja Haji Abdullah (d. 1858) expanded the reach of the Naqshbandiyyah tariqah in his kingdom. His son, Raja Muhammad Yusuf (d. 1889), succeeded him as the murshid. Both figures were learned in Islamic sciences and established large collections of books on different Islamic disciplines.[73] Indeed, many rulers in Southeast Asia were riveted by Sufi teachings, and some were seen as Insanul Kamil or dignified themselves as khalifahs of Sufi brotherhoods in their states.[74]

Colonialism weakened the authority of rulers but did not remove their functions as the patrons of Islam. As guardians of the shari'a, rulers maintained strategic coalitions with religious functionaries who were consulted in deliberations over the selection of rulers. The current

---

[69] Anon., *Hikayat Merong Mahawangsa* (Kuala Lumpur: Yayasan Karyawan dan Penerbitan Universiti Malaya, 1998), 109.

[70] Tariq Ramadan, *In the Footsteps of the Prophet: Lessons from the Life of Muhammad* (New York: Oxford University Press, 2007), 177.

[71] William Forster (ed.), *The Voyages of Sir James Lancaster to Brazil and the East Indies, 1591–1603* (London: Hakluyt Society, 1934), 165.

[72] Al-Attas, Mysticism of Hamzah Fansuri, 15–17.

[73] Rosnaanini Hamid, *Tuan Haji Muhammad Yatim Haji Ismail: Tokoh Tarekat Naqshabandiyyah* (Kedah: UUM Press, 2015), 16.

[74] Anthony C. Milner, 'Islam and the Muslim State', in *Islam in South-East Asia*, ed. M. B. Hooker (Leiden: Brill, 1983), 41–44.

ruler of Perak, Raja Nazrin Shah, maintained the tradition of having Sufi advisers. A member of the Naqshbandi-Haqqani Sufi order, Raja Nazrin was initiated into the tariqah via encouragement from his brother, Raja Ashman Shah (1958–2012), who received ijazah from Shaykh Nazim 'Adil al-Haqqani (1922–2014). The two royals sponsored regular visits by Shaykh Nazim and Shaykh Hisham Kabbani to Malaysia. Mass dhikrs, mawlids, and burdahs were organized during these visits. The Naqshbandi-Haqqani tariqah has been censured as heterodox by several Southeast Asian Muslim states, including Sufi scholars in Malaysia.[75] With advice by the Perak state mufti and other Sufi leaders, Raja Nazrin refuted negative reception towards the tariqah, asserting that its teachings of tariqah could be practiced with "the condition that it does not contradict the foundations of belief and the shari'a."[76]

The advent of Western modernity not only decentred the power of the royals but also provoked the rise of a new form of politics in which Sufis became active participants. By the early twentieth century, Southeast Asia entered the era of democratic politics which "involves endless bargaining in order to influence government policy, which is nothing more than a compromise between the differing interest groups involved in the political process."[77] Decolonization and the establishment of nation-states augmented the pursuit of democracy by the masses. In most Southeast Asian nations, kings were reduced to constitutional monarchs. Faced with pressures from modernist Muslim intellectuals and populist activists, Sufis in Southeast Asia indulged in civil society movements and in parties to carve a space for themselves in the new political terrain. Because many Sufis were already involved in anti-colonial resistance, adjusting to the new realities was generally smooth. Many emerged as influential political actors, advocating their versions of democratic politics clothed in Sufi vocabularies, supported by Sufi institutions and movements.[78]

---

[75] Luthfi Makhasin, "The Politics of Contending Piety: Naqshbandi-Haqqani Sufi Movement and the Struggle for Islamic Activism in Contemporary Indonesia" (PhD Dissertation, Canberra, Australian National University, 2015).

[76] Saifullah Ahmad, "Perak Benar Amal Tarekat Naqsyabandiah Bersyarat," accessed August 3, 2022, https://www.sinarharian.com.my/Article/214557/Berita/Nasional/Perak-Benar-Amal-Tarekat-Naqsyabandiah-Bersyarat.

[77] Kate Nash, *Contemporary Political Sociology: Globalization, Politics, and Power* (Chichester: Wiley-Blackwell, 2010), 14.

[78] Martin van Bruinessen, "Saints, Politicians and Sufi Bureaucrats: Mysticism and Politics in Indonesia's New Order," in *Sufism and the "Modern" in Islam,* eds. Martin van Bruinessen and Julia Day Howell (London: I.B. Tauris, 2007), 111.

The transition among Sufis in Southeast Asia from royalist to democratic politics can be said to have been sparked by modernist and ethno-nationalist pulses. In Java in 1912, an organization called Sarekat Islam (SI, or Islamic Association) attracted leaders of tariqahs to preside over their branches. With backing from the tariqahs, SI began with the desire to empower Muslims through businesses to break the Chinese dominance. The movement grew rapidly, with members agitating for the reformation of Muslim traditions and independence from colonial rule. However, collaboration between Sufis and modernists faltered. By 1926, after the *Moe'tamar 'Alam Islami* (International Islamic Congress) held in Makkah, fissures between these groups emerged over Islamic practices the Saudis regarded as un-Islamic. Sufis splintered and formed their own organization, the NU, on 31 January 1926. NU's overall ideological thrust was traditionalist, and the subsequent disbandment of the SI provided NU with the void to carve a Sufi variant of democratic politics. NU utilized newspapers, rallies, and strikes to magnify its visibility across Indonesia.[79]

K.H. Hasyim Asy'ari, the founding father of NU organization: https://en.wikipedia.org/wiki/Hasyim_Asy%27ari#/media/File:Hasyim_Asyari.jpg

---

[79] John T. Sidel, *Republicanism, Communism, Islam Cosmopolitan Origins of Revolution in Southeast Asia* (Ithaca, NY: Cornell University Press, 2021), 120–145.

Within a few decades, the NU had millions of registered members. Its growth can be attributed to their use of modern political apparatuses while remaining ideologically traditionalist and Sufistic. NU was part of Masyumi (*Partai Majelis Syuro Muslimin Indonesia*, or Council of Indonesian Muslim Associations), a major Islamic political party in Indonesia until it was banned in 1960. Many NU leaders and ulama encouraged their members to enter politics. They supported and maintained uneasy alliances with the ruling GOLKAR Party (*Parti Golongan Karya*, or Party of Functional Groups) and founded several civil society organizations during Suharto's long reign (1966–1998). Abdurrahman Wahid, the grandson of one of NU's founders, was elected President of Indonesia between 1999 and 2001. A champion of democratic politics, religious inclusivity, and Muslim cosmopolitanism, his *Partai Kebangkitan Bangsa* (PKB, or National Awakening Party) mobilized forty-five Sufi tariqahs for elections. PKB's stronghold was in rural Indonesia.

Sufis in Southeast Asia admit both women and men in their political echelons. NU was not only in support of male presidential candidates but also has been successful in mobilizing women to widen its political support. Highly educated members such as Rustriningsih, Siti Qomariyah, and Ratna Ani Lestari rose to high positions as regents and governors in Java.[80] Leading up to the Indonesian general elections on April 2019, 200 NU organized their members to support the incumbent president, Joko Widodo, while assisting the candidature of a prominent NU leader, Ma'ruf Amin, who eventually became the Vice-President of Indonesia. Joko–Ma'ruf's partnership and victory in the elections exhibit the potency of Sufi participation in democratic politics.[81]

A similar combination of modern political tools and Sufi ideology occurred in Sumatra. In Minangkabau, teachers from the Naqshbandiyyah tariqah founded PERTI (Persatuan Tarbiyah Islamiyah, or Islamic Education Organization) in 1928, a religious organization which became a political movement. Hundreds of circulatory institutions, the first being Madrasah Tarbiyah Islamiyah (MTI), united Sufi scholars to achieve religio-political ends. MTI also deepened public knowledge about Islam and acted as a bulwark against corrupting influences. The members trained Islamic missionaries who were tasked to enjoin Muslims to

---

[80] Kurniawati Hastuti Dewi, *Indonesian Women and Local Politics Islam, Gender and Networks in Post-Suharto Indonesia* (Singapore: NUS Press, 2015).
[81] Irfan Teguh, "Sejarah Politisasi Agama ala Nahdlatul Ulama," accessed 11 February 2019, https://tirto.id/sejarah-politisasi-agama-ala-nahdlatul-ulama-dgck

preserve their customs and make the adat congruent with the shari'a (*adat nan kawi, syara' nan lazim*). Critical of the Kaum Muda activists in Sumatra, PERTI defended strict adherence to the Shafi'ite jurisprudence. Under the leadership of a charismatic and prolific author, Sulaiman Ar-Rasuly (1871–1970), PERTI swelled its membership through a network of suraus. By the 1970s, PERTI transformed into a political party.[82]

Al-Rasuly's transformation from an educator to a participant in democratic politics was shared by another prominent member of the Naqshbandiyyah tariqah in Aceh, Abuya Syech Amran Waly al-Khalidy. Amran, a known scholar whose grassroots work and links with many Sufi seminaries, was elected as a legislator from 1982 to 1987. He led the Darul Ihsan dayah, and wrote several popular books on Sufism. After his successful stint in politics, his influence grew through an organization he founded, the *Majelis Pengkajian Tauhid Tasawuf* (Monotheistic Sufi Study Council). With branches in Malaysia and other parts of Indonesia, Amran emerged as transnational Sufi master in the region, officiating conferences for Sufi ulama in Aceh and Malaysia. In late 2009, Amran published a booklet discussing Al-Jili's concept of Insanul Kamil and Ibn Arabi's Wahdatul Wujud. State-linked ulama accused Amran of heresy and promoting dangerous ideas espoused by Hamzah Fansuri and Syamsuddin Sumatrani. A fatwa was issued banning his books. This made Amran more popular. Although he failed to gain the political backing he wanted, his Tauhid-Tasawuf movement lived on under the watchful eye of the shari'a state.[83]

Different from preceding Sufis who remained generally traditionalistic in their worldviews, some Sufis in Southeast Asia espoused modern ideologies and sought to balance these ideas with their tasawwuf commitments and democratic forays. A significant sample was the late Burhanuddin Al-Helmy (1911–1969). A medical doctor turned anticolonial activist, Burhanuddin was also a Sufi ideologue who became the third President of the most formidable Islamic party in Malaysia, PAS. Similar to the aforementioned Sufis, Burhanuddin belonged to the Naqshbandiyyah tariqah and enjoined Sufis to unite in the road to liberate the Malay world from British rule. His conceptualization of Sufism went beyond spiritual purification. Sufis, to him, must keep

---

[82] Baharuddin Ar-Rasuly, *Sejarah Lengkap Persatuan Tarbiyah Islamiyah* (Candung, 1979).

[83] Moch Nur Ichwan, "Neo-Sufism, Shariatism, and Ulama Politics: Abuya Shaykh Amran Waly and the Tauhid-Tasawuf Movement in Aceh," in *Islam, Politics and Change: The Indonesian Experience after the Fall of Suharto,* eds. Kees van Dijk and Nico J. G. Kaptein (Leiden: Leiden University Press, 2016), 221–246.

Politics **163**

up with the times and shape democratic politics.[84] He epitomized that vision. A founding leader of the Parti Kebangsaan Melayu Malaya (PKMM, or The Malay Nationalist Party), his radical political stance earned him two spells of imprisonment during British rule. Upon the independence of Malaysia, Burhanuddin distanced himself from the leftist movements he once steered to focus on Islamic activism.

Under his leadership, from 1956 till 1965, PAS campaigned for the establishment of an Islamic state and union of the Muslim states in Southeast Asia. In the 1959 elections, PAS took control of legislative assemblies in the northern states of Trengganu and Kelantan, raising much anxiety among the ranks of the Alliance government in Malaysia then. In January 1965, he was arrested under the Internal Security Act (ISA) for suspicions of conspiring to topple the government. He was among the many leftist activists, opposition politicians, and Sufis detained during the confrontation between Malaysia and Indonesia. Gone too soon while behind bars, his radical activism was pivotal in rallying succeeding generations of Sufis in Malaysia to consider democratic politics as a lifetime vocation.[85]

CONCLUSION

Sufis in Southeast Asia have made incessant contributions in politics. They were political beings par excellence. They obtained a large following from the masses through state endorsement of their scholarly pursuits, missionary work, institutions, and brotherhoods. By placing themselves within the orbit of politics in Southeast Asia, Sufis structured the fates of states and societies. They played transformative roles in conversion politics, creatively transforming Malay minds to adopt Islam as a dominant frame of thought. This change was gradual to ensure harmony, allowing pre-Islamic practices and concepts to endure and become congruent with the spirit of Islam. And yet, Sufi scholars also corrected many practices and understandings of Islam among the already converted population. They critiqued pantheistic and monistic tendencies and punished other Sufis for their heterodox beliefs.

---

[84] Burhanuddin Al-Helmi, *Simposium Tasawwuf Dan Tariqat* (Pulau Pinang: The United Press, 1971).

[85] Khairudin Aljunied, *Radicals: Resistance and Protest in Colonial Malaya* (Dekalb: Northern Illinois University Press, 2015), 190.

As advisers of power elites and grassroots activists, Sufis shaped the configurations of royalist and democratic politics. Politics, to the Sufis, were instruments to create a spiritually inclined and highly ethical society. Ideally, Sufis hoped for a revolution of "the Malay-Indonesian worldview, turning it away from a crumbling world of mythology...to the world of intelligence, reason and order."[86] Then again, politics is rife with dissensions and discords. Many Sufis found themselves entangled in such trappings or were complicit in using worldly power to overwhelm competitors and enemies, including their own brethren. Most skilfully navigated their way through the circuits of powerful structures and figures, asserting their places in the changing Southeast Asian political terrain. Contemplating over the histories of Sufis and their active participation in various spheres of politics inform us of how they remodelled Southeast Asia into a mesmerizing domain where Sufism as a dialogical tradition interacted and intersected with the politically powerful.

---

[86] Syed Muhammad Naquib Al-Attas, *Some Aspects of Sufism as Understood and Practised by the Malays* (Kuala Lumpur: Malaysian Sociological Research Institute, 1963), 4.

Epilogue: Contemplating Sufism

We have travelled with the Sufis in Southeast Asia across many realms, into many domains, through many experiences. In this journey spanning many centuries, Sufis have survived shifting constellations of power, navigated various mazes of beliefs, adapted to cultural changes, and outlived restraints and impositions of all kinds. They lived through multiple waves of global revolutions. How did the Sufis in Southeast Asia implant their ways of life and their currents of thought into almost every corner of the region? What made Sufism so resilient?

Sufism has been a powerful force in Southeast Asian history because it has been a dialogical tradition. This tradition can only be properly discerned through the prism of contemplative histories, a fresh methodology that empathizes with the spiritual and metaphysical and that recognizes the plurality of Sufi pasts. Contemplative histories encourage empathy with seemingly irrational ways of life from the actors' perspectives. It is an approach that puts into sharp relief how Sufism was personified and articulated in different times and spaces into a single frame of analysis, with a view of flashing out patterns of behaviour and trends of thought. Contemplative histories uncover the relationship between Muslim piety and secular pursuits, showcasing how Sufis explained, expressed, and enhanced their beliefs and practices, especially through power play.

Contemplative histories circumvent the errors of assigning "golden ages" and "declines" to the history of Sufism. Instead, it acknowledges the varying challenges Sufis faced in each era, their reasoning for certain actions, and the impact of their decisions on their futures. Rather than offering a linear view of Sufi pasts, this methodology trains us to view Sufi histories from the vantage points of the calmness of everyday life and transformations wrought by significant events. Both perspectives are equally important. A contemplative historian is akin to a

---

Contemplating Sufism: Dialogue and Tradition Across Southeast Asia, First Edition. Khairudin Aljunied.
© 2025 John Wiley & Sons Ltd. Published 2025 by John Wiley & Sons Ltd.

traveller on a boat in the boundless ocean of Sufism, aware of gradual ripples and occasional storms, but always discerning of the vast terrain and persistent interchanges interposing between peoples and places. Such a historian identifies with the environment and internalizes what Zygmunt Bauman describes as being "always on the outside even when inside, examining the familiar as if it was a foreign object of study, asking questions no one else asked, questioning the unquestionable and challenging the unchallengeable."[1]

In contemplating Sufism in Southeast Asia as a dialogical tradition, I found that Sufis enchanted the *rasa* of Southeast Asians. They used supplicative and figurative mediums to stir emotions. Discerning of local cultural tastes, they creatively deploy *burdahs, mawlids, ratibs, sha'irs,* and *hikayats* to instil Muslim norms. These mediums narrated the intriguing lives of prophets, Sufi masters, and dedicated preachers. The dialogue with feelings introduced new religious imaginaries and possibilities of conceiving spiritual life, bringing Southeast Asians closer to Islam. With *rasa* came the love for the divine and humankind. Having captured the laity's feelings, Sufis offered moral lessons drawn from the deep wells of Islamic scriptures to build hybridized civilizations with Muslims and non-Muslims.

But feelings, like thoughts, come and go. One way to lodge feelings deep into the sensibilities of the people was to embellish the dead to embroider the living. Sufis monumentalized the *karamah* of saints and the *barakah* they believed flowed through mausoleums. Divided over assigning divinity over the dead, with some branding such rituals as *bid'ah* and *shirk* and others seeing honouring of saints as blameless, Sufis in Southeast Asia remained fond of marvelling at miracles. Rules and rituals, protocols and marks of honour, elegant aesthetics, and unique localities transformed ordinary burial places into sanctified tombs. Splashed with enigmatic stories, graves became sites of collective memories and markers of shared identities. Incredible tales of dead saints gifted with superhuman feats, appearing as they did in mysterious dreams, dazzled the rational minded. These mythologies gave karamah and barakah dialogical qualities that constantly piqued those who encountered them. These mythologies prompted opposition within the Sufi fraternity who regarded sanctified tombs as significant yet far from being places of worship and veneration, practices they deemed contrary to the authentic dialogical tradition.

---

[1] Zygmunt Bauman, *Modernity and the Holocaust* (Ithaca: Cornell University Press, 2001), 53.

Epilogue: Contemplating Sufism **167**

Sufism retained its significance in Southeast Asia through various establishments, particularly Sufi seminaries known as *pesantrens, pondoks, madrasahs*, and *dayahs*. As circulatory institutions where organic texts – the kitab kuning – were memorized and debated by scholars of deep learning, Sufi seminaries preserved *silsilahs* and accorded *ijazahs*, binding Sufis in Southeast Asia with their brethren long gone and far-flung in other edges of the Muslim world. These organic texts were taught by peripatetic spiritual mediators who spent their energies not only as teachers but also as healers, enforcers, businesspersons, and counsellors to the devout communities who upheld them. The support given and the participation of devout communities in these institutions turned Sufi seminaries into lively hubs where *iman*, *'ilm*, and *amal* were internalized. Indeed, through the partnership between spiritual mediators and devout communities, new cohorts of learners and teachers were produced and reproduced. These communities widely read, appreciated, and circulated organic texts across the Southeast Asian region and beyond.

More than just persons who appealed to feelings, or believers purveying miraculous tales, or builders of thriving institutions, Southeast Asian Sufis were also fierce warriors. For them, the dialogical tradition must be peacefully disseminated and ardently defended. They employed *jihad* or *perang* sabil as ideological vocabularies to wage holy struggles against opposing factions and colonizing armies. They expanded budding sultanates, safeguarded treasured traditions, and imposed forgotten norms and laws. Holy struggles, even at the cost of their lives, may not have always yielded triumphs, but their sacrifices roused Muslim publics and inspired generations of Sufis to be martially equipped. An accepted maxim among Sufis has been that they must be ever engaged in the inner jihad – disciplining the *nafs* from immoralities. They must also be ready to defend their faith and homeland. The outer jihad is an expression of Sufi love for God, justice, liberty, and the creed above the self.

To state then that Sufis in Southeast Asia have "never been known to exhibit religious militarism" ignores an important component of their dialogues with religious texts and conflictual contexts.[2] Besides serving as soldiers in the path of God, Sufis were political beings and experts in realpolitik. They were conspicuous in halls of power. They engaged in reform and renewal to rid societies of interpretations of Sufism that contradicted the *shari'a*. They were active in the service of states. Delving

---

[2] Syed Muhammad Naquib Al-Attas, *Some Aspects of Sufism as Understood and Practised among the Malays* (Singapore: Malaysian Sociological Research Institute, 1963), 99.

in politics won them many converts and allies but placed the Sufis in perilous zones. For Southeast Asian Sufis, *siasah* was war by other means, proselytization in another guise, and purification with different names. Politics were tools for achieving other-worldly salvation.

I conclude by highlighting two dominant problems in studies of Sufism in Southeast Asia that this book hopes to demystify: the issue of "homogenization" and the fallacy of "segmentizing Sufism." Many analysts tend to paint Sufis as either "placid" or "highly tolerant." From such a vantage point, Sufism is as an alternative to the more literalist, legal-oriented, and strict currents of Islam. In today's academic parlance, Sufis are regarded as opposites to Salafis and modernists. However, this binary is tenuous and artificial.[3] The story of Sufism in Southeast Asia complicates this homogenizing assumption. Undeniably, there were many Sufis who showed highly tolerant attitudes towards non-Muslim beliefs, cultures, and societies. They transplanted much of ancient and Hindu-Buddhist philosophies and rituals into the nub of Sufism in the region and were excellent creators of creolized beliefs and practices.

Equally, there were Sufis who abided fully to the shari'a and interpreted it in firmest terms. While they accepted preceding cultures in as long as such cultures remained congruent to the Islamic spirit, they were unwilling to compromise the idea of tawheed with any pantheistic philosophies or bend Islamic laws to fit totally with local exigencies. The burning and banning of Wujudiyyah written doctrines and their permutations, the execution of Shaykh Siti Jenar, the purist battles waged by Padris in Sumatra, and the scores of fatwas passed against wayward Sufis were among many examples of muscular and rule-driven Sufism in Southeast Asian history. This variant of Sufism was by no means exception to the rule. For these Sufis, religious indiscretions were worthy of punitive and corrective actions. Sufis were not necessarily gentle beings. They were stalwarts of laws and were staunch in their promotion of their dogmas. They were belligerent in the face of transgressions of Islamic precepts. They asserted the superiority of Islam while maintaining tolerance, respect, and protection of other faiths and belief systems. They were devoted traditionalists and committed reformists.[4]

Linked to the issue of homogenization is the idea of Sufism as a unique and separate offshoot of Islam, which I call the fallacy of "segmentizing

---

[3] Mark Woodward et al., "Salafi Violence and Sufi Tolerance? Rethinking Conventional Wisdom," *Perspectives on Terrorism* 7, no. 6 (2013): 58–78.

[4] See Azyumardi Azra, *The Origins of Islamic Reformism in Southeast Asia* (Honolulu: University of Hawai'i Press, 2004).

Epilogue: Contemplating Sufism **169**

Sufism." Writers caught in this line of reasoning decouple Sufism from the faith it originated. Their supposition is as follows: one can be a "Sufi" without necessarily being Muslim. One can be an adherent of Sufism without accepting the Qur'an and the Sunnah as fundamental and indispensable sources. Sufism is thus dislodged from its origins. It becomes a stand-alone ideology, a belief with its own essence. Such ways of looking at Sufism run in contrary to the thinking of generations of Sufi scholars and masters in Southeast Asia. As Armando Salvatore observes: "Several Western scholars have attempted since the nineteenth century to reduce Sufism to an odd component within Islam, often even surmising, without providing cumulative evidence, that it originated from extra-Islamic sources. Yet a quite solid scholarly consensus now maintains that Sufism's remote roots are as old as the translation of Muhammad's message into pious practice by his companions."[5]

For the majority who affiliate themselves to Islam, Sufism is an expression and the ultimate embodiment of the vision of the Qur'an and the Sunnah. There is no Sufism without Islam as its bedrock. There is no Sufism without a firm belief in Allah, the one true God. Thus, no one can be regarded as Sufi without first being Muslim. Moving beyond the mistake of segmentizing Sufism would make us more sensitive to the fact that, for Sufis in Southeast Asia, the term "Sufism" is laden with genealogies, histories, communities, scriptures, practices, and dogmas that are traced back to the Prophet Muhammad. For Sufis in Southeast Asia, the word "Sufism" is packed with transcendental elements, transmitted from one Sufi master to another for over a millennium, often through multiple networks, to achieve transformational intents and purposes. As such, Sufism is not an offshoot of Islam. It *is* Islam. Sufis in Southeast Asia did not endeavour to transcend all faiths. They dedicated their lives fully to one faith and underlined the distinctiveness of that faith above others. At the same time, they emphasized universal values such as love, peace, righteous conduct, compassion, justice, equality, and mercy that binds all of humankind.[6]

The ventures of Sufis in shaping rasa, in mythologizing karamah and barakah, in circulating 'ilm and pieties, in waging jihad, and in playing with siasah reveal how Sufis were scarcely world-renouncing. Sufism in Southeast Asia and in the world over has always been very

---

[5] Armando Salvatore, *The Sociology of Islam: Knowledge, Power and Civility*, The Sociology of Islam: Knowledge, Power and Civility (Oxford: Wiley-Blackwell, 2016), 78.
[6] Muhammad Uthman El-Muhammady, *Ajaran Tasawwuf Ulama' Nusantara* (Kota Bharu: Majlid Agama Islam dan Adat Istiadat Melayu Kelantan, 2016), 209–228.

worldly, utterly activistic, and constantly altering both seen and unseen realms of life. Sufis appealed to the souls while brandishing power. Sufis touched many hearts while making and breaking structures of oppression. Sufis hypnotized minds and shaped the mundane verves of societies. Sufis in Southeast Asia have fulfilled many functions and served many roles, both for and against the forces of their time. They were intellectuals and popular preachers, saints and warriors, social activists and politicians, merchants and wanderers, poets and philosophers. They have been agents of a multitude of societal changes. They were pioneers and participants of ever-expanding networks. Their failings were many, and yet, their successes were plenty. They epitomized and bequeathed upon us all a dialogical tradition that demands our fullest attention. Our deepest contemplation.

And God knows best.

Bibliography

A. G. Muhaimin. *The Islamic Traditions of Cirebon: Ibadat and Adat among Javanese Muslims*. Canberra: ANU E Press, 2006.

Abaza, Mona. "A Mosque of Arab Origin in Singapore: History, Functions and Networks." *Archipel* 53 (1997): 61–83.

Abd. Madjid, Hilman Latief, and Aris Fauzan. "Honoring the Saint through Poetry Recitation: Pilgrimage and the Memories of Shaikh Abdurrahman Siddiq Al-Banjari in Indragiri Hilir." *Religions* 13, no. 3 (2022): 1–12.

Abdul Aziz bin Juned. *Keramat Wali-Wali Allah*. Brunei Darussalam: Jabatan Pejabat Mufti, 2011.

Abdul Razak Abdul Rahman. *Tradisi Ratib Al-Haddad Di Alam Melayu: Manuskrip, Sanad, Kitab Dan Pembudayaannya*. Kuala Lumpur: Akademi Jawi Malaysia, 2021.

Abdullah Al-Haddad, *Nasihat Agama dan Wasiat Iman* (trans. Syed Ahmad Semait) (Singapore: Pustaka Nasional, 1989).

Abdullah Gymnastiar. *Aa Gym Apa Adanya: Sebuah Qolbugrafi*. Bandung: Khas MQ, 2006.

Abdullah, Wan Mohd Shaghir. *Penyebaran Thariqat-Thariqat Shufiyah Mu'tabarah di Dunia Melayu*. Khazanah Fathaniyah, 2000.

———. *Syeikh Daud Bin Abdullah Al-Fatani: Ulama' Dan Pengarang Terulung Asia Tenggara*. Selangor: Hizbi, 1990.

Abdurrahman Wahid. "Principles of Pesantren Education." In *The Impact of Pesantren in Education*, eds. Manfred Oepen and Wolfgang Karcher. Jakarta: Fredrich-Naumann Stiftung, Technical University Berlin and P3M Jakarta, 1988.

Abu Hassan Sham. *Puisi-Puisi Raja Ali Haji*. Kuala Lumpur: Dewan Bahasa dan Pustaka, 1993.

Abubakar Aceh. *Pengantar Sejarah Sufi and Tasawwuf*. Solo: Ramadhani, 1989.

Ach. Fatchan, and Basrowi. *Pembelotan Kaum Pesantren Dan Petani Di Jawa*. Surabaya: Yayasan Kampusina, 2004.

Acri, Andrea, and Verena Meyer. "Indic-Islamic Encounters in Javanese and Malay Mystical Literatures." *Indonesia and the Malay World* 47, no. 139 (2019): 277–84.

Contemplating Sufism: Dialogue and Tradition Across Southeast Asia, First Edition. Khairudin Aljunied.
© 2025 John Wiley & Sons Ltd. Published 2025 by John Wiley & Sons Ltd.

Adhi Maftuhin. *Sanad Ulama Nusantara Transmisi Keilmuan Ulama Al-Azhar & Pesantren Disertai Biografi Penulis Kitab Kuning*. Bogor: Sahifa Publishing, 2018.

Agama, Kementerian. *Mu'tabara Tariqas (Notable Sufi Orders) in Indonesian Islam*. Jakarta: Badan Litbang Agama dan Diklat Keagamaan, 2011.

Ahmad, Abdul Samad. *Kesenian Adat, Kepercayaan Dan Petua*. Melaka: Associated Educational Distributors, 1990.

Ahmad Daudy. *Allah Dan Manusia Dalam Konsep Nuruddin Al-Raniri*. Jakarta: Rajawali Press, 1983.

Ahmad Fauzi Abdul Hamid. "From Darul Arqam to the Rufaqa' Corporation: Change and Continuity in a Sufi Movement in Malaysia." In *Islamic Thought in Southeast Asia: New Interpretations and Movements*, eds. Kamaruzzaman Bustamam-Ahmad and Patrick Jory, 45–65. Kuala Lumpur: University of Malaya Press, 2013.

———. "Malay Anti-Colonialism in British Malaya: A Re-Appraisal of Independence Fighters of Peninsular Malaysia." *Journal of Asian and African Studies* 42, no. 5 (2007): 371–98.

Ako, Mashino. "Frame Drum Ensemble in Muslim Balinese Culture." In *Drums and Drum Ensembles Along the Great Silk Road*, eds. Xiao Mei and Gisa Jahnichen, 113–27. Berlin: Logos Verlag, 2019.

Alam, Muzaffar. *The Mughals and the Sufis: Islam and Political Imagination in India, 1500–1750*. Albany: State University of New York Press, 2021.

Alatas, Ismail Fajrie. *What Is Religious Authority?: Cultivating Islamic Communities in Indonesia*. Princeton, N.J.: Princeton University Press, 2021.

Al-Attas, Syed Muhammad Naquib. *A Commentary on the Hujjat Al-Siddiq of Nur Al-Din Al-Raniri*. Kuala Lumpur: Ministry of Culture, 1986.

———. *Prolegomena to the Metaphysics of Islam*. Kuala Lumpur: ISTAC, 2001.

———. *Raniri and the Wujudiyyah of 17th Century Acheh*. Singapore: Malaysian Branch of the Royal Asiatic Society, 1966.

———. *Some Aspects of Sufism as Understood and Practised among the Malays*. Singapore: Malaysian Sociological Research Institute, 1963.

———. *The Mysticism of Hamzah Fansuri*. University of Malaya Press, 1970.

Al-Fatani, Syeikh Daud. *Wasiat Abrar, Peringatan Akhyar (ed. H.W.M. Saghir Abdullah)*. Shah Alam: Penerbit Hizbi, 1992.

Al-Ghazali, Abu Hamid. *The Book of Contemplation: Book 39 of the Ihya' 'ulum al-Din*. Louisville, USA: Fons Vitae, 2021.

Al-Haddad, Abdullah Alwi. *Nasihat Agama Dan Wasiat Iman* (trans. Anwar Rasyidi and Mama' Fatchullah). Semarang: Thoha Putra, 2012.

Al-Haddad, Sayyid Alwi bin Tahir. *Fatwa-Fatwa Mufti Kerajaan Johor, Vol.2*. Johor Bharu: Jabatan Agama Johor, 1981.

Al-Helmi, Burhanuddin. *Simposium Tasawwuf Dan Tariqat*. Pulau Pinang: The United Press, 1971.

Al-Jawi, Syaikh Muhammad Nawawi ibnu Umar. *Nashaihul 'Ibad* (trans. Abu Mujaddidul Islam Mafa). Surabaya: Gitamedia Press, 2008.

Al-Jilani, Abd al-Qadir, *al-Fath al-rabbani wa-l-fayd al-rahmani* (Cairo: Al-Maktabah al- Sya'biyyah, 1988),

Aljunied, Khairudin. *Shapers of Islam in Southeast Asia*. New York: Oxford University Press, 2022.

———. *Hamka and Islam*. Cornell University Press, 2018.

———. *Islam in Malaysia: An Entwined History*. Oxford University Press, 2019.

———. *Muslim Cosmopolitanism: Southeast Asian Islam in Comparative Perspective*. Edinburgh University Press, 2017.

———. *Radicals: Resistance and Protest in Colonial Malaya*. Dekalb: Northern Illinois University Press, 2015.

Al-Raniri, Nuruddin. *Al-Fawa'id Al-Bahiyyah Fi Al-Ahadith Al-Nabawiyyah* (trans. and ed. Mohd Muhiden Abd. Rahman). Kuala Lumpur: Dewan Bahasa dan Pustaka, 2009.

Al-Zubaidi, Khairi O. "The Main Characteristics of Arabic Borrowed Words in Bahasa Melayu." *AWEJ for Translation & Literary Studies* 2, no. 4 (2018): 232–60.

Andani, Khalil. "Metaphysics of Muhammad The Nur Muhammad from Imam Ja'far al-Sadiq (d. 148/765) to Nasir al-Din al-Tusi (d. 672/1274)." *Journal of Sufi Studies* 8 (2019): 99–175.

Andaya, Barbara Watson. "Islam and Christianity in South-East Asia 1600-1700." In *Christian-Muslim Relations. A Bibliographical History Volume 11 South and East Asia, Africa and the Americas (1600–1700)*, eds. David Thomas and John A. Chesworth, 15–27. Leiden: Brill, 2017.

———. *The Flaming Womb: Repositioning Women in Early Modern Southeast Asia*. University Hawai'i Press, 2006.

———. "The Glocalization of Christianity in Early Modern Southeast Asia." In *Early Modern Southeast Asia, 1350–1800*, ed. Ooi Keat Gin and Hoang Anh Tuah, 233–49. London: Routledge, 2015.

Andaya, Leonard Y. *Leaves of the Same Tree: Trade and Ethnicity in the Straits of Melaka*. Honolulu: University of Hawai'i Press, 2008.

Anjum, Tanvir. "Vernacularization of Islam and Sufism in South Asia: A Study of the Production of Sufi Literature in Local Languages." *Journal of the Research Society of Pakistan* 54, no. 1 (2017): 190–207.

———. "Sufism in History and Its Relationship with Power." *Islamic Studies* 45, no. 2 (2006): 221–68.

Anon. "A Malay Legal Digest Compiled for 'Abd al-Ghafur Muhaiyu'd-Din Shah Sultan of Pahang 1592–1614 A.D." ed. John E. Kempe and Richard O. Winstedt." *Journal of the Malayan Branch of the Royal Asiatic Society* 21, no. 1 (144) (1948): 1–67.

———. "Hikayat Raja-Raja Pasai, ed. and trans, by A. H. Hill." *Journal of the Malayan Branch of the Royal Asiatic Society* 33, no. 2 (190), (1960): 1–215.

———. *Babad Dipanagara: A Surakarta Court Poet's Account of the Outbreak of the Java War (1825–30)*, (ed. and trans. Peter Carey). Kuala Lumpur: Malaysian Branch of the Royal Asiatic Society, 2019.

———. *Babad Sultan Agung*. Jakarta: Departemen Pendidikan dan Kebudayaan, 1980.

———. *Babad Tanah Jawi: The Chronicle of Java (ed. and tsrans. by Willem Remmelin)*. Leiden: Leiden University Press, 2022.

———. *Hikayat Iskandar Zulkarnain. Kuala Lumpur*: Dewan Bahasa dan Pustaka, 1986.

———. *Hikayat Merong Mahawangsa*. Kuala Lumpur: Yayasan Karyawan dan Penerbitan Universiti Malaya, 1998.

———. *Hikayat Patani, eds. A. Teuww and D. K. Wyatt*. The Hague: Nijhoff, 1970.

———. *Hikayat Raja Pasai, ed. Russell Jones*. Kuala Lumpur: Dewan Bahasa dan Pustaka, 2016.

———. *Inilah Hikayat Nur Muhammad Dan Nabi Bercukur Dan Nabi Wafat*. Pulau Pinang: Dar al-Maarif, 19–

———. "The Miracle Worker of Old Singapore." *New Nation*, September 1, 1972.

Archer, Raymond LeRoy. "Muhammadan Mysticism in Sumatra." *Journal of the Malayan Branch of the Royal Asiatic Society* 15, no. 2 (128) (1937): 1–126.

Arif Zamhari. *Rituals of Islamic Spirituality: A Study of Majlis Dhikr Groups in East Java*. Canberra: ANU E Press, 2010.

Ar-Rasuly, Baharuddin. *Sejarah Lengkap Persatuan Tarbiyah Islamiyah*. Candung, 1979.

As'ad, Muhammad. "Salafi's Criticism on the Celebration of the Birthday of Prophet Muhammad." *Teosofi: Jurnal Tasawuf Dan Pemikiran Islam* 9, no. 2 (2019): 353–79.

Asad, Talal. *Formations of the Secular: Christianity, Islam, Modernity*. Stanford University Press, 2003.

———. "Thinking About Tradition, Religion, and Politics in Egypt Today." *Critical Inquiry* 42, no. 1 (2015): 166–214.

Asher, Catherine B. "The Sufi Shrines of Shahul Hamid in India and Southeast Asia." *Artibus Asiae* 69, no. 2 (2009): 247–58.

Asna Husin. "Leadership and Authority: Women Leading Dayah in Aceh." In *Gender and Power in Indonesian Islam Leaders, Feminists, Sufis and Pesantren Selves*, eds. Bianca J. Smith and Mark Woodward, 49–66. London: Routledge, 2014.

As-Sanariy, Muhadir Bin Haji Joll. *Pesona Ahli Syurga*. Petaling Jaya: Galeri Ilmu, 2016.

Asy'ari, Hasyim. *Koreksi Peringatan Maulid Nabi Muhammad Saw Tanbihat al Wajibat Li Man Yashna'al Maulid Bi al Munkarat* (trans. Rosidin). Malang: Bayu Media Publishing, 2013.

Atif Khalil, *Repentance and the Return to God: Tawba in Early Sufism* Albany: State University of New York Press, 2018.

Avery, Kenneth S. *A Psychology of Early Sufi Sama: Listening and Altered States.* Abingdon: RoutledgeCurzon, 2002.

Azmi bin Omar. "In Quest of An Islamic Ideal of Education: A Study of the Role of the Traditional Pondok Institution in Malaysia." Ph.D, Temple University, 1993.

Azra, Azyumardi. "Sufism in Indonesian Islam: A Brief History and a New Typology." In *Knowledge, Tradition, and Civilization: Essays in Honour of Professor Osman Bakar*, ed. Khairudin Aljunied, 231–42. Oldham: Beacon Press, 2022.

———. *Islam in the Indonesian World An Account of Institutional Formation* (Jakarta: MIzan Press, 2006),

———. *The Origins of Islamic Reformism in Southeast Asia.* Honolulu: University of Hawai'i Press, 2004.

———. *Surau: Pendidikan Islam Traditional Dalam Transisi Dan Modernisasi.* Jakarta: Logos, 2003.

Azyumardi Azra, Dina Afrianty, and Robert W. Hefner. "Pesantren and Madrasa: Muslim Schools and National Ideals in Indonesia." In *Schooling Islam: The Culture and Politics of Modern Muslim Education*, eds. Robert W. Hefner and Muhammad Qasim Zaman. Princeton, NJ: Princeton University Press, 2007.

Badran, Muhammad Abu l-Fadl. *Adabiyat Al-Karamat al-Sufiya: Dirasa Fi l-Shakl Wal-Madmun.* al-'Ayn, United Arab Emirates: Markaz Zayid li-t-turath wa-t-tarikh, 2001.

Badri, Malik. *Contemplation: An Islamic Psychospiritual Study.* Herndon: International Institute of Islamic Thought, 2018.

Badriyah Haji Salleh. *Kampung Haji Salleh Dan Madrasah Saadiah-Salihiah, 1914–1959.* Kuala Lumpur: Dewan Bahasa dan Pustaka, 1984.

Baihaqi AK. *Ulama Dan Madrasah di Aceh.* Jakarta: Lembaga Ilmu Pengetahuan Indonesia, 1976.

Bakar, Osman. "Sufism in the Malay-Indonesian World." In *Islamic Spirituality: Manifestations*, ed. Seyyed Hossein Nasr, 259–89. New York: Crossroad, 1991.

Bang, Anne. *Sufis and Scholars of the Sea: Family Networks in East Africa, 1860–1925.* London: Routledge, 2003.

Barzanji, Ja'far bin Hassan al-. *The Barzanji Mawlid: The Jewelled Necklace of The Resplendent Prophet's Birth* (trans. Muhammad Shakeel Qaadari Ridawi). London: Self-Publishing, 2018.

Bashir, Shahzad. "Narrating Sight: Dreaming as Visual Training in Persianate Sufi Hagiography." In *Dreams and Visions in Islamic Societies*, eds. Özgen Felek and Alexander D. Knysh, 233–49. Albany: State University of New York Press, 2012.

———. *Religion and Society in Medieval Islam.* New York: Columbia University Press, 2011.

Bauman, Zygmunt, *Modernity and the Holocaust.* Ithaca: Cornell University Press, 2001.

Beattie, Hugh. "The Mahdi and the End-Times in Islam." In *Prophecy in the New Millennium When Prophecies Persist*, eds. Suzanne Newcombe and Sarah Harvey, 89–104. London: Routledge, 2013.

Beck, Herman. "Islamic Purity at Odds with Javanese Identity: The Muhammadiyah and the Celebration of the Garebeg Maulud Ritual in Yogyakarta." In *Studies in Ritual Behaviour*, edited by Jan Platvoet and Jan van der Toorn, 261–84. Leiden: Brill, 1995.

———. "The Contested State of Sufism in Islamic Modernism: The Case of the Muhammadiyah Movement in Twentieth-Century Indonesia." *Journal of Sufi Studies* 3 (2014): 183–219.

Berg, L. W. C. van den. "Het Mohammedaansche Godsdienstonderwijs Op Java En Madoera En de Daarbij Gebruikt Arabische Boeken." *Tijdschrift Voor In- Dische Taal-, Land-, En Volkenkunde* 31 (1886): 519–55.

Birchok, Daniel Andrew. "Women, Genealogical Inheritance and Sufi Authority: The Female Saints of Seunagan, Indonesia." *Asian Studies Review* 40, no. 4 (2016): 583–99.

Blagden, Charles O. "Review of: The Peninsular Malays. I: Malay Beliefs by R. J. Wilkinson, of the Civil Service of the Federated Malay States. (London: Luzac & Co. Leiden: Late E. J. Brill, 1906.)." *Journal of the Royal Asiatic Society* 38, no. 4 (2011): 1029–33.

Blair, Sheila S. "Sufi Saints and Shrine Architecture in the Early Fourteenth Century." *Muqarnas* 7 (1990): 35–49.

Boland, B.J. *The Struggle of Islam in Modern Indonesia*. Nijhoff: The Hague, 1971.

Bonan, Sunan. *The Admonitions of Seh Bari (ed. and trans. G.W.J. Drewes)*. Martinus NIjhoff: The Hague, 1969.

Bougas, Wayne. "Some Early Islamic Tombstones in Patani." *Journal of the Malaysian Branch of the Royal Asiatic Society* 59, no. 1(250) (1986): 85–112.

Bourdieu, Pierre. "Legitimation and Structured Interests in Weber's Sociology of Religion." In *Max Weber, Rationality and Modernity*, eds. Sam Whimster and Scott Lash, 119–36. London: Routledge, 1987.

Bousfield, John. "Adventures and Misadventures of the New Sufis: Islamic Spiritual Groups in Contemporary Malaysia." *Sojourn: Journal of Social Issues in Southeast Asia* 8, no. 2 (1993): 328–44.

Braginsky, Vladimir. *The Heritage of Traditional Malay Literature: A Historical Survey of Genres, Writings and Literary Views*. Leiden: KITLV Press, 2004.

Braginsky, Vladimir I. *The System of Classical Malay Literature*. Leiden: KITLV Press, 1993.

———. *The Turkic-Turkish Theme in Traditional Malay Literature: Imagining the Other to Empower the Self*. Leiden: Brill, 2015.

Brown, Rajeswary Ampalavanar Brown. *Islam in Modern Thailand: Faith, Philanthropy and Politics*. London: Routledge, 2014.

Bruckmayr, Philipp. *Cambodia's Muslims and the Malay World: Malay Language, Jawi Script, and Islamic Factionalism from the 19th Century to the Present*. Leiden: Brill, 2019.

Bruinessen, Martin van. "Controversies and Polemics Involving the Sufi Orders in Twentieth-Century Indonesia." In *Measuring the Effect of Iranian Mysticism on Southeast Asia*, ed. Imtiyaz Yusuf, 129–62. Bangkok: Cultural Centre, 2004.

———. "Kitab Kuning; Books in Arabic Script Used in the Pesantren Milieu; Comments on a New Collection in the KITLV Library." *Bijdragen Tot de Taal-, Land- En Volkenkunde* 146, no. 2/3 (1990): 226–69.

———. *Kitab Kuning: Pesantren Dan Tarekat*. Jakarta: Mizan Press, 1995.

———. *Mullas, Sufis, and Heretics: The Role of Religion in Kurdish Society: Collected Articles*. New Jersey: Gorgias Press, 2011.

———. "Saints, Politicians and Sufi Bureaucrats: Mysticism and Politics in Indonesia's New Order." In *Sufism and the "Modern" in Islam*, eds. Martin van Bruinessen and Julia Day Howell, 92–112. London: I.B. Tauris, 2007.

———. "Sufism, 'Popular' Islam and the Encounter with Modernity." In *Islam and Modernity: Key Issues and Debates*, eds. Muhammad Khalid Masud, Armando Salvatore and Martin van Bruinessen, 125–57. Edinburgh: Edinburgh University Press, 2009.

———. *Tarekat Naqsyabandiyya Di Indonesia: Survei Histories, Geografis Dan Sosiologis*. Penerbit Mizan, 1992.

———. "The Origins and Development of Sufi Orders (Tarekat) in Southeast Asia." *Studia Islamika: Indonesian Journal for Islamic Studies* 1, no. 1 (1994): 1–23.

———. "Traditionalist and Islamist Pesantrens in Contemporary Indonesia." In *The Madrasa in Asia Political Activism and Transnational Linkages, eds. Farish A. Noor, Yoginder Sikand & Martin van Bruinessen*, 217–45. Amsterdam: Amsterdam University Press, 2008.

Bubandt, Nils. *Democracy, Corruption and the Politics of Spirits in Contemporary Indonesia*. London: Routledge, 2014.

Buckley, Charles B. *An Anecdotal History of Old Times in Singapore*. Kuala Lumpur: University of Malaya Press, 1965.

Buehler, Arthur F. *Recognizing Sufism*. London: I.B. Tauris, 2016.

Bulletin Nasional. "Gus Dur: Saya Nggak Percaya Sama Yang Masih Hidup, Kalau Yang Sudah Mati Kan Nggak Punya Kepentingan Apa-Apa Lagi!!!," March 31, 2022. https://www.buletinterkini.com/2022/03/31/gus-dur-saya-nggak-percaya-sama-yang-masih-hidup-kalau-yang-sudah-mati-kan-nggak-punya-kepentingan-apa-apa-lagi/.

Burhanpuri, Muhammad ibn Fadl Allah. *The Gift Addressed to the Spirit of the Prophet (ed. and trans. Anthony H. Johns)*. Australian National University, 1965.

Bush, Robin. *Nahdlatul Ulama and the Struggle for Power within Islam and Politics in Indonesia*. Singapore: ISEAS Press, 2009.

Busiri, Sharaf al-din al-. *The Burdah: The Singable Translation of Busiri's Classic Poem in Praise of the Prophet* (trans. Mostafa Azzam). Atlanta: Al-Madina Institute, 2016.

Carey, Peter. *The Power of Prophecy: Dipanagara and the End of an Old Order in Java, 1785-1855*. Leiden: KITLV, 2008.

Cesar Adib Majul. "The General Nature of Islamic Law and Its Application in the Philippines." *Philippine Law Journal* 52 (1977): 374–94.

Chabbi, Jacqueline. "'Abd al-Qâdir al-Djîlânî Personnage Historique: Quelques Éléments de Biographie." *Studia Islamica* 38 (1973): 75–106.

Chalmers, Ian. "The Islamization of Southern Kalimantan: Sufi Spiritualism, Ethnic Identity, Political Activism." *Studia Islamika - Indonesian Journal for Islamic Studies* 14, no. 3 (2007): 371–417.

Chambert-Loir, Henri. "Saints and Ancestors: The Cult of Muslim Saints in Java." In *The Potent Dead: Ancestors, Saints and Heroes in Contemporary Indonesia*, eds. Henri Chambert-Loir and Anthony Reid, 132–40. Crows Nest, Australia: Allen and Unwin, 2002.

Clancy-Smith, Julia A. *Rebel and Saint: Muslim Notables, Populist Protest, Colonial Encounters (Algeria and Tunisia, 1800-1904)*. Berkeley: University of California Press, 1997.

Clifford, Hugh C. "Report: Expedition to Trengganu and Kelantan." *Journal of the Malayan Branch of the Royal Asiatic Society* 34, no. 1 (1961): xi–119.

Coedès, George. *Indianized States of Southeast Asia, trans. Sue Brown Cowing*. Honolulu: University of Hawai'i Press, 1996.

Cook, David. "Sufism, the Army, and Holy War." In Sufi Institutions, ed. *Alexandre Papas*, 315–21. Leiden: Brill, 2021.

———. *Understanding Jihad*. Berkeley: University of California Press, 2005.

Cooke, Miriam and Lawrence, Bruce B. "Introduction," in *Muslim Networks from Hajj to Hip Hop*, eds. Miriam Cooke and Bruce Lawrence Chapel Hill: The University of North Carolina Press, 2005, 1–28.

Dadoo, Yousuf, and Auwais Rafudeen eds. *Spiritual Path, Spiritual Reality: Selected Writings of Shaykh Yusuf of Macassar*. Durban: University of South Africa, 2021.

Da-Sheng, Chen. "A Brunei Sultan in the Early 14th Century: Study of an Arabic Gravestone." *Journal of Southeast Asian Studies* 23, no. 1 (1992): 1–13.

Delorenzo, Yusuf Talal. "Translator's Introduction." In *A Sufi Study of Hadith: Haqiqat al-Tariq Min al-Sunna al-'Aniqa*, 11–21. London: Turath Publishing, 2010.

Dindin Solahudin. *The Workshop for Morality: The Islamic Creativity of Pesantren Daarat Tauhid in Bandung, Java*. Acton: ANU E Press, 2008.

Dobbin, Christine. *Islamic Revivalism in a Changing Peasant Economy: Central Sumatra, 1784-1847*. London: Curzon Press, 1983.

Doorn-Harder, Nelly van, and Kees de Jong. "The Pilgrimage to Tembayat: Tradition and Revival in Indonesian Islam." *The Muslim World* 91 (2001): 325–54.

Drewes, G. W. J. "A Note on Muhammad Al-Samman, His Writings, and 19th Century Sammàniyya Practices, Chiefly in Batavia, According to Written Data." *Archipel* 43 (1992): 73–87.

———. *An Early Javanese Code of Ethics*. The Hague: Nijhoff, 1978.

———. *Een 16de Eeuwse Maleise Vertaling van de Burda van Al-Būsiri: Arabisch Lofdicht Op Mohammad*. Nijhoff: 's-Gravenhage, 1955.

———. "Further Data Concerning Abd Al-Samad al-Palimbani." *In: Bijdragen Tot de Taal-, Land- En Volkenkunde* 132, no. 2/3 (1976): 267–92.

———. "Short Notice on the Story of Haji Mangsur of Banten." *Archipel* 50 (1995): 119–22.

Drewes, G.W.J. *Directions for Travellers on the Mystics Path*. The Hague: Martinus NIjhoff, 1977.

Drewes, G.W.J. and Poerbatjakara. *Kisah-Kisah Ajaib Syekh Abdulkadir Jailana* (trans. M. Amir Sutaarga). Jakarta: Pustaka Jaya, 1990.

Eaton, Richard Maxwell. *The Sufis of Bijapur*. Princeton: Princeton University Press, 1978.

Eden, Jeff. *Warrior Saints of the Silk Road*. Leiden: Brill, 2019.

Editorial. "USIM Iktiraf Sumbangan Roslan Madun Martabat Syair." *Berita Harian*, May 2, 2019.

Eickelman, Dale F., and James Piscatori. *Muslim Politics*. Princeton: Princeton University Press, 2004.

Eka Srimulyani. "Muslim Women and Education in Indonesia: The Pondok Pesantren Experience." *Asia Pacific Journal of Education* 27, no. 1 (2007): 85–99.

———. *Women from Traditional Islamic Educational Institutions in Indonesia Negotiating Public Spaces*. Amsterdam: Amsterdam University Press, 2012.

El-Muhammady, Muhammad Uthman. *Ajaran Tasawwuf Ulama' Nusantara*. Kota Bharu: Majlid Agama Islam dan Adat Istiadat Melayu Kelantan, 2016.

Endang Turmudi. *Struggling for the Umma: Changing Leadership Roles of Kiai in Jombang, East Java*. Canberra: ANU E Press, 2006.

Entji' Amin. *Syair Perang Mengkasar: The Rhymed Chronicle of the Macassar War* ed. and trans. Cyril Skinner. The Hague, 1963.

Ephrat, Daphna, and Paula G. Pinto. "Sufi Places and Dwellings." In *Sufi Institutions*, ed. Alexandre Papas, 105–44. Leiden: Brill, 2021.

Ephrat, Daphna, Ethel Sara Wolper, and Paula G. Pinto. "Introduction: History and Anthropology of Sainthood and Space in Islamic Contexts." In *Saintly Spheres and Islamic Landscapes: Emplacements of Spiritual Power across Time and Place*, eds. Daphna Ephrat, Ethel Sara Wolper and Paulo G. Pinto, 1–34. Leiden: Brill, 2021.

Ernst, Carl. "Muhammad as the Pole of Existence." In *The Cambridge Companion to Muhammad*, ed. Jonathan E. Brockopp, 123–38. New York: Cambridge University Press, 2010.

———. *Refractions of Islam in India: Situating Sufism and Yoga*. Thousand Oaks: Sage, 2016.

Ewing, Katherine P. "Dreams from a Saint: Anthropological Atheism and the Temptation to Believe." *American Anthropologist* 96, no. 3 (1994): 571–83.

Fansuri, Hamzah. *The Poems of Hamzah Fansuri* trans. G.W.J Drewes and L.F. Brakel. Leiden: Royal Institute of Linguistics and Anthropology, 1986.

Farouk Yahya. *Magic and Divination in Malay Illustrated Manuscripts*. Leiden: Brill, 2016.

Farrer, Douglas S. *Shadows of the Prophet Martial Arts and Sufi Mysticism*. New York: Springer, 2009.

Faudzinaim Badaruddin, and Muhammad Mahyuddin. "Autoriti Sanad Tarekat Dan Peranannya Dalam Ilmu Tasawuf." *International Journal of Islamic Thought* 20 (2021): 34–44.

Federspiel, Howard M. "Islam and Muslims in the Southern Territories of the Philippine Islands during the American Colonial Period (1898 to 1946)." *Journal of Southeast Asian Studies* 29, no. 2 (1998): 340–56.

———. *Sultans, Shamans, and Saints: Islam and Muslims in Southeast Asia*. University of Hawai'i Press, 2007.

Florida, Nancy K. "Shattariya Sufi Scents: The Literary World of the Surakarta Palace in Nineteenth-Century Java." In *Buddhist and Islamic Orders in Southern Asia: Comparative Perspectives*, eds. R. Michael Feener and Anne M. Blackburn, 153–84. Honolulu: University of Hawai'i Press, 2019.

———. *Writing the Past, Inscribing the Future: History as Prophesy in Colonial Java*. Durham, NC: Duke University Press, 1995.

Fogg, Kevin W. *Indonesia's Islamic Revolution*. Cambridge: Cambridge University Press, 2020.

Foley, Sean. "The Naqshbandiyya-Khalidiyya, Islamic Sainthood, and Religion in Modern Times." *Journal of World History* 19, no. 4 (2008): 521–45.

Formichi, Chiara. *Islam and the Making of the Nation: S.M. Kartosuwiryo and Political Islam in 20th Century Indonesia*. Leiden: KITLV Press, 2012.

Forster (ed.), William. *The Voyages of Sir James Lancaster to Brazil and the East Indies, 1591-1603*. London: Hakluyt Society, 1940.

Fox, James J., and Pradjarta Dirjosanjoto. "The Memories of Village Santri from Jombang in East Java." In *Observing Change in Asia*, eds. Ronald J. May and William J. O'Mallay, 94–110. Bathurst: Crawford House Press, 1989.

Gaddis, John Lewis. *The Landscape of History*. New York: Oxford University Press, 2002.

Gade, Anna M. *Perfection Makes Practice: Learning, Emotion, and the Recited Quran in Indonesia*. Honolulu: University of Hawai'i Press, 2004.

———. "Sunan Ampel of the Javanese Wali Songo." In *Tales of God's Friends: Islamic Hagiography in Translation*, ed. John Renard, 341–58. Berkeley: University of California Press, 2009.

Gaffney, Patrick D. "Popular Islam." *The Annals of the American Academy of Political and Social Science* 524 (1992): 38–51.

Geertz, Clifford. "The Javanese Kijaji: The Changing Role of a Cultural Broker." *Comparative Studies in Society and History* 2, no. 2 (1960): 228–49.

Gibson, Thomas. *Islamic Narrative and Authority in Southeast Asia: From the 16th to the 21st Century*. Basingstoke: Palgrave Macmillan, 2007.

Gibson, William L. *A Complete Catalog of Keramat in Singapore*. Singapore: National Library of Singapore, 2022.

Gilsenan, Michael. "On Conflict and Violence." In *Exotic No More: Anthropology on the Front Lines, ed.* Jeremy MacClancy, 99–114. Chicago: Chicago University Press, 2002.

Glazer, Sidney. "The Alfiyya of Ibn Malik." *The Muslim World* 31, no. 3 (1941): 274–79.

Gowing, Peter G. *Muslim Filipinos: Heritage and Horizon*. Manila: New Day Publishers, 1979.

Graaf, Hermanus Johannes de. *De Regering van Sultan Agung, Vorst van Mataram (1613–1645) En Die van Zijn Voorganger Panembahan Séda-Ing-Krapjak (1601–1613)*. Leiden: Brill, 1958.

Graaf, Hermanus Johannes de, and Theodore G.Th. Pigeaud. *Chinese Muslims in Java in the 15th and 16th Centuries: The Malay Annals of Semarang and Cerbon*. Melbourne: Monash University, 1984.

Green, Nile. *Sufism: A Global History*. Oxford: Wiley-Blackwell, 2012.

Gullick, John Michael. *Malay Society in the Late Nineteenth Century: The Beginnings of Change*. Singapore: Oxford University Press, 1987.

Gunn, Geoffrey C. *History Without Borders: The Making of an Asian World Region*. Hong Kong: Hong Kong University Press, 2011.

H.M. Amin Syukur, *Zikir Menyembuhkan Kanker* Jakarta: Emir, 2016.

Hadler, Jeffrey. *Muslims and Matriarchs: Cultural Resilience in Indonesia through Jihad and Colonialism*. Ithaca: Cornell University Press, 2008.

Haji Matussein bin Haji Jumat, and Wan Zailan Kamaruddin Wan Ali. "Tarekat Abdul Razak: Analisis Intipati Pengharamannya Di Brunei Darussalam." *Borneo Research Journal* 10 (2016): 30–53.

Haji, Mohamed B Haji Abdul Kadir @ S. Mohdir. *Visual Arts*. Vol. Reel/Disc 9 of 20, Accession Number 003431, 2009.

Hall, Kenneth R. *A History of Early Southeast Asia: Maritime Trade and Cultural Development, 100-1500*. Lanham, Md: Rowman & Littlefield, 2011.

Hallaq, Wael B. *The Impossible State: Islam, Politics, and Modernity's Moral Predicament*. Columbia University Press, 2013.

Hamid, Abu. *Syeikh Yusuf: Seorang Ulama, Sufi, Dan Pejuang*. Jakarta: Yayasan Obor Indonesia, 1994.

Hamid, Ismail. *The Malay Islamic Hikayat*. Bangi: Penerbit Universiti Kebangsaan Malaysia, 1983.

Hamidi, Muhammad. *Mitos-Mitos Dalam Hikayat Abdulkadir Jailani*. Jakarta: Yayasan Obor Indonesia, 2003.

Hamidy, U.U. *Pengislaman Masyarakat Sakai Oleh Tarekat Naksyahbandiyah Babussalam*. Pekanbaru: UIR Press, 1992.

Hamka. *Mengembalikan Tasawuf Ke Pangkalnya*. Jakarta: Pustaka Panjimas, 1973.

———. *Pelajaran Agama Islam*. Jakarta: Gema Insani, 2018.

———. *Tasauf: Perkembangan Dan Pemurniannya*. Seventh Edition. Medan: Yayasan Nurul Islam, 1978.

Hans-Georg, Gadamer. *Truth and Method* trans. Joel Weinsheimer and Donald G. Marshall. London: Continuum, 2006.

Harnish, David D. "Tensions between Adat (Custom) and Agama (Religion) in the Music of Lombok." In *Divine Inspirations: Music and Islam in Indonesia*, eds. David D. Harnish and Anne K. Rasmussen, 80–109. New York: Oxford University Press, 2011.

Harnish, David D., and Anne K. Rasmussen. "Introduction." In *Divine Inspirations: Music and Islam in Indonesia*, eds. David D. Harnish and Anne K. Rasmussen, 5–42. New York: Oxford University Press, 2011.

Harrison, Rodney. *Heritage: Critical Approaches*. London: Routledge, 2013.

Harry S. Neale. *Sufi Warrior Saints: Stories of Sufi Jihad from Muslim Hagiography*. London: I.B. Tauris, 2022.

Harun, Mohd Faizal. *Tasawuf Dan Tarekat Sejarah Perkembangan Dan Alirannya Di Malaysia*. Kedah: UUM Press, 2017.

Hassan Madmarn. *The Pondok and Madrasah in Patani*. Bangi: UKM Press, 1999.

———. "Traditional Muslim Institutions in Southern Thailand: A Critical Study of Islamic Education and Arabic Influence in the Pondok and Madrasah Systems in Pattani." PhD Dissertation, University of Utah, 1990.

Hasanuddin Yusof (ed.), *Karya Jihad Ulung Syeikh Abdul Samad Al-Palimbani: Nasihat al-Muslimin Wa Tazkirat al-Mukminin* Seremban: Dr. Mohd Hasanuddin Mohd Yusof, 2023.

Heck, Paul L. "Introduction." In *Sufism and Politics: The Power of Spirituality*, ed. Paul L. Heck, 1–22. Princeton: Markus Wiener Publishers, 2007.

Hefner, Robert W. "Introduction: The Culture, Politics, and Future of Muslim Education." In *Schooling Islam: The Culture and Politics of Modern Muslim Education*, eds. Robert W. Hefner and Muhammad Qasim Zaman, 1–39. Princeton NJ: Princeton University Press, 2007.

———. "Introduction: The Politics and Cultures of Islamic Education in Southeast Asia." In *Making Modern Muslim: The Politics of Islamic Education in Southeast Asia*, ed. Robert W. Hefner, 1–54. Hawai'i: University of Hawai'i Press, 2009.

Helius Sjamsuddin. *Pegustian Dan Temenggung Akar Sosial, Politik, Etnis Dan Dinasti Perlawanan Di Kalimantan Selatan Dan Kalimantan Tengah 1859–1906*. Jakarta: Balai Pustaka, 2001.

Helman, Sarit. "The Javanese Conception of Order and Its Relationship to Millenarian Motifs and Imagery." *International Journal of Comparative Sociology XXIX*, no. 1–2 (1988): 126–38.

Hew, Wai-Weng. "Expressing Chineseness, Marketing Islam: The Hybrid Performance of Chinese Muslim Preachers." In *Chinese Indonesians Reassessed:*

History, Religion and Belonging. eds. Siew-Min Sai and Chang-Yau Hoon, 178–99. London: Routledge, 2012.

Hijjas, Mulaika. "The Trials of Rabiʿa Al-ʿAdawiyya in the Malay World: The Female Sufi in the Hikayat Rabiʿah." *Bijdragen Tot de Taal-, Land- En Volkenkunde* 174, no. 2/3 (2018): 216–43.

Ho, Engseng. "Empire through Diasporic Eyes: A View from the Other Boat." *Comparative Study of Society and History* 46, no. 2 (2004): 210–46.

Hodgson, Marshall G. S. *The Venture of Islam: Conscience and History in a World Civilization, Vol. 3.* Chicago University Press, 1974.

Honerkamp, Kenneth Lee. "The Spirituality of Invocations and Litanies in Islam." In *The Wiley Blackwell Companion to Islamic Spirituality*, eds. Vincent J. Cornell and Bruce B. Lawrence, 61–73. Chichester: Wiley-Blackwell, 2023.

Horikoshi, Hiroko. "The Dar Ul-Islam Movement in West Java (1948062): An Experience in the History Process." *Indonesia* 20 (1975): 58–96.

Howell, Julia D. "Revitalised Sufism and the New Piety Movements in Islamic Southeast Asia." In *Routledge Handbook of Religions in Asia*, eds. Bryan S. Turner and Oscar Salemink, 276–92. London: Routledge, 2015.

Hukum Sambut Maulid Nabi - Dr Rozaimi / Dr Maza / Maulana Asri / Maulana Fakhrurrazi, 2022. https://www.youtube.com/watch?v=1_KqyjI1RkI.

Hurgronje, C. *Snouck.* Kumpulan Karangan Snouck Hurgronje. Jakarta: INIS, 1993.

———. *Mekka in the Latter Part of the 19th Century: Daily Life, Customs and Learning. The Moslims of the East-Indian Archipelago, trans. J.H. Monahan.* Leiden: Brill, 2007.

———. *The Achehnese Vols. I & II* (trans. A.W.S. O'Sullivan). Leiden: Brill, 1906.

Hurley, Vic. *Swish of the Kris: The Story of the Moros.* Seattle: Ceberus Books, 2010.

I. Rofi'ie Ariniro. *Panduan Wisata Religi Ziarah Wali Sanga.* Yogyakarta: Saufa, 2016.

Ibn al-Arabi. *Futuhat Al-Makkiyya, Vol. II.* Beirut: Dar al-Kutub al-'Ilmiyya, 1991.

Ibrahim, Ahmad, and Ahilemah Joned. *The Malaysian Legal System.* Dewan Bahasa dan Pustaka, 1987.

Ibrahim Syukri. *Sejarah Kerajaan Melayu Patani.* Bangi: Universiti Kebangsaan Malaysia, 2002.

Ibrahim, Teuku Alfian. *Perang Di Jalan Allah: Perang Aceh, 1873-1912.* Jakarta: Pustaka Sinar Harapan, 1987

———. *Sastra Perang: Sebuah pembicaraan mengenai Hikayat Perang Sabil.* Jakarta: Balai Pustaka, 1992

Imran T. Abdullah. "Ulama Dan Hikayat Perang Sabil Dalam Perang Belanda Di Aceh." *Humaniora* 12, no. 3 (2000): 239–52.

Isa Anshori. *Dinamika Pesantren Muhammadiyah & Nahdatul Ulama: Perspektif Sosial, Ideologi Dan Ekonomi.* Sidoarjo: Nizamia Learning Center, 2020.

Jappie, Saarah. *"Between Makassars: Site, Story, and the Transoceanic Afterlives of Shaykh Yusuf of Makassar."* PhD Dissertation, Princeton University, 2018.

Jelani Harun. "Bustan Al-Salatin, 'the Garden of Kings': A Universal History and Adab Work from Seventeenth-century Aceh." *Indonesia and the Malay World* 32, no. 92 (2004): 21–52.

Johns, Anthony H. "Islam in the Malay World: An Exploratory Survey with Some Refe- Rence to Quranic Exegesis." In *Islam in Asia, Vol. II Southeast and East Asia*, eds. Raphael Israeli and Anthony H. Johns, 115–61. Jerusalem: The Magnes Press, 1984.

———. "Islamization in Southeast Asia: Reflections and Reconsiderations with Special Reference to the Role of Sufism." *Journal of Southeast Asian Studies* 31, no. 1 (1993): 43–61.

———. "Sufism in Southeast Asia: Reflections and Reconsiderations." *Journal of Southeast Asian Studies* 26, no. 1 (1995): 169–83.

———. "The Role of Sufism in the Spread of Islam to Malaya and Indonesia." *Journal of the Pakistan Historical Society* 9, no. 3 (1961): 143–60.

Joll, Christopher Mark. *Muslim Merit-Making in Thailand's Far-South.* New York: Springer, 2012.

Jones. *Hikayat Sultan Ibrahim Ibn Adham.* Lanham, MD: University Press of America, 1985.

Jones, Russell. "Ten Conversion Myths from Indonesia." In *Conversion to Islam*, eds. Nehemia Levtzion, 129–58. New York: Holms and Meier, 1979.

Juned, Awang Abdul Aziz bin. *Raja Brunei: Pelopor Penggunaan Vaksin Ketuhanan.* Bandar Seri Begawan: Jabatan Mufti Kerajaan, 2021.

Kahn, Joel S. "The Inner Lives of Javanese Muslims: Modern Sufi Visions in Indonesian Islam." *Social Imaginaries* 3, no. 2 (2017): 15–36.

Kaptein, Nico N. J. *Islam, Colonialism and the Modern Age in the Netherlands East Indies: A Biography of Sayyid 'Uthman (1822–1914).* Leiden: Brill, 2014.

———. *Muhammad's Birthday Festival.* Leiden: Brill, 1993.

———. "The Berdiri Mawlid Issue among Indonesian Muslims in the Period from circa 1875 to 1930." *Bijdragen Tot de Taal-, Land- En Volkenkunde* 149, no. 1 (1993): 124–53.

———. *The Muhimmat Al-Nafa'is: A Bilingual Meccan Fatwa Collection for Indonesian Muslims from the End of the Nineteenth Century.* Jakarta: Indonesian-Netherlands Cooperation in Islamic Studies (INIS), 1997.

Karim, Wazir Jahan. "Prelude to Madness: The Language of Emotion in Courtship and Early Marriage." In *Emotions of Culture: A Malay Perspective*, ed. Wazir Jahan Karim, 21–63. Singapore: Oxford University Press, 1990.

Kartodirdjo, Sartono. "Agrarian Radicalism in Java: Its Setting and Development." In *Culture and Politics in Indonesia*, ed. Claire Holt, 71–125. Jakarta: Equinox Publishing Ltd, 2007.

Bibliography **185**

————. *Protest Movements in Rural Java: A Study of Agrarian Unrest in the Nineteenth and Early Twentieth Centuries*. Singapore: Oxford University Press, 1973.

————. *Ratu Adil*. Penerbit Sinar Harapan, 1984.

————. *The Peasants' Revolt of Banten in 1888*. Nijhoff: 's-Gravenhage, 1966.

Kartosoewirjo, S.M. *Haloen Politik Islam*. Malangbong: Dewan Penerangan Masjoemi Daerah Priangan, 1946.

Kathirithamby-Wells., Jeyamalar. "Ahmad Shah Ibn Iskandar and the Late 17th Century 'Holy War' in Indonesia." *Journal of the Malayan Branch of the Royal Asiatic Society* 43, no. 1 (217) (1970): 48–72.

Katz, Jonathan G. "Dreams and Their Interpretation in Sufi Thought and Practice." In *Dreams and Visions in Islamic Societies*, eds. Özgen Felek and Alexander D. Knysh, 181–98. Albany: State University of New York Press, 2012.

Katz, Marion Holmes. *The Birth of the Prophet Muhammad Devotional Piety in Sunni Islam*. Abingdon: Routledge, 2007.

Keddie, Nikki. "The Revolt of Islam, 1700 to 1993: Comparative Considerations and Relations to Imperialism." *Comparative Studies in Society and History* 36, no. 3 (1994): 463–87.

Kermani, Navid. *God Is Beautiful: The Aesthetic Experience of the Quran (trans. Tony Crawford)*. Cambridge: Polity, 2015.

Khoo, Betty L. "The Land of Long Graves." *New Nation*, August 24, 1974.

Kiefer, Thomas M. "Parrang Sabbil: Ritual Suicide among the Tausug of Jolo." *Bijdragen Tot de Taal-, Land- En Volkenkunde* 129, no. 1 (1973): 108–23.

Kingsley, Jeremy. "Redrawing the Lines of Religious Authority in Lombok, Indonesia." *Asian Journal of Social Science* 42 (2014): 657–77.

Knysh, Alexander. *Islamic Mysticism: A Short History*. Leiden: Brill, 2000.

————. *Sufism: A New History of Islamic Mysticism*. New Jersey: Princeton University Press, 2017.

Kooria, Mahmood. *Islamic Law in Circulation: Shafi'i Texts across the Indian Ocean and Mediterranean*. Cambridge: Cambridge University Press, 2022.

Kugle, Scott. *Sufis and Saints' Bodies: Mysticism, Corporeality, and Sacred Power in Islam*. Chapel Hill: University of North Carolina Press, 2007.

Kull, Ann. "At the Forefront of a Post-Patriarchal Islamic Education: Female Teachers in Indonesia." *Journal of International Women's Studies* 11, no. 1 (2009): 25–39.

Kunhali, V. *Sufism in Kerala*. Calicut: University of Calicut, 2004.

Kurniawati Hastuti Dewi. *Indonesian Women and Local Politics Islam, Gender and Networks in Post-Suharto Indonesia*. Singapore: NUS Press, 2015.

Laffan, Michael F. "A Sufi Century? The Modern Spread of the Sufi Orders in Southeast Asia." In *Global Muslims in the Age of Steam and Print, eds. James L. Gelvin and Nile Green*, 25–39. Berkeley: University of California Press, 2013.

————. "From Alternative Medicine to National Cure: Another Voice for the Sufi Orders in the Indonesian Media." *Archives de Sciences Sociales Des Religions* 51, no. 135 (2006): 91–115.

———. *Islamic Nationhood and Colonial Indonesia: The Umma below the Winds*. Routledge, 2003

———. *The Makings of Indonesian Islam: Orientalism and the Narration of a Sufi Past*. Princeton University Press, 2011.

———. *Under Empire: Muslim Lives and Loyalties Across the Indian Ocean World, 1775–1945*. New York: Columbia University Press, 2022.

Latief M Hasyim. *Laskar Hizbullah: Berjuang Menegakkan Negara RI*. Surabaya: Lajnah Ta'lif wan Nasyr, 1995.

Lau, Alberto. *A Moment of Anguish: Singapore in Malaysia and the Politics of Disengagement*. Singapore: Eastern Universities Press, 2003.

Lefèvre, Raphaël. *Jihad in the City: Militant Islam and Contentious Politics in Tripoli*. Cambridge: Cambridge University Press, 2021.

Lukens-Bull, Ronald. *A Peaceful Jihad: Negotiating Identity and Modernity in Muslim Java*. Basingstoke: Palgrave Macmillan, 2005.

Luthfi Makhasin. *"The Politics of Contending Piety: Naqshbandi-Haqqani Sufi Movement and the Struggle for Islamic Activism in Contemporary Indonesia."* PhD Dissertation, Australian National University, 2015.

M. Dawam Rahardjo. "The Life of Santri Youth: A View from the Pesantren Window at Pabelan." *Sojourn: Journal of Social Issues in Southeast Asia* 1, no. 1 (1986): 32–56.

M. Idwar Saleh, and Sri Sutjiatiningsih. *Pangeran Antasari*. Jakarta: Departemen Pendidikan dan Kebudayaan, 1993.

Madun, Roslan. "Roslan Madun Syair Berbuat Jasa." Accessed April 29, 2022. https://www.youtube.com/watch?v=AMrsaY8UibM.

Mahbib Khoiron. "Mencium Batu Nisan Saat Ziarah, Bolehkah?," November 16, 2018. https://islam.nu.or.id/jenazah/mencium-batu-nisan-saat-ziarah-bolehkah-onZfU.

Mahmood, Saba. *The Politics of Piety: The Islamic Revival and the Feminist Subject*. Princeton, N.J.: Princeton University Press, 2004.

Mahmood Zuhdi Haji Abd. Majid. "Mazhab Syafi'i Di Malaysia: Sejarah, Realiti Dan Prospek Masa Depan." *Jurnal Fiqh* 4 (2007): 1–38.

Mahmud H. Yunus. *Sejarah Pendidikan Islam Di Indonesia*. Jakarta: Mutiara, 1979.

Mahmud Saedon Awang Othman. *Ajaran Sesat Di Negara Brunei Darussalam: Satu Tinjauan*. Pusat Da'wah Islamiah: Brunei Darussalam, 2002.

Majul, Cesar Adib. "Islamic and Arab Cultural Influences in the South of the Philippines." *Journal of Southeast Asian History* 7, no. 2 (1966): 61–73.

———. *Muslims in the Philippines*. University of the Philippines Press, 1999.

Makdisi, George. *The Rise of Colleges: Institutions of Learning in Islam and the West*. Edinburgh: Edinburgh University Press, 1981.

Makin, Al. "Unearthing Nusantara's Concept of Religious Pluralism: Harmonization and Syncretism in Hindu-Buddhist and Islamic Classical Texts." *Al-Jami'ah: Journal of Islamic Studies* 54, no. 1 (2016): 1–30.

Mandal, Sumit. "The Indian Ocean in a Malay Text: The Hikayat Mareskalek in Transregional Perspective." *Indonesia and the Malay World* 43, no. 120 (2013): 237–54.

Mansur, Fadlil Munawwar. "Interpretation and Overinterpretation of Ja'far Ibn Hasan Al-Barzanji's Mawlid Al-Barzanji." *Humaniora* 29, no. 3 (2017): 316–26.

Mansurnoor, Iik A. "Muslims in Modern Southeast Asia: Radicalism in Historical Perspectives." *Taiwan Journal of Southeast Asian Studies* 2, no. 2 (2005): 3–54.

Marzuki Abu Bakar. *Pesantren Di Aceh: Perubahan, Aktualisasi Dan Pengembangan.* Yogyakarta: Kaukaba Dipantara, 2015.

"Masjid Sunan Muria Kudus." Accessed July 11, 2022. https://duniamasjid. islamic-center.or.id/1313/masjid-sunan-muria-kudus/.

Matheson, Virginia. "Questions Arising from a Nineteenth Century Riau Syair." *Review of Indonesian and Malayan Affairs* 17 (1983): 1–61.

Matheson, Virginia, and M. B Hooker. "Jawi Literature in Patani: The Maintenance of an Islamic Tradition." *Journal of the Malaysian Branch of the Royal Asiatic Society* 61, no. 1 (254) (1988): 1–86.

Matusky, Patricia, and Tan Sooi Beng. *The Music of Malaysia: The Classical, Folk and Syncretic Traditions.* London: Routledge, 2017.

Mawardi. *Practica Politika NU: Mendajung Ditengah Gelombang.* Jakarta: Jajasan Pendidikan Practica, 1967.

Mayeur-Jaouen, Catherine. "Sufi Shrines." In Sufi Institutions, ed. *Alexandre Papas*, 145–56. Leiden: Brill, 2021.

McCargo, Duncan. *Tearing Apart the Land: Islam and Legitimacy in Southern Thailand.* Ithaca, NY: Cornell University Press, 2008.

Mee, Wendy. "The Ebb and Flow of Popular Islamic Music Forms: Zikir Maulud Amongst Sambas Malays." *Asian Journal of Social Science* 40, no. 2 (2012): 203–33.

"Mega Mawlid 2013: Habib Syech Assegaf," June 2, 2013. https://www.youtube. com/watch?v=c_Bi3Sg4t6c.

Metcalf, Peter. "Meaning and Materialism: The Ritual Economy of Death." *Man* 16, no. 4 (1981): 563–78.

Millie, Julian. "Creating Islamic Spaces: Tomb and Sanctity in West Java." *ISIM Review* 17 (2006): 12–13.

———. "Khâriq Ul-'Âdah Anecdotes and the Representation of Karâmât: Written and Spoken Hagiography in Islam." *History of Religions* 48, no. 1 (2008): 43–65.

Milner, Anthony C. "Islam and the Muslim State. " In *Islam in South-East Asia*, ed. M. B. Hooker, 23–49. Leiden: Brill, 1983,

———. "Islam and Malay Kingship." *Journal of the Royal Asiatic Society of Great Britain and Ireland* 1 (1981): 46–70.

———. *The Invention of Politics in Colonial Malaya: Contesting Nationalism and the Expansion of the Public Sphere.* Cambridge: Cambridge University Press, 1995.

Misno BP, Abdurrahman. *Mari Ziarah Kubur*. Jawa Barat: Penerbit Adab, 2020.

Moch Nur Ichwan. "Neo-Sufism, Shariatism, and Ulama Politics: Abuya Shaykh Amran Waly and the Tauhid-Tasawuf Movement in Aceh." In *Islam, Politics and Change: The Indonesian Experience after the Fall of Suharto*, eds. Kees van Dijk and Nico J.G. Kaptein, 221–46. Leiden: Leiden University Press, 2016.

Moh. Toriqul Chaer, and Wahyudi Setiawan. *Ziarah, Barakah, Dan Karamah: Tinjauan Etnografi Dan Psikologi Pendidikan Islam*. Ponorogo: Wade Publishing, 2018.

Mohammad Taib Osman. *Malay Folk Beliefs: An Integration of Disparate Elements*. Kuala Lumpur: Dewan Bahasa dan Pustaka, 1989.

Mohammad Z. Sabuj. *The Legitimacy of Use of Force in Public and Islamic International Law*. Basingstoke: Palgrave Macmillan, 2021.

Mohammed Gamal Abdelnour, *The Higher Objectives of Islamic Theology* (New York: Oxford University Press, 2022).

Mohd. Nor bin Ngah. *Kitab Jawi: Islamic Thought of the Malay Muslim Scholars*. Singapore: ISEAS Press, 1983.

Mohd. Shuhaimi bin Haji Ishak, and Osman Chuah Abdullah. "Islamic Education in Malaysia: A Study of History and Development." *Religious Education* 108, no. 3 (2013): 298–311.

Moosa, Ebrahim. *Ghazali and the Poetics of Imagination*. Chapel Hill: University of North Carolina Press, 2005.

Moris, Zailan. *Revelation, Intellectual Intuition and Reason in the Philosophy of Mulla Sadra: An Analysis of the al-Hikmah al-'arshiyyah*. London: Routledge, 2013.

Morris, Megawati. *Al-Ghazzali's Influence on Malay Thinkers: A Study of Shaykh 'Abd-Samad Al-Palimbangi*. Islamic and Strategic Studies Institute Berhad, 2016.

Muedini, Fait. *Sponsoring Sufism How Governments Promote "Mystical Islam" in Their Domestic and Foreign Policies*. Basingstoke: Palgrave Macmillan, 2015.

Muhaimin Sulam. "Menjejak Maqam Ulama, Sejarah Yang Tenggelam Tidak Dicatat." *Accessed* July 19, 2022. https://nextstepmalaysia.com/menjejaki-maqam-ulama/.

Muhammad Abdul-Rauf. *A Brief History of Islam with Special Reference to Malaya*. Kuala Lumpur: Oxford University Press, 1964.

Muhammad bin Abdullah bin Malik, *Matan Alfiyah Ibnu Malik* (Maktabah Dar al-Arubah li Nashr wa Tawazi: Kuwait, 2006).

Muhammad bin Abu Bakar. "Sayyid Muhammad Abdul Rahman Al-Idrus." In *Islam Di Malaysia*, 34–51. Kuala Lumpur: Persatuan Sejarah Malaysia, 1979.

Muhammad Rizal. *Pendidikan Dayah Dalam Bingkai Otonomi Khusus Aceh*. Lhokseumawe: Sefa Bumi Persada, 2016.

Muhammad Samman Kati. *Kitab Tasawwuf*. Kuala Lumpur: Akademi Jawi Malaysia, 2018.

Mulder, Niels. *Mysticism in Java: Ideology in Indonesia*. Amsterdam: The Pepin Press, 1998.

Muljana, Slamet. *Runtuhnya Kerajaan Hindu-Jawa Dan Timbulnya Negara-Negara Islam Di Jawa*. Yogyakarta: LKiS, 2005.

Mulyati, Sri. *Tasawuf Nusantara: Rangkaian Mutiara Sufi Terkemuka*. Jakarta: Kenchana, 2017.

Nabhani, Yusuf ibn Isma'il al-. *Jami' Karamat Al-Awliya'*. Beirut: al-Maktaba al-Thaqafiyya, 1991.

Nagata, Judith A. "Alternative Models of Islamic Governance in Southeast Asia: Neo-Sufism and the Arqam Experiment in Malaysia." *Global Change, Peace & Security* 16, no. 2 (2004): 99–114.

Nash, Kate. *Contemporary Political Sociology: Globalization, Politics, and Power*. Chichester: Wiley-Blackwell, 2010.

Nasr, Seyyed Hossein. *Living Sufism*. London: Unwin Paperbacks, 1980.

———. "Oral Transmission and the Book in Islamic Education." In *The Book in the Islamic World: The Written Word and Communication in the Middle East*, ed. George N. Atiyeh, 57–70. State University of New York Press: Albany, 1995.

———. *Sufi Essays*. Albany: State University of New York Press, 1972.

Nasution, Khoo Salma. "Colonial Intervention and Transformation of Muslim Waqf Settlements in Urban Penang: The Role of the Endowments Board." *Journal of Muslim Minority Affairs* 22, no. 2 (2002): 299–315.

Neale, Harry S. *Jihad in Premodern Sufi Writings*. New York: Palgrave Macmillan, 2017.

Nieuwenhuijze, C.A.O. van. *Samsu'l-Din van Pasai: Bijdrage Tot de Kennis Der Sumatraansche Mystiek*. Leiden: Brill, 1945.

Nik Abdul Aziz, Tuan Guru. *Peranan Ulama Dalam Politik*. Kuala Lumpur: GG Edar, 1994.

Nilan, Pam. "The 'Spirit of Education' in Indonesian Pesantren." *British Journal of Sociology of Education* 30, no. 2 (2009): 219–32.

Nocheseda, Elmer I. "Palapas Vernacular: Towards an Appreciation of Palm Leaf Art in the Philippines." *Philippine Quarterly of Culture and Society* 32, no. 1 (2004): 1–72.

Noer, Deliar. *The Modernist Muslim Movement in Indonesia, 1900-1942*. Singapore: Oxford University Press, 1973.

Nourse, Jennifer W. "The Meaning of Dukun and Allure of Sufi Healers: How Persian Cosmopolitans Transformed Malay–Indonesian History." *Journal of Southeast Asian Studies* 44, no. 3 (2013): 400–422.

O'Fahey, Rex S. "Small World: Neo-Sufi Interconnexions between the Maghrib, the Hijaz and Southeast Asia." In *The Transmission of Learning in Islamic Africa*, ed. Scott Reese, 274–88. Leiden: Brill, 2004.

Oldenburg, Ray. *The Great Good Place: Cafes, Coffee Shops, Bookstores, Bars, Hair Salons, and Other Hangouts at the Heart of a Community*. New York: Marlowe & Company, 1999.

Oman Fathurahman. "A New Light on the Sufi Network of Mindanao (Philippines)." *Indonesia and the Malay World* 47, no. 137 (2019): 108–24.

———. "Female Indonesian Sufis: Shattariya Murids in the 18th and 19th Centuries in Java." *Kyoto Bulletin of Islamic Area Studies* 11 (2018): 40–67.

Ong, Walter J. *Orality and Literacy*. New York: Routledge, 2002.

Overbeck, Hans. "Shaer Ta'bir Mimpi." *Malaysian Branch of the Royal Asiatic Society* 7, no. 2 (107) (1929): 338–75.

Papas, Alexandre. "Sufism and Worldly Powers." In *Sufi Institutions*, ed. Alexandre Papas, 255–92. Leiden: Brill, 2021.

Patmawati, and Elmansyah. *Sejarah Dan Eksistensi Tasawuf Di Kalimantan Barat*. Pontianak: IAIN Pontianak Press, 2019.

Pejabat Mufti Negeri Sarawak. *Adab & Larangan Ketika Menziarahi Kubur*. Kuching: Pejabat Mufti Sarawak, 2020.

Pemberton, Kelly. *Women Mystics and Sufi Shrines in India*. Columbia: University of South Carolina Press, 2010.

Pigeaud, Theodore Gauthier Th. *Islamic States in Java 1500-1700: Eight Dutch Books and Articles by H. J. de Graaf / as Summarized by Theodore G. Th. Pigeaud*. The Hague: Nijhoff, 1976.

Pires, Tomé. *The Suma Oriental of Tomé Pires (ed. and trans. Armando Cortesao)*. Hakluyt Society, 1994.

Pitsuwan, Surin. *Islam and Malay Nationalism: A Case Study of Malay-Muslims of Southern Thailand*. Bangkok: Thai Khadi Research Institute, Thammasat University, 1985.

Pogadaev, Victor A. "Folk Singer Roslan a Hit at Russian Festival." *The New Straits Times*, August 22, 2021.

Poljarevic, Emin. "Jihad." In *Encyclopedia of Indian Religions, eds. Zayn R. Kassam, Yudit Kornberg Greenberg and Jehan Bagli*, 392–402. New York: Springer, 2018.

Porpora, Douglas V. "Methodological Atheism, Methodological Agnosticism and Religious Experience." *Journal for the Theory of Social Behaviour* 36, no. 1 (2006): 57–75.

Potter, Laurence. "Sufis and Sultans in Post-Mongol Iran." *Iranian Studies* 27, no. 1–4 (1994): 77–102.

Presidential Decree No. 1083 (1977). https://pcw.gov.ph/assets/files/2020/03/PRESIDENTIAL-DECREE-No-1083.pdf.

Purwadaksi, Ahmad. "Ratib Samman Dan Hikayat Syekh Muhammad Samman." PhD Dissertation, Universitas Indonesia, 1992.

Pusat Data Dan Analisa Tempo. *Budaya Ziarah Makam Wali Dan Tokoh Sakti Di Jawa*. Jakarta: Tempo Publishing, 2020.

Quinn, George. "The Veneration of Female Saints in Indonesia." In *Encyclopedia of Women and Islamic Cultures, ed. Suad Joseph et. Al.* Leiden: Brill, 2012. http://www.brill.com/publications/encyclopedia-women-islamic-cultures.

Qushayri, Abu'l Qasim al-. *Al-Qushayri's Epistle on Sufism* (trans. Alexander D. Knysh). Reading: Garnet Publishing Limited, 2007.

Qushayri, Muslim ibn al-Hajjaj al-. *Sahih Muslim, Vol. 4*. Lahore: Sh. Muhammad Ashraf, 1975.

Rahman Arifai, and Ishak Saat. "Al-Arqam: Pioneer of Nasyid Art in Malaysia, 1975-1997." *International Journal of Academic Research in Business and Social Sciences* 11, no. 4 (2021): 685–94.

Raphael, Vincente L. *Contracting Colonialism: Translation and Christian Conversion in Tagalog Society Under Early Spanish Rule*. Durham, NC: Duke University Press, 1993.

Redzuan Othman. "The Role of Makka-Educated Malays in the Development of Early Islamic Scholarship and Education in Malaya." *Journal of Islamic Studies* 9, no. 2 (1998): 146–57.

Rees A., Mark. "Monumental Landscape and Community in the Southern Lower Mississippi Valley During the Late Woodland and Mississipi Periods, ed. Timothy R. Pauketat, 483–97. New York: Oxford University Press, 2012.

Reid, Anthony. *An Indonesian Frontier: Acehnese and Other Histories of Sumatra*. Singapore: NUS Press, 2005.

Reinhart, A. *Kevin, Lived Islam: Colloquial Religion in a Cosmopolitan Tradition*. New York: Cambridge University Press, 2020.

Republika. "Di Indonesia, Jumlah Santri Ponpes Mencapai 3,65 Juta." July 19, 2011.

Ricklefs, Merle C. *Jogjakarta under Sultan Mangkubumi, 1749-1792: A History of the Division of Java*. London: Oxford University Press, 1974.

———. *Mystic Synthesis in Java*. Norwalk: Signature Books, 2006.

Riddell, Peter G. "'Abd Al-Samad All-Palimbani." In *Christian-Muslim Relations: A Bibliographical History, Vol 12, Asia, Africa, and the Americas*, eds. David Thomas and John Chesworth, 614–20. Leiden: Brill, 2018.

Rijali. Historie van Hitu. *Een Ambonse Geschiedenis Uit de Zeventiende Eeuw* (trans. Hans Straver, Chris van Fraassen and Jan van Der Putten). Utrecht: LSEM (Landelijk Steunpunt Educatie Molukkers), 2004.

Rinkes, Douwe A. *Nine Saints of Java* (trans. H.M. Froger, ed. Alijah Gordon, intro. G.W.J. Drewes.) Kuala Lumpur: Malaysian Sociological Research Institute, 1996.

Rivers, P.J. "Keramat in Singapore in the Mid-Twentieth Century." *Journal of the Malaysian Branch of the Royal Asiatic Society* 76, no. 2 (2003): 93–119.

Roff, William R. "Pondoks, Madrasahs and the Production of 'Ulama in Malaysia." *Studia Islamika* 11, no. 1 (2004): 1–21.

Rogers, Carl. *On Becoming a Person: A Therapist's View of Psychotherapy*. Boston: Houghton Mifflin, 1995.

Ronkel, Ph. S. van. "Account of the Six Malay Manuscripts of the Cambridge University Library." *Bijdragen Tot de Taal-, Land- En Volkenkunde van Nederlandsch-Indië* 46, no. 1 (1996): 1–53.

———. "Het Heiligdom Te Oelakan." *Tijdschrift Voor Indische Taal-, Land- En Volkenkunde* 56 (1914): 281–316.

Ronnit, Ricci. *Islam Translated: Literature, Conversion, and the Arabic Cosmopolis of South and Southeast Asia.* Chicago: University of Chicago Press, 2011.

Ropi, Ismatu. "Wali Songo Festival: Tracking Islamic Heritage and Building Islamic Brotherhood." *Studia Islamika: Indonesian Journal for Islamic Studies* 6, no. 3 (1999): 197–202.

Rosnaanini Hamid. *Adab-Adab Selepas Suluk: Tarekat Naqshabandiyyah.* Kedah: UUM Press, 2019.

———. *Tuan Haji Muhammad Yatim Haji Ismail: Tokoh Tarekat Naqshabandiyyah.* Kedah: UUM Press, 2015.

Rubin, Uri. "Pre-Existence and Light—Aspects of the Concept of Nūr Muḥammad." *Israel Oriental Studies* 5 (1975): 62–119.

Rudnyckyj, Daromir. *Spiritual Economies: Islam, Globalization, and the Afterlife of Development.* Cornell University Press, 2010.

S. Soebardi. "Kartosuwiryo and the Darul Islam Rebellion in Indonesia." *Journal of Southeast Asian Studies* 14, no. 1 (1983): 109–33.

———. "Santri Religious Elements as Reflected in the Serate Tjentini." *Bijdragen Tot de Taal-, Land-, En Volkenkunde* 127, no. 3 (1971): 331–49.

S. Soebardi. *The Book of Cabolèk: A Critical Edition with Introduction, Translation and Notes.* Dordrecht: Springer, 1975.

Sabri Haji Said. *Madrasah Al-Ulum Al-Syariah Perak 1937-1977: Satu Kajian Pendidikan Islam.* Kuala Lumpur: Dewan Bahasa dan Pustaka, 1983.

Sahara Ramadhani, and Shofia Trianing Indarti. *Kisah Penyejuk Jiwa Syaikh Abdul Qodir Jaelani.* Yogyakarta: Penerbit Anak Hebat Indonesia, 2021.

Sahib, Muzdalifah. *Sheikh Yusuf Al-Makassary, His Life Story as a National Hero from Gowa, South Sulawesi to Cape Town, South Africa and a Reformer in Islamic Mystic World.* Makassar: Alauddin University Press, 2011.

Saifuddin Zuhri. *Guruku Orang-Orang Dari Pesantren.* Bandung: PT Alma'arif, 1974.

Saifullah Ahmad. "Perak Benar Amal Tarekat Naqsyabandiah Bersyarat." *Https://Www.Sinarharian.Com.My/Article/214557/Berita/Nasional/Perak-Benar-Amal-Tarekat-Naqsyabandiah-Bersyarat,* August 3, 2022.

Salvatore, Armando, *The Sociology of Islam: Knowledge, Power and Civility, The Sociology of Islam: Knowledge, Power and Civility* Oxford: Wiley-Blackwell, 2016.

Samsul Munir Amin. *Karomah Para Kiai.* Yogyakarta: Pustaka Pesantren, 2008.

Sato, Tsugitaka. "The Sufi Legend of Sultan Ibrahim Bin Adham." *Orient XLII* (2007): 41–54.

Saynee Mudmarn. "Language Use and Loyalty among the Muslim-Malays of Southern Thailand." PhD Dissertation, State University of New York, 1988.

Schielke, Samuli. "Hegemonic Encounters: Criticism of Saints-Day Festivals and the Formation of Modern Islam in Late 19th and Early 20th-Century Egypt." *Die Welt Des Islams* 47, no. 3/4 (2007): 319–55.

Schimmel, Annemarie. "Aspects of Mystical Thought in Islam." In *The Islamic Impact*, eds. Yvonne Y. Haddad, Byron Haines, and Ellison Findly, 113–36. Syracuse: Syracuse University Press, 1984.

———. *Mystical Dimensions of Islam*. Chapel Hill: University of North Carolina Press, 1978.

Scott, James C. *Seeing Like a State: How Certain Schemes to Improve the Human Condition Have Failed*. New Haven: Yale University Press, 1998.

Sedgwick, Mark. *Sufism: The Essentials*. New York: Oxford University Press, 2003.

———. *Western Sufism: From the Abbasids to the New Age*. New York: Oxford University Press, 2017.

Sells, Michael A (ed. and trans.). *Early Islamic Mysticism: Sufi, Qur'an, Mi'raj, Poetic, and Theological Writings*. New York: Paulist Press, 1997.

Sevea, Teren. *Miracles and Material Life: Rice, Ore, Traps and Guns in Islamic Malaya*. New York: Cambridge University Press, 2020.

Shah, Niaz A. "The Use of Force under Islamic Law." *European Journal of International Law* 24, no. 1 (2013): 343–65.

Sharma, Sunil. *Mughal Arcadia: Persian Literature in an Indian Court*. Boston: Harvard University Press, 2017.

Shaykh 'Abdullah Arif. *Bahr Al-Lahut*. Johor Bahru: Jahabersa, 2022.

Sidel, John T. *Republicanism, Communism, Islam Cosmopolitan Origins of Revolution in Southeast Asia*. Ithaca, NY: Cornell University Press, 2021.

Sila, Muhammad Adlin. *Maudu': A Way of Union with God*. Acton: ANU Press, 2015.

Sirriyeh, Elizabeth. *Dreams and Visions in the World of Islam: A History of Muslim Dreaming and Foreknowing*. London: I.B. Tauris, 2015.

Sjamsuddin, Helius. "Islam and Resistance in South and Central Kalimantan in the Nineteenth and Early Twentieth Centuries." In *Islam in the Indonesian Social Context*, ed. Merle C. Ricklefs, 7–17. Melbourne: Centre of Southeast Asian Studies, Monash University, 1991.

Skeat, Walter W. "Report of Cambridge Exploring Expedition to the Malay Provinces of Lower Siam." *The Journal of the Anthropological Institute of Great Britain and Ireland* 30 (1900): 73–77.

Smith, Holly S. *Aceh: Art and Culture*. Kuala Lumpur: Oxford University Press, 1997.

Soemarsaid Moertono. *State and Statecraft in Old Java: A Study of the Later Mataram Period, 16th to 19th Century*. Singapore: Equinox Publishing Ltd, 2009.

Solahudin. *The Roots of Terrorism in Indonesia: From Darul Islam to Jema'ah Islamiyah*. Ithaca, NY: Cornell University Press, 2013.

Stange, Paul. "Legitimate Mysticism in Indonesia." *Review of Indonesian and Malaysian Affairs* 22, no. 2 (1986): 76–117.

———. "The Logic of Rasa in Java." *Indonesia* 38 (1984): 113–34.

Steenbrink, Karel A. *Pesantren, Madrasah, Sekolah, Pendidikan Islam Dalam Kurun Modern* trans. Karel A. Steenbrink Dan Abdurrahman. Jakarta: LP3ES, 1994.

Straits Echo. "Mohammedan Cemeteries." April 16, 1904.

Sturrock. *Annual Report of British Adviser, Trengganu for the Years A.H. 1346 to 1347*. Singapore: Government Printing Office, 1929.

Suen-Oltmanns, Angela. "A Historical Survey of the Keramat Phenomenon (with Special Reference to Singapore)." Unpublished Honours Thesis, Department of History, National University of Singapore, 1993.

Sukardi (ed.). *Kuliah-Kuliah Tasawwuf*. Bandung: Pustaka Hidayah, 2000.

Surattee, Muhammad Ghouse Khan. *The Grand Saint of Singapore: The Life of Habib Nuh Bin Muhammad Al-Habshi*. Singapore: Masjid Al-Firdaus, 2008.

Suwardi Endaswara. *Mistik Kejawen: Sinkrestime, Simbolisme Dan Sufisme Dalam Budaya Spiritual Jawa*. Yogyakarta: Penerbit Narasi, 2006.

Sweeney, Amin. "Malay Sufi Poetics and European Norms." *Journal of the American Oriental Society* 112, no. 1 (1992): 88–102.

———. "Some Observations on the Malay Sha'ir." *Journal of the Malaysian Branch of the Royal Asiatic Society* 44, no. 1 (219) (1971): 53–70.

Syafiq Hasyim. *The Politics of the Council of Indonesian Ulama (Majelis Ulama Indonesia, MUI)*. Leiden: Brill, 2022.

Syed Salim Syed Shamsuddin et. al. "Kitab Turath Fiqh Syafie Jawi Sebagai Medium Penyampaian Ilmu Fardu Ain Di Malaysia: Analisis Metodologi Penulisan Kitab Hidayat Al-Sibyan Fi Ma'rifat Al-Islam Wa Al-Iman," 752–74. Malaysia: Universiti Sains Islam Malaysia, 2020.

Tanti Handriana, Praptini Yulianti, and Masmira Kurniawati. "Exploration of Pilgrimage Tourism in Indonesia." *Journal of Islamic Marketing* 11, no. 3 (2020): 783–95.

Tariq Ramadan. *In the Footsteps of the Prophet: Lessons from the Life of Muhammad*. New York: Oxford University Press, 2007.

Thanvi, Maulana Ashraf Ali. *A Sufi Study of the Hadith, trans. Yusuf Talal DeLorenzo*. London: Turath Publishing, 2010.

"The Singapore Free Press." August 2, 1866.

The Straits Times. "Goodwill Committees Established in All 51 Constituencies." July 27, 1964.

Tibbets, Gérald R. *A Study of the Arabic Texts Containing Material on South-East Asia*. Brill, 1979.

"Tiga Makam Keramat Objek Wisata Religi Di Lombok." June 11, 2020. https://muslim.okezone.com/read/2020/06/11/615/2228359/tiga-makam-keramat-objek-wisata-religi-di-lombok.

Triyoga A. Kuswanto. *Jalan Sufi Nurcholish Madjid: Neo Sufisme*. Yogyakarta: Pilar Media, 2007.

Tschacher, Torsten. *Race, Religion, and the 'Indian Muslim' Predicament in Singapore*. London: Routledge, 2018.

Van Dijk, Cornelius. *Rebellion under the Banner of Islam: The Darul Islam in Indonesia*. The Hague: Martinus Nijhoff, 1981.

Veth, Pieter Johannes. "Het Beratip Beamal in Bandjermasin." *Tijdschrift Voor Nederlandsch-Indië* 3, no. 2 (1870 1869): 197–202.

Vikør, Knut S. "Sufism and Colonialism." In *The Cambridge Companion to Sufism*, ed. Lloyd Ridgeon, 212–32. Cambridge: Cambridge University Press, 2015.

Voll, John O. *Islam: Continuity and Change in the Modern World*. Syracuse University Press, 1994.

Vuckovic, Brooke Olson. *Heavenly Journeys, Earthly Concerns: The Legacy of the Mi'raj in the Formation of Islam*. London: Routledge, 2005.

Waardenburg, Jacques. "Islam as a Vehicle of Protest." In *Islamic Dilemmas: Reformers, Nationalists and Industrialization in the Southern Shore of the Mediterranean*, ed. Ernest Gellner, 22–48. Amsterdam: Mouton Publishers, 1985.

Wan, Meng Hao. *Heritage Places of Singapore*. Singapore: Marshall Cavendish, 2009.

Werenfels, Isabelle "Beyond Authoritarian Upgrading: The Re-Emergence of Sufi Orders in Maghrebi Politics." *The Journal of North African Studies* 19, no. 3 (2014): 275–295.

Winstedt, Richard O. "A History of Malay Literature." *Journal of the Malayan Branch of the Royal Asiatic Society* 17, no. 3 (135) (1940): i–iv and 1–243.

———. "'Karamat': Sacred Places and Persons in Malaya." *Journal of the Malayan Branch of the Royal Asiatic Society* Vol. 2, no. 3 (92) (1924): 264–79.

———. *Shaman, Saiva and Sufi: A Study of the Evolution of Malay Magic*. London: Constable, 1925.

Winzeler, Robert L. "Traditional Schools in Kelantan." *Journal of the Malaysian Branch of the Royal Asiatic Society* 48, no. 1 (227) (1975): 91–103.

Woodward, Mark, Muhammad Sani Umar, Inayah Rohmaniyah, and Mariani Yahya. "Salafi Violence and Sufi Tolerance? Rethinking Conventional Wisdom." *Perspectives on Terrorism* 7, no. 6 (2013): 58–78.

Wright, Zachary Valentine Realizing Islam: *The Tijaniyya in North Africa and the Eighteenth-Century Muslim World* Chapel Hill: University of North Carolina Press, 2020.

Yilmaz, Hüseyin. *Caliphate Redefined: The Mystical Turn in Ottoman Political Thought*. New Jersey: Princeton University Press, 2018.

Yusriadi. *Identitas Orang Melayu Di Hulu Sungai Sambas*. Pontianak: IAIN Pontianak Press, 2019.

Zamakhsyari Dhofier. "Kinship and Marriage among the Javanese Kyai." *Indonesia* 29 (1980): 47–58.

———. *Tradisi Pesantren: Studi Tentang Pandangan Hidup Kiyai*. Jakarta: LP3ES, 1980.

———. "Traditional Islamic Education in the Malay Archipelago: Its Contribution to the Integration of the Malay World." *Indonesia Circle* 19, no. 53 (1990): 19–34.

Ziemek, Manfred. *Pesantren Dalam Perubahan Sosial* trans. Butche B. Soendjojo. Jakarta: Perhimpunan Pengembangan Pesantren dan Masyarakat, 1986.

Zuhri Saifuddin. *Berangkat Dari Pesantren*. Yogyakarta: LkiS, 2013.

Index

A

Aa Gym (Abdullah Gymnastiar), 74
Abdul Malik bin Abdul Karim Amrullah (Hamka), 3, 5
Abdul Razak Tarekat, 146–147
Abdul Wahab Rokan, 42
Abdul Wahid Hashim, 85
Abdurrahman Wahid (Gus Dur), 50, 51, 72
Abuya Syech Amran Waly al-Khalidy, 162
Aceh, Acehnese, 1, 20, 26–27, 35–36, 39, 44, 54, 78, 81, 84–86, 92, 100, 143, 151, 158, 162
Adab, 92, 153
Adat, 83, 127–128, 162
Afghanistan, 44, 108
Africa, 2, 34, 108, 118, 126
Ahlul bait, 74
Ahlus sunnah wal jama'ah (The People of the Sunnah and the Majority), 146
Ahmad Hassan, 30
Ahmad Khatib Sambas, 22
Ahmad Shah ibn Iskandar, 119–120
Air mawar (scented water), 64
Ajaran sesat (deviant teachings), 6
Ajengan, 79
Akhlaqul karimah (noble character), 15
Alawiyyah, 36
Aljunied, Syed Omar 54
Aljunied, Syed Hussein, 59
Al-Ahwal Asy-Syaithaniyyah (Devilish States), 51
al-Azhar University, 90
al-Bantani, Nawawi, 30, 88
al-Burhanpuri, Fadhlullah, 92
al-Busiri, Sharaf al-Din, 22, 23
al-Fatani, Daud, 88, 91, 112, 113
al-Ghazali, Abu Hamid, 6, 7, 13, 90
al-Haqqani, Nazim 'Adil 159
al-Haddad, Abdullah bin Alawi, 33, 34
al-Haddad, Alwi bin Thahir, 144
al-Helmy, Burhanuddin, 162–163
al-Jailani, Abdul Qadir 66, 67, 72, 147
al-Jawi, Nawawi,13
al-Jawi al-Rumi, Daud, 81
al-Junaid al-Baghdadi, 44

al-Kurani, Ibrahim 145
al-Madrasah al-Idrisiah, 85
al-Mahdi (or Imam Mahdi): the prophesized Muslim messianic hero, 109, 129, 140, 154
al-Mandili, Abd al-Qadir, 91
al-Nawawi, Abu Zakariyya, 64, 90, 154
al-Palimbani, Abdul Samad Al-Palimbani, 112–113
al-Qushayri, Abu'l Qasim, 12
al-Raniri, Nuruddin, 41, 91, 112, 143–4, 152
al-Samman, Muhammad bin 'Abd al-Karim, 33–36, 46
al-Sinkili, Abd al-Rauf (Abdur-Ra'uf Singkel), 81
al-Sumatra'i, Daud 41
Alexander Knysh, 3, 12
Aliran kepercayaan, 139, 152
Anthony Johns, 157
Anthony Milner, 136
Aqeedah, 88
Aql (reason), 13
Arab, 18, 47
Arabic, 6, 13, 19, 20, 23, 28, 36, 37, 43
Arab-Persian, 19, 21, 39, 44, 45
Arthur Buehler, 15
Ary Ginanjar Agustian, 156
Asad, Talal, 10–12
Ashaari Muhammad, 143, 147
Ashiq (burning love for the divine), 41
Ayer tawar (healing water), 100
Azimat (amulets), 100, 109, 128
Azra, Azyumardi, 6, 13, 16

B

Babad, 67, 115, 122, 138, 151
Baghdad, 44, 66, 157
Bali, 25, 54
Bandongan, 92
Banjarmasin Sultanate, 128–129
Banten, 1, 69, 70, 88
Barakah or berkat (blessings), 15, 50, 51, 56, 63, 75
Bauman, Zygmunt, 166
Bay'ah, 14, 131
Bid'ah (innovations), 29, 125, 146
Bolkiah, Sultan, 57

Contemplating Sufism: Dialogue and Tradition Across Southeast Asia, First Edition. Khairudin Aljunied.
© 2025 John Wiley & Sons Ltd. Published 2025 by John Wiley & Sons Ltd.

Index　　　　**197**

Borneo, 63, 123
Brunei, 35, 57, 86, 146
Buka kitab, also Tadah Kitab, 92
Burdah (Poem of the Cloak): use in Southeast Asia, 21–26, 29, 30, 32, 34
Burdahs, Mawlids, Ratibs, Sha'irs, Hikayats, 166

C

Cairo, 84, 89–90
Cambodia, 83, 86
Cape of Good Hope, 2
Caucasus, 108
Celebes islands, 25
Ceylon (Sri Lanka), 2
Chau Doc, 53
Chistiyyah, 36, 115
Cilegon, 128
Circulatory institutions 79–83, 86, 91–98, 102–106
Circumambulation of tombs, 64
Colonial modernity, 77
Colonialism, 83
Contemplative histories, 6–10, 17, 165–166
Conversion politics, 136–148
Critical appraiser approach, 5–6

D

Dajjals (deceitful messiahs), 146
Damascus 1, 84, 111
Dargah, 52, 65, 66
Darul 'Ulum (Madrasah) 84
Darul Arqam movement 142–143, 147
Darul Islam movement 127–131
Dato' Bahaman, 124
Dawam Raharjo, 95
Dayah Kan'an (first dayah in Aceh), 81
Dayahs, see also Pesantren, 81–82
Deccan 108
Decolonization, 159
Delhi 111, 149
Democratic politics, 156–164
Devout advocate approach, 3–6
Devout communities 80, 102, 103, 104, 105
Dhawq, see also Rasa, 19
Dhikr (remembering), 15, 21–22, 36, 46, 78, 95, 98
Dialogical tradition, 6–17, 165–167, 170
Dihliz, 6
Dikir barat, 140
Diponegoro, 123
Dosa 19
Dream encounters, 66, 72, 73, 74, 75
Dream interpretation, also *ta'bir al-ru'ya*, 41, 42
Du'a, 21

E

Ebrahim Moosa, 6
Economic dislocation, 118
Effendi Sa'ad, Shaykh Muhammad, 73–74

Eickelman, Dale, 135
Emotional Spiritual Quotient(ESQ), 156
Empathy, 7, 8, 165
Enlightenment, 7
Erbe Sentanu, 156
Erving Goffman 78
European colonialism, 112, 118, 128

F

Fana' (annihilation of the self), 41
Fatwas, 143, 146, 152
Feelings (rasa), 18–23, 26, 31, 37, 39, 48
Female saints, 54–55
Female spiritual mediators, 97–101
Female Sufi warriors, 123
Figurative mediums, 37–49, 166
Fiqh 150, 154
Flag-raising ceremonies 65
Folk mysticism, 139
Foucault, Michel, 78
Fratricide 119

G

Gadamer, Hans-Georg, 10, 11
Ghazal (amatory poems) 39
Ghazalian ethics, 92
Guerrilla force 124
Guilds 77
Gujerat 1
Gunungan, 28

H

Habaib (singular: habib, beloved ones), 4, 148
Habib Nuh, 59, 61, 71
Habib Soleh bin Muhsin al-Hamid 4
Hadith, 47, 56, 84, 87, 88, 89, 90, 96
Hadith Jibril, 89
Hadrah, 22, 30
Hadramaut, 84, 111
Hadrami-Arabs, 26, 32–33, 36, 43, 45, 53–54, 58–59
Haji Abdul Rahman Limbong 124
Haji Mohammed bin Abdul Kadir, 32
Halal (permissible), 48
Halaqah (study circle), 92
Hamzah Fansuri, 5, 39, 40, 42
Haqiqah, 13
Harfiyah (word by word), 92
Hasyiyah (glosses) of Shafi'i, 154
Haul, 104
Healing powers, 66, 67, 68, 69
Hejaz, 89
Heritagization, 60, 61
Hidayatullah, Pangeran, 129
Hijab (veil), 15
Hijaz, 83
Hikayat 38, 42, 43, 44, 45, 46, 47, 48
Hikayat Merong Mahawangsa, 157

198 INDEX

Hikayat Prang Sabi, 114, 119
Hikayat Raja-Raja Pasai, 48
Hodgson, Marshall, 127
Holy war, also jihad, perang sabil, parrang sabbil, 108, 112, 114, 116, 117, 119, 120, 123, 128, 129
Homogenization, 168
Hukum Kanun Pahang(Pahang Digest), 153
Hulul (incarnation), 144
Hybridized pugilistic tradition, 110
Hybridized institutions see also
    Madrasah Dayah, 85

I

Ibadah (acts of worship), 15
Ibn 'Arabi, 144
Ibn Sirin, Muhammad, 41
Ihsan(excellence), 15
Ijazah (licenses), 36, 37, 79, 89, 97, 101, 159, 167
Ikhas (sincerity), 15
Ilmu laduni (direct knowledge from God), 99
Imam Bonjol, 127
Imam Mahdi 109, 129
Iman (faith), 15, 167
Incredible tales, 66–76
India subcontinent, 108
Indonesia, 27
Indonesian revolution, 124–125
Inner jihad, 107
Insanul Kamil 158, 162
Insurgencies, 111
Invasion of the Deccan region, 108
Islah (reform), 136
Supra-Islamic ideas, 109
Islamic law 114, 127
Islamic reformism 84, 89
Islamic revivalism, 128
Islamic state 129–131
Islamic Youth Corps also Kaikyo Seinen
    Teishintai, 124
Islamization of Southeast Asia, 108
Istanbul, 1, 84, 148
Istidraj (reaping bounties that lead to gradual
    destruction), 51
Ittihad (union with Allah), 144

J

Jacques Waardenburg, 132
James Lancaster, 158
James Piscatori, 135
Janissaries, 123
Java War, 124
Java 1, 4,15, 117, 129, 130
Jawi ecumene, 20
Jawi script, 92
Jawiyyin 145
Jerusalem 108
Jihad, 107, 108, 109, 110, 111, 112, 113, 167

Joko Widodo, 161
Jong Islamieten Bond (JIB), 130
Julian Millie, 66
Juramentado, 121, 123
Juru kunci (keepers of the keys), 60

K

K.H. Hasyim Asy'ari, 154
Kalimah syahadah (declaration of faith), 48
Kalimantan, 24–25, 73, 83, 101, 128, 131, 146
Karamah (Miracles), 51–52, 56, 58, 60–63, 65, 68, 71, 75, 76, 166, 169
Kaum Muda, 29
Kebatinan movements , 139
Kedah 56, 83, 157
Keddie, Nikki, 111
Kejawen (Javanism), 139
Kejiwaan 139
Kelantan 14, 53, 83, 98
Kerajaan (kingdoms), 111, 134
Khaddam (servants), 98
Khadim (Caretaker), 60
Khalafi seminaries, 85
Khalidiyyah-Naqshbandiyyah, 125
Khalifahs of Sufi Brotherhood, 158
Khalwatiyyah, 14
Khidr, Prophet, 69
Kiai Salleh, 124
Kiai Wasyid bin Muhammad Abbas, 128
Kitab gundul (bare books), 88
Kitab jawi, 88
Kitab kuning (yellow book), 88
Kiyai, also tok guru, tuan guru, shaykh, ajengan, buya (highly respected teachers), 79, 85, 96, 98, 104
Klinik rawatan Islam, also Klinik Ruqyah, 99
Knut S. Vikør 132
Krabi, 68
Kusu Island, 56
Kyai (Sufi teachers), 93, 101, 102
Kyai Fuad Hasyim Buntet, 71
Kyai Hussein Muhammad, 101

L

Learning hubs, 77
Lebai Deraman, 124
Leonard Andaya, 39
Lodges, 77
Lombok, 58, 101, 104
Long graves, 56

M

Ma'rifah (interior knowledge), 13, 41
Ma'ruf Amin, 161
Madrasah dayah, 85
Madrasah Shaulatiyah, 84
Madrasah system, 84, 85

Index   **199**

Madura, 101
Mahabbah (love), 15
Mahmood Kooria, 79
Mahmud Yunus, 81
Majelis Ulama Indonesia (Indonesian Ulama
  Council), 153
Majelis Pengkajian Tauhid Tasawuf (Monotheistic
  Sufi Study Council), 162
Majlis ta'lim also majelis taklim, Islamic forum, 22
Makam Loang Baloq, 58
Makam Sunan Muria, 58
Makassar 2, 26, 123
Makkah, 1–2, 22, 26, 29, 30, 45, 69–71, 80–84, 112,
  119, 121, 124, 126, 128, 151, 154, 160
Malay peninsula, also Malaya, 26, 56, 91, 116
Malaysia, 14, 42, 53, 64, 86, 91, 103, 139–140, 143,
  147, 159, 162–163
Malfuzat (oral discourse), 66
Malik Badri, 6
Manaqib(s) (hagiographies, virtuous
  deeds), 4, 65, 66
Manfuzh at-Tarmasi, 154
Mantiq (logic), 88
Maqam (Sanctified Tomb), 50, 52, 53, 60
Maqamat (spiritual stations), 15
Martabat tujuh (seven stages of being), 92, 146
Martial arts 109, 113
Martyrdom, 119, 132
Masyumi (Partai Majelis Syuro Muslimin
  Indonesia, Council of Indonesian Muslim
  Associations), 161
Mat Kilau, 124
Mat Salleh, 124
Mataram 117, 122
Mausoleums 52, 60
Mawlid, 21, 22, 25, 26, 27, 28, 29, 30, 31, 32, 34, 35
Mega Mawlid or Superstar Mawlid, 33
Messianic 140, 147
Metahuman explanations or supernatural
  reasonings, 7
Methodological atheism, 7
Mevlevi, 108
Mi'raj (ascension), 69
Militant campaigns, also qital, ghazwah 111, 130
Minangkabau, 30, 78, 120, 126, 161
Mindanao 114, 120, 121
Nation-states, 159
Mohammed Gamal Abdelnour, 89
Monumentalization, 52, 54, 58, 61, 62
Moosa, Ebrahim: concept of dihliz, 6
Mortifications of the self, 78
Mosques 23, 27, 28, 32, 34, 35, 50, 58, 59, 77, 81, 98,
  103, 128, 131, 138, 144, 150
MTI (Madrasah Tarbiyah Islamiyah), 161
Muhammad Abduh, 29
Muhammad Samman Kati, 150
Muhammadiyah movement, 31

Muhsinun, 15
Mujahadah, 15
Mujahid, 120
Mukhtasar (abridgements), 154
Munadarah or muzakarah, 93
Murid, 14, 26, 38, 79, 97
Murshid, 14, 32
Murshidul 'Am (Spiritual Guide), 14
Murtad (apostates), 144
Muslim cosmopolitanism, 161
Muslim revolts, 111
Musyahadah (witnessing), 41
Mystic synthesis, 139
Mystical powers, 117

N

Nafs, 13
Nahdlatul Ulama (NU), 160
Nahu and Sharaf, 88
Nakhoda Ragam, 57
Nakorn Si Thammarak, 68
Naqshbandi-Haqqani, 159
Naqshbandiyyah, 83, xx, xxi, 14, 26, 42, 49, 101, 125,
  128, 146, 158, 162
Naqshbandiyyah-Mazhariyyah,101
Naquib Al-Attas, Syed Muhammad, 4, 5, 13
Narathiwat, 121
Nasyid 32, 141
Negara Islam Indonesia (NII), 130
Neo-Sufism, 149
Nik Abdul Aziz Bin Haji Nik Mat, 14
North Africa 118, 126
Nur (divine light), 15
Nur Muhammad (Light of Muhammad):
  theological debates, 151–152
Nur Muhammad 29, 30
Nurcholish Madjid, 97, 156
Nyai Ageng Serang, 123

O

Oldenburg, Roy 103
Omar Fathurrahman, 100
Organic texts, 79, 80, 85, 87, 88, 89, 90, 91, 92, 95,
  96, 98, 104, 105, 106
Outer jihad, 107

P

Padri Wars, 126, 127
Pam Nilan, 78
Pangeran Dakar (Haji Mangsur), 69
Pangnga, 69
Pantun 35, 38, 39
Paramadina University, 156
Parang Sabil Kissa, 114
Partai Kebangkitan Bangsa (PKB), 161
Patani, 20, 46, 57, 68, 83, 88, 91, 92
Patani Malays, also Orang Melayu, 121

Patani United Liberation Movement (PULO), 86
Patriarchal structures in Sufi seminaries, 97, 100
Peasant revolt in Cilegon, 128
Pelajar also santri, murid, 79
Pelajar sepenuh masa, 104
Penang 54, 58, 61, 71
Pengawas Aliran Kepercayaan Masyarakat (Coordinating Board for Monitoring Mystical Beliefs in Society), 152
People's Religious Schools (Sekolah Agama Rakyat, SAR), 86
Perak, 56, 85, 150, 153
Perang kafir (war against disbelievers), 108
Perang sabil, see also jihad, parrang sabbil 108, 112, 116, 120, 123, 125, 132
Perarakan mawlid (mawlid marches), 31
Persian, Arab-Persian, 13, 19, 21, 29, 38, 39, 43, 44–45, 52, 62, 88, 90–91, 151
PERSIS (Persatuan Islam), 30
PERTI (Persatuan Tarbiyah Islamiyah), 161, 162
Pesantren, 78–89, 90–95, 101–102
Phra Ong Mahawangsa, 157
Phuket, 69
Pilgrimage tourism, 60
Politik, 136
Polyvocality, 80
Pondok, see also Dayah and Pesantren, 78–79, 83–86, 91–93, 103
Populist da'wa, 139–148
Processions, 65
Prophet Muhammad: Night Journey and Ascension (Al-Isra' wal-Mi'raj), 69
Prophet Muhammad, 87, 94, 95
Protectionist Sufi warriorism, 120, 121, 122
Pulau Besar Island, 56
Purist Sufi warriorism, 125, 126, 127

Q

Qadiriyyah xxi, 14, 83, 125, 128, 150
Qalb (heart), 13
Qana'ah(contentment), 15
Qasidah al-Burdah, 22
Qasidah rebana, 22, 25
Qiyam(standing), 30
Qur'an, Qur'anic, 12, 16, 18, 20, 25, 38, 39, 48, 65, 81, 87, 90, 96, 100, 109, 120, 121, 135, 139, 140, 142, 146, 151, 169

R

Rabiah al-Adawiyah, 43, 44
Raden Ayu Yudakusuma, 123
Raja Ali Haji, 41
Raja Ashman Shah, 159
Raja Haji Abdullah, 158
Raja Hassan, 41
Raja Muhammad Yusuf, 158
Raja Nazrin Shah, 159

Rasa (dhawq, perasaan), 18, 19, 20, 22, 23, 26, 31, 37, 39, 48, 166
Rashidiyyah 14
Rashid Rida, 29
Ratib, 21–28, 41–45, 130
Ratib al-Attas, 33
Ratib al-Haddad, 33
Ratib Samman, 33, 34, 35, 36
Ratib, 21, 22, 33
Ratna Ani Lestari, 161
Realpolitik, 167
Redha (acceptance), 15
Reflexive admirer approach, 4–6
Reformist politics, 136, 149–152, 155, 156
Religious polarization, 118
Religious-educated Muslims see also santri, murid, pelajar, 79
Revolutionary, 112, 130
Riau islands 42, 65, 155
Ribats, 60
Ricklefs, Merle 139
Rifa'iyyah 14
Ritual economy, 63
Riyadhah (spiritual practices), 15
Roslan Madun, 42
Royalist politics, 156
Ruba'i (poetry with four lines of rhyming verse), 39
Ruqyah, 8
Rustriningsih, 161

S

Sabr (patience), 15
Salafi, 85
Salafiyyah movement, 89
Sama' (listening), 22
Sammaniyyah, 14, 26, 34, 36, 129, 150
Sanad (lineage), 79, 80, 94
Sanctified tombs, see also Maqam, 52, 53, 54, 55, 56, 57, 58, 59, 60
Sanskrit, 18
Santri, also murid, pelajar, 79, 95, 99, 102, 104
Sarawak, 65, 66
Sarekat Islam (Islamic Association), 160
Saudi Arabia 31
Sayyid Muhammad Al-Baghdadi 58
Sayyid Uthman bin Yahya, 36
Sayyid Yasin, 53, 54
Segmentizing Sufism, 168–169
Sekolah Arab (Arabic school) 77, 79
Sembahyang (to pray to the divine), 19
Seyyed Hossein Nasr, 19, 87
Shadhiliyyah, 14, 36, 147
Sha'ir (poem), 38, 39, 40 , 41, 42, 43
Shafi'ite school, 79, 92, 153–155, 162
Shahadah (profession of faiths), 58
Shahadah (simple testimonials), 94
Shamsuddin al-Sumatra'i 13, 91, 115, 143, 158

Index

Sharaf (Arabic grammar), 88
Sharaf al-Din al-Busiri, 22, 24
Shari'a 12–14, 31, 49, 105, 113, 119, 124–126, 129, 130
Shari'a-minded Sufi(s), 127–128
Shattariyyah, 83
Shaykh(s) see also kiyai, tok guru, tuan guru, ajengan, buya, 79, 80, 91, 92, 94, 96, 97
Shaykh Abdul Rahim, 56
Shaykh Abdul Rahman, 56
Shaykh Abdullah Arif, 151, 157, 158
Shaykh al-Islam, 39
Shaykh Dalem Arif Muhammad, 55
Shaykh Hisham Kabbani, 159
Shaykh Ismail 47, 48
Shaykh Karang, 69–70
Shaykh Muhammad Effendi Sa'ad, 73, 74
Shaykh Siti Jenar, 144
Shi'ite, 25, 151
Shirk (idolatrous polytheism), 53
Siasah also siyasa, 168, 169
Silat (Malay combative art), 110, 128
Silsilah (lineage), 14, 80, 94
Singapore 31–34, 41, 52, 54, 56, 59, 61, 65–66, 71, 96
Sinta Nuryiah, 101
Sirat ul-awliya' (biographies of the saints), 66
Siti Musdah Mulia, 101
Siti Qomariyah, 161
Social injustice, 109
Soekarmadji Maridja Kartosuwiryo, 130
Songkhla, 68
Sorongan, 93
South Sulawesi, 26
South Thailand 78, 85, 91, 103, 121, 129
Spiritual mediators, 79–80, 96–106
State Religious Schools (Sekolah Agama Negeri, SAN), 86
Structural transformations in Muslim societies, 118
Sufi cosmology, 19, 39, 118
Sufi ethics,154, 156
Sufi resistance, 9
Sufi seminaries, 79–86
Sufi tradition, 3, 9
Sufi warriorism, 109, 110, 114–130
Sufi-inflected mysticism, 16, 139, 140, 146
Sulaiman Ar-Rasuly, 162
Sultan Abu Sa'id, 44
Sultan Ageng (Tirtayasa), 1, 119
Sultan Alauddin Ri'ayat Shah 143, 158
Sultan Haji, 1, 119
Sultan Ibrahim bin Adham, 44, 45
Sultan Iskandar Muda, 143
Sultan Iskandar Tsani, 143
Sultan Malikul Saleh (Merah Silu), 47, 48
Suluk (journey), 13
Suluk Garwa Kencana, 117
Sumatra 34, 42, 46, 83, 116, 119, 120, 127

Sunan Bonan(g), 15
Sunnah (words and acts of Prophet Muhammad), 12
Supernatural power 142, 151
Supplicative mediums, 20–22, 29, 34
Surau (prayer places), 78, 81, 93
Sword-plays, 65
Syech Amran Waly al-Khalidy, 162
Syed Muhammad Naquib Al-Attas: perspective on Sufi militarism, 167
Syekh Abdul Qadir As Saggaf, 32

T

Tabaqat (ranks or classes), 84
Tabarruk, 65
Tadah kitab or buka kitab, 92
Tadhkirah (memorial, memento), 66
Tafakkur, 6, 7, 15
Tafsir (Qur'anic exegesis), 88, 89
Tahlil (litany in praise of God), 65
Tajdid (renewal), 136
Tamassuh (touching), 64
Taqlid, 93
Taqwa (piety), 15
Tariqah (Sufi Brotherhood), see also Sufi Orders, 1, 5, 9, 13, 14, 26, 31–36, 42, 54, 65, 71–74, 83, 86, 97, 98–102, 109, 110–111, 115, 119, 121–125, 127, 128, 129, 136, 140, 143, 145–147, 150, 152, 155, 158–162,
Tariqah sufiyah mu'tabarah, 6
Tasauf moderen also modern Sufism, 156
Tasawwuf (Sufism), 1, 4, 5, 12, 77, 88, 90, 105, 140, 145, 149, 150
Tasawwur, 19
Tawakkal (trust in God), 15
Tawassul (intercession), 50
Tawbah, 15
Tawheed (oneness of God), 13, 168
Tazkiya (purifying), 16
Teleportation 69, 71
Textual cords and textual families, 79
Tijaniyyah, xxi, 83, 150
Tok Gajah, 124
Tok guru (respected teachers, 4, 14, 78, 79, 85, 93, 96–98, 104
Tok Janggut, 124
Tok Kenali, 83
Tok Ku Paloh, 123
Tomé Pires, 144
Total institutions, 78–79
Traditionalist(s), 160, 161
Transcendental, transmittal, transformational (elements of Sufism), 13–17, 169
Transoxiana, 108
Trengganu 83, 124, 163
Tuan guru see also kiyai, 79
Tuanku Nan Renceh, 127

Tuanku Nan Tuo, 127
Tuanku Rao, 127
Tuon Kosem, 53
Tuon Ku Umar, 53
Turath (heritage of Muslim thought), 12

U

Undang-undang Sembilan Puluh Sembilan Perak
    (Ninety-Nine Laws of Perak), 153
Universal values, 169
Usul al-din, 88
Usul al-fiqh, 88
Uzlah(seclusion), 15

V

van Bruinessen, Martin, 5
Vernacular occultism, 110
Vietnam, 53
Violence, 109, 126, 131, 133

W

Wahdatul wujud, 43, 92, 144, 146, 162
Wasaya (testaments), 66

Wali hidup (living saints), 111
Wali Songo, 52, 62, 82
Wan Ali Kutan, 83
Wara' (scrupulousness), 15
Wayang kulit, 140
Wirid, 21
Wujudiyyah, 143–144

Y

Yala, 121
Ya-Sin (Qur'anic chapter 36), 66
Yusuf Al-Makassari: life story, exile, and influence,
    1, 2, 3, 9

Z

Zamakshari Dhofier, 102
Zawiya see also khanqah (large and integrated
    devotional complexes), 77
Zikrzamman, 21
Ziyarah (Visitation), 15, 50
Zuhud (renunciation of the world), 15
Zuhri, Saifuddin: leader of Laskar Hizbullah, 125